STEPS TO IMMATURITY

By the same author

THE YOUNG MAN (A NOVEL)

D. H. LAWRENCE: A FIRST STUDY
THE NONESUCH COLERIDGE
MINNOW AMONG TRITONS:
THE LETTERS OF MRS S. T. COLERIDGE
COLERIDGE AND S.T.C.
THE MUSE IN CHAINS

GAMESMANSHIP
LIFEMANSHIP
ONE-UPMANSHIP
SUPERMANSHIP

SENSE OF HUMOUR: AN ANTHOLOGY
POTTER ON AMERICA
THE MAGIC NUMBER

On the sea-wall east of Worthing. This photograph, taken by Father, rather well illustrates our characters. S. P. is independent, determined to be leader, but conscious of the four-foot drop on the far side. Muriel affectionately accepts the situation. Mother is anxious about the possibility of my falling. Uncle Jim, pleased to be in the party, is anxious not to be conspicuous. Uncle Josh knows how to stand, and might have preferred us all facing the other way.

Stephen Potter

STEPS TO
IMMATURITY

★

RUPERT HART-DAVIS
SOHO SQUARE LONDON
1959

Printed in Great Britain by Richard Clay and Company, Ltd.,
Bungay, Suffolk.

Dedicatory Letter

MY DEAR MURIEL

I am, of course, dedicating this book to you—and not only because you have helped me with difficult bits and filled up gaps in my memory. You were with me during most of this Vol. I, when we were children together in that unprepossessing and happy house. The book I hope therefore is certain to be interesting to you, probably also to A. and J. and some day L., and even to such less closely connected blood relations as L.P.G. Whether these essentially small-scale events of this first volume will seem worth reading to many other people is something which I know you doubt. So do I—in fact were it not for the approval and advice of my possibly too optimistic friends Rupert H.-D. and Richard G., I might not have gone ahead with publication. At the same time the truth is always supposed to be interesting; and I have done my best to say what really happened, reminding you that truth has many layers, the most revealing of which are the least accessible and often beyond my powers to find.

I have been haunted by a metaphor as I write this autobiography and plan future volumes (taking it for granted that these will be forthcoming). I believe that children are born grown-up. They are mature adults from the start, but tied up in a parcel the binding of which is much too tight for them and only gradually released. Not only their movements, but their personality and thoughts are always struggling, sometimes actually with an air of apologetic amusement, to get free from the handicap. This explains the occasional glimpses of something only to be called grown-up—one of us—which I have been observing recently, even in your nephew L., now that he has reached the decidedly immature age, as it is officially supposed to be, of three. One by one the wrappings are untied. You, as well as anybody, know how the right kind of teaching is really helping to untie knots, or putting "tin openers" as you will remember I used to call them, within reach. I seem to have spent a lot of time in this book complaining that when I was at school some of the knots were actually tightened. My own personal grown-up-hood came through very patchily and very late—long after the close of this book, where I am really describing the steps towards the general immaturity I achieved in my twenties.

At the other end of life, the potential maturity is still there: but the binding up begins all over again, both physically and mentally. Before I have returned completely to the cocoon stage I want to give myself the enjoyment of trying to recall something of the bad angels attendant on my failure to come of age; and those good angels, our parents, uncles and aunts, who seemed to us so much bigger than life then, such tender and vanishing spirits now.

STEPHEN

October, 1959

6

Contents

Illustrations

CHAPTER ONE

Fixed Faces

IT is difficult for a child to realise that things may have been different before he was born. The grown-up people, his older relations, seem to have been created as permanently grown-up, forever older relations. Time moves so slowly that everything seems fixed. "Your aunt was exquisitely pretty as a girl"; "Uncle Jim used to keep us in fits of laughter"; "They went to Paris for their honeymoon"—it's not that these remarks are not believed: they give so little interest that they are scarcely even heard.

It is true there are the family albums, and it is true that these give evidence that there were once younger people of the same names. "Rose," "Lucy," "Jim at Bryn Cottage," are written underneath; but "Uncle" or "Aunt" has been cut out of them: moreover, the characters are so immovable, the clothes so strange, that the figures look like actors in amateur theatricals. It is not possible to see a real connection.

My father's family album, the Potter album, is particularly fixed and solemn in appearance. The most recent photograph is well before 1900, the date of my birth. The covers are stuffed and heavy. There is padding inside as well, for next to a great-aunt covered in lace is unexpectedly set the severe countenance of Mr Hood, the family doctor: while still more surprisingly there are likenesses in the following folios of John Bright, Tennyson, the first Lord Brassey and the Empress Eugénie. Lord Brassey had some right to a page all to himself because he was considered the benefactor of my father and his elder brother, my uncle James; but the rest of the notables were put in to fill up space and give at least some sort of interest to a page devoid of Potters. The pictures go back through the first collodion positives on glass, back through

calotypes, to the photographic Dark Ages. With the majestic simplicity of monumental brasses, each expressive phase of Victorian
costume is illustrated. The quiet, still look of the Victorian ladies
is contrasted with the slightly contemptuous lounging of the gentlemen. I see repeated in successive generations my own face with
censorious-looking congenital frown (which first becomes a furrow
at the age of three) gazing with gravity at the world of Gladstone,
Palmerston or even of Melbourne: and side by side the decidedly
more intellectual, faintly sarcastic faces of the Rawlingses, my
grandmother's family, the successful ones, the men who made a
little money, or at any rate enough to have it swindled and
dwindled away from them. I remember only one of the Rawlingses, the handsome and dark-bearded Walter, who, with an
amused display of keeping a reverent distance, was romantically
attentive to my mother and enjoyed the most beautiful new cloth
in his frock-coats, and had the silkiest of top-hats, in the nap of
which at the age of four I loved, when alone and unobserved, to
make railway tracks with my finger. He was not good at tricks
with coins, but I was glad to watch him trying, because he had a
splendidly pronounced tremor of the hands, and Mother used to
whisper to me that it was due to his over-smoking. I was later
to become familiar with Mother's highly personal medical approach. It was these dark and bearded Rawlingses, with their thin,
straight noses and dashing looks, whom I used to feel a little proud
of when I first began to associate myself with the fixities. I used
to scan their faces for signs of a tendency to make daring breaks
from the conventional, a trait which in the most conventional
period of my own life, my youth, I used to imagine was obvious
in myself.

The Potter faces are somewhat more plebeian, with good big
fleshy noses, and peculiar long heads and an expression which
seems to want to say, "I am being good." My grandparents
appear only dimly, blanketed underneath mountains of clothes,
their features dimmed by these earliest photographic processes
(my grandmother was born a week or two before the death of
Pitt, near the beginning of 1806). Father, of course, is there as a

good little boy, an expression which he retained throughout his life. James, his brother, is the naughty one, the sprite.

Nostalgia is the least helpful of all moods in which to try to remember, but there are two faces, particularly, I now look at with that feeling uppermost. One is my father's sister Lucy, my favourite aunt—"Auntie Herbert," as I called her (and shall continue to call her to avoid confusion with my mother's sister, who shared the delightful eighteen-fiftyish name Lucy). The other suggests a real beauty, the face of Anne Thorpe—features which I myself was to know and admire because their structure was so delicately firm that they remained almost untouched when she was an old lady. Father knew and kept this picture. His own family and the Thorpes lived at Belvedere near Erith. Anne became his first great object of love—never declared, I would guess, except by an increase of respectful attentiveness. Father was too young, was too soon banished to London to earn his living. Before anybody knew it was happening the handsome and piratical Tom Gash turned up in Belvedere to woo and marry her. Father was romantic but not dashing, and certainly not even microscopically piratical—least of all at this period of his life. There is a photograph of him at this time looking particularly serious and defencelessly youthful, though his look of dependable goodness must have been intensified by the necessity of standing very still and looking the camera straight in the eye. Whenever he was having his photograph taken Father always looked as if he was outstaring Honesty itself, whether he was seventeen or seventy-six.

James, nine years older, looked more a man of the world. He was much better dressed, his neckties were thicker and more elegant; his hair was parted fashionably just to the left of the middle line. And James's education was completed. He had studied modern languages at Lausanne and Nuremberg. He was already somewhat splendidly earning his living as secretary to that largest fixture in the Potter family album with the page to himself—Sir Thomas Brassey, the maker of railways, afterwards the first Lord Brassey. There was an aura of wonderful success about James. No doubt his younger brother admired him; but the admiration must have been wistful. There was to be no foreign travel, no university life for Frank. For it was at this time that his father, the breadwinner, began to sicken for the illness which eventually killed him. There was nothing to keep the family going except the carefully guarded portion of Rawlings money which my grandmother had inherited. Frank, the youngest son, had to plunge into work immediately. For the junior clerk in a warehouse and junior in a firm of stockbrokers, happy country days at Belvedere were over, and the romantic mists of Dickens's *Great Expectations* country were exchanged for the grimness and perpetual fog of a Dickens office buried in the City.

Meanwhile a new set of frozen glimpses, a more up-to-date family album, was being collected round a different kind of household altogether. The Reynolds album, my mother's, which sets the scene of my father's ultimate destiny, is in complete contrast to the Potter book. There are no solemn faces staring, solitary, in the photographer's studio. There are no celebrated contemporaries or noble patrons shoved in to make up weight, no old ladies in elaborate lace caps. Instead there are outdoor groups mostly taken in the sun by the keen young gentlemen who were fortunate enough to possess the new "hand camera," with which, by exposing film for an amazingly short space of time, it was possible to take admirable photographs of the attractive Misses Reynolds screwing their eyes up in the dazzle and leaning hard on their parasols as an aid to stillness. First come picnics and tennis parties: the wedding groups were to follow later, with the great "Josh" himself included, occasionally in the full glory of his uniform—Captain Reynolds, my mother's father, from whom (always excepting the fact that he was perennially a little short of cash) all blessings flowed.

The Reynolds family had been on the full Victorian scale. If only some of these photographs could be made to move and come alive again. My mother, with the special dignity of being "the pretty one" and her father's favourite daughter as well—or her own favourite, her young brother Willie, who stands up so straight

14

and manly in the photograph, already acting the part of Josh the Second, preparing himself to be the great Uncle Josh of my boyhood.

Court Lodge was a happy house. The building itself was mid-Victorian and on the cheap; the richness was in the characters of the inhabitants. Mother's brothers and sisters ran to eleven or so, nine surviving. They were sufficient to themselves as a unit, and the longer they lived together, the more their various roles were intensified. Differentiation was speeded up, like evolution on a solitary island. The home was at Caterham in Surrey, and the front gate of the house still opens on to Caterham Church and the Caterham cemetery, which sweeps down in a cataract of tombstones to the Warlingham valley. The chalk of that airy slope is riddled with the graves of my aunts and uncles, parents and grandparents; and nearly a dozen times I have stood fidgeting by, tearful and bored, while the earth thudded down on family coffins, all the exuberant differences of the inhabitants put tidy at last.

Presiding over Court Lodge, with a noble pair of moustaches cascading down from a big curved nose, was my grandfather, Captain Reynolds, the true original Josh, holding that affectionate nickname unchallenged to his death. I know only one thing for certain about his character: he had an exaggerated aversion to severity. Ridiculously unsuitable as this trait was in a soldier, he could not bear to be concerned with any kind of reprimand or punishment. Perhaps this was a reaction from a particularly intensive nineteenth-century father, who used the buckle-end of his strap with muscular relish. His son was strong enough to answer back; but as soon as he had made sure that his brothers were old enough to look after themselves, my grandfather walked stolidly out of this house forever.

Family history records that he was as big as a man when he was still not quite seventeen, so that by faking his age he was able to enlist at Wellington Barracks, convinced that in a few weeks (since the Brigade of Guards was already in action) he would be marching to glory in the Crimea. It also records that his father came storming up to London, but that with great foresight and insight the Army refused to disgorge, turning the son, his true age revealed, into the most junior possible kind of Coldstream Guard. He loved the Army, and the Army loved him, and the recruit became a corporal, who became a sergeant, who became a sergeant-major, who became a regimental sergeant-major, who became chief warrant officer in the Brigade of Guards, with a speed which broke the peace-time promotion record. While still young he even made the leap—possible in the Brigade only for a Quartermaster—to commissioned rank, and became Captain Reynolds, loved and liked by everybody, a sort of martinet by kindness, plenty of bark but no bite, outwardly fierce and disciplinary but always stealthily countermanding punishments or rigging ameliorating alternative sentences; and known through all ranks as Josh and indeed occasionally receiving, when stationed in the eighties at St James's Palace, a guttural "Good morning, Josh," from the Prince of Wales himself.

Predictably, this easy-goingness, which succeeded so surprisingly in the Army, was taken advantage of by his retinue of sons and daughters. His wife was very pretty, very young, with an Irish tendency to side-step difficulties, and a blazing Irish temper. Like many of her kind, she never grew up herself. Her mixture of hard cuffs and harder caresses was disregarded by her children. When she told the Captain that "Arthur is in his bedroom and must be spanked immediately," Josh would stride up the stairs and the sound of slaps would satisfactorily be audible below. But Josh was using the flat of his hand on the banister rail. The family had long since grown too disordered even for the stony barracks of the Brigade. Only my mother (who was born in the Tower of London) and the first few children went the rounds. They must be crammed into some kind of permanent house. Court Lodge it was, within walking distance of the Guards Depot—and even this small miracle of inconvenience was more than a captain's pay could afford.

Life at Court Lodge must have been explosive. There must have been a constant sense of pressure. In earlier days Walter, the

A first photograph
of my father.

Captain Reynolds
—"the great Josh,"
my grandfather.

From a painting by W. Cheesman. East Hill, Wandsworth, in 1882, just before my mother and father separately came to live in this country suburb.

eldest son, had been in genial control of admiring sisters; but in Court Lodge a crop of younger brothers were making their appearance. Three of the girls were stuffed into one small bedroom together. At full complement, Percy had to sleep with Arthur, the baby. Percy was the gentlest of all the brothers, but even he felt that Arthur, the adored pet, was sometimes also the last straw, the unnecessary eleventh. One day Percy lowered him into the water-butt and left him there; then rushed into the house to confess. Perhaps on this same Saturday on the tennis lawn (a size too small for its tennis court) the elder girls, their healthy young waists squeezed into tight, wide waistbands, would be rehearsing, for the Court Lodge Orchestral and Dramatic Society, the Casket Scene from *The Merchant of Venice*, Willie in charge as producer, organiser, chief prince and fanfare on a trumpet all in one. From across the verandah, Lilla, my mother, would be heard practising "Angels ever Bright and Fair" for her L.R.A.M. Intermediate—a contralto "Keep, O keep me," deep and strong. Giggles and Handel it was, with old military uniforms and helmets fished out for fancy dress or acting, distant parade ground effects from the Depot, Willie standing up stiff and dignified, trying out his delivery of the "Old Mel" speech from H. J. Byron's new play at the Folly Theatre, *The Upper Crust*, which he had seen twice. Crunchings on the drive of large military feet of orderlies with messages for the Captain. Three dogs, their different and unusual breeds clearly reflected in their voices. And somewhere on the perimeter the plaintive remonstrances and childish threats of Mrs Reynolds, and the genial boomings of the Captain, background effects which made no more difference to the suffused turbulence of the house than the bugle-calls, distant but so clear that they seemed to be printed on the connecting air, made to the punctuality of Court Lodge's complicated time-table. It was all part of the general sound, as far away now as the breaking of waves on a distant seashore, of Court Lodge on any fine Saturday afternoon.

At first the eldest brother, Walter, as firm and dependable as his father, had been the centre of order. But Walter left early, to work in London. The Lodge needed his help. It was left to Lilla to keep some sanity in the confusion. Indeed, Lilla, before she was twelve years old, had assumed the position of mother-in-chief to the rest of the family. It was she who bound up Arthur's nasty cut or pulled Ethel's head out of the railings; she who made sure that Willie was sent to school on time, noticed that Lucy was inclined to droop unbecomingly when she sat at table and that Percy was inattentive ("tail off the ear, Percy"); she who saw that Matty, the delicate one, with the tendency to catch colds, got her extra glass of milk and slept, even at the height of summer, with her window opened not more than two inches.

Above all, it was on the second boy of the family that she bestowed her love and protection. It was Willie, "the little Josh," whose clothes were best mended, who was sent best brushed out of the house, who was pulled most sympathetically out of the tangles of the bicycle-spokes' monkey-puzzle of the penny-farthing after a fall. It was Willie she encouraged, trying somehow to bat tennis balls over the net for first games lessons; it was Willie with whom she Wandered down the Mountain Side or Called the Cattle Home, playing his accompaniments on the piano, and building up the idea that it was he who was the really musical one, though her own singing voice was truly fine, ten times better. This really was the shaping of Willie, the forming of his role in the dramatis personae, for he returned her love with adoration and soon established himself as knight protector of his sister. He tried to make some kind of order for her in the rabble, for Court Lodge was becoming a problem of the survival of the tidiest, like life on a small yacht. It would help her, perhaps, if he put the Mendelssohn and the old volumes, and the modern music like Parry, in different piles. In his shared bedroom he made Percy clear away the top surface, at any rate, of their bedroom floor. If he had to share a hair-brush with Percy, he would have his own comb, burnished bright and exactly placed in his own drawer, in military alignment with his diary, his *Theatrical Almanack* and his ruler. It was he who organised the chain gang for laying the table and clearing away again; and if his father, the great Josh, was often away, he could become bit by bit, now that Walter had gone, the minor Josh, the natural Prince Regent.

In time, of course, Court Lodge tidied itself up; for as everybody got older, everybody had to work. Lilla had long ago taken up her scholarship at the Royal Academy of Music; now Willie had got his foot in at the Bank, as the youngest and surely the most dependably serious-sounding junior in the profession. He began even on the lowest salary-rung to save, never able to forget that after his first month he had blued his whole earnings on an extravagance (as he was to tell his nephew fifty times in future years as a warning). There had been the pair of enamelled scissors for Lilla. That was right. What was so unwise was the new hairbrushes for himself, two of them, with his initials on the back.

Court Lodge on working days was sadly not what it used to be; but at week-ends it was as full as ever. And the Sunday population had gone up, because, however exclusive the family ring, there came a time when interested or interesting young ladies and gentlemen had to be admitted.

Lilla, the daughter in charge, maintaining her dignified beauty in the maelstrom, was the centre of attention: two of the four other sisters were particularly pretty in a vivacious way. At any rate among the groups in the Reynolds album strange young men begin to make their appearance. As with all front-line warfare, it must have been the gentler, more sensitive and therefore the more adaptable of these gentlemen who had the best chance of running the Court Lodge gauntlet. The conditions were not favourable for tête-à-têtes. Kittens must be removed from a special nest between the exposed and prolapsed springs of the sofa. Lucy must be somehow wafted from the piano-stool and Percy dug out from his lair behind the curtain. Arthur, the youngest, must be encouraged to say "Hallo" without staring at his boots.

On weekdays Lilla was in London, renting a small house with Walter. It was a pity Walter had to live south of the river, for the Royal Academy of Music was more than a little way north, and a good deal of the journey had to be taken on foot. But Wandsworth, destined to become the Potter country, had one great advantage: it was reasonably near to London, and yet it was almost, if not quite, countrified. For by historical time-scale this wedge of traffic and trolley-bus was truly country only the day before yesterday. In 1885, when my mother arrived, Wandsworth High Street was a sleepy little road, with a few small shops, and sheep or cows walking peacefully down the middle. Garratt Lane looked across meadows to the Wandle, flowing slowly between banks of water-mint and angelica, and still, or recently, an admirable trout-stream in its upper reaches. And what splendid country walks could be taken, by footpath all the way, from Dunsford Farm past the lake of Wimbledon Park straight up the hill to the commodious residences dotted along the edge of Wimbledon Common, and thence to the windmill.

The morning journey to the Royal Academy was not so pleasant, but flushed with her walk Lilla did not look less pleasing at the piano—nor any less pretty when she was singing. Her position as she played showed off her figure perfectly. Mother would reveal to us, in confessional moments, that Walter Macfarren, the Principal of the Academy, used to find it politic suddenly to appear round the door of the music-lesson room.

"I hope your pupil is behaving herself, Mr Simmonds," he would say genially. For of course it was youthful Mr Simmonds who was leaning forward a little too attentively, even if he was only gently shaking Miss Reynolds's forearm to make sure it was relaxed and flexible.

I do not know whether Mr Simmonds was ever reprimanded for these attentions; but Mother did not encourage them. Yet later another pupil became the object of Mr Simmonds's interest, a Miss Tempest, a girl whom Mother never liked, never admired (even when later she became *the* Miss Marie Tempest) and was never able to speak of patiently. Miss Tempest used geranium petals on her cheeks. For all the gentle kindness of her attitude to her family, Mother never had very much forbearance for such people. Perhaps this side of her character, this firmness which showed even in her singing voice, was born of the Court Lodge struggle.

"Now ladies——"

It would be the great Garcia for the latter half of the Academy morning. Garcia in charge of the mezzo-sopranos.

"Now ladies—'I know.' Strongly now."

I know that my Redeemer liveth. Fifteen young ladies sound the phrase in unison, the key transposed to fit their voices, the word "liveth" in a downward cadence, F E, not E repeated, in accordance with the Handel interpretation of the period.

"No, no, NO. I *know* . . . I *know.* You sing it as if you say 'Please pass the cup of tea.' "

The ladies stood as meek as Dickens heroines.

"Now, Miss Reynolds, please. Alone."

Then from the throat of Miss Reynolds, who looked the mildest of them all, would come the notes so firm and strong, and all thoughts of the unexemplary behaviour of Miss Tempest were lost in the beauty of the music.

It was this voice which first caused Father to realise the existence of Miss Reynolds.

Father used to commute to his office from the same part of Wandsworth, two leafy lanes and two little rows of new houses away. On the Saturday before Easter there was a performance of the *Messiah* at St Mark's, and Mother was singing the contralto solo from the gallery over the south transept.

Then shall the eyes of the blind be opened.

Father's eyes lifted reverently to the young woman in white.

And the ears of the deaf unstoppéd.

A beautiful girl singing Handel. To Father Handel was the musical equivalent of God, and something which he had recently been actually able to partake of himself, when he played, as a member of the Wandsworth Common Orchestral Society, in the massed orchestras of the Handel Festival at the Crystal Palace, where the slight squeakiness of his violin-notes merged and was drowned in the vast satisfactory echo of Crystal Palace Handel.

The first introduction took place at the tennis club, where the Potter brothers made keen appearances on Saturday afternoons. How James, the eldest, made Lucy laugh! The photograph, in the album, of a somewhat overwhelmingly noble mansion is a reminder of thrilling talk of the week-end James had just spent at Normanhurst, the Brassey residence, as big as the biggest military barracks and teeming with menservants. Apparently there were actually "two capital tennis courts," and Jim had played on one of them with Lady Idina before sitting down to a "perfectly ordinary luncheon party for eighteen people." Perfectly ordinary —and a footman standing behind practically everybody.

Tennis had been the cue for Frank and Lilla's first conversation. Mother remembered the dialogue, at their first introduction:

"Do you play tennis, Miss Reynolds?"

"No, I don't, but I'd like to, thank you very much."

Frank wanted to go on talking to Lilla, indeed it was obvious that he should; but, being younger and shyer than James, he expressed this inclination by talking particularly hard to Walter—a technical discussion on the introduction of overhead play and the "Doherty smash."

James used to do a wonderful take-off of this meeting, which took place at the gates of the new Allfarthing Lane Lawn Tennis Club, laid out beside the two remaining fields of Dunsford's Farm.

What did Miss Reynolds think of Frank Potter? Mother used to say, strangely, that he had often seen her in the train but that she had never seen him. After tennis Father would be asked back to the little house which Walter and Lucy were sharing. Walter gave them brawn and cheese, and, for the men, beer. But even before this happened, Mother "was quite sure," as she loved to tell us.

"I remember seeing him walking down the Lane after he had left and thinking 'that is the man for me.'"

Father was equally sure that she was the woman for him; but

first that fatal gene in the Potter–Reynolds blood-stream, financial haemophilia, had to be combated. True, Mother was earning a few guineas by teaching and by professional appearances. Or occasionally she would appear as the singer who mingled with the guests after a dinner-party in one of the big residential houses in Harley Street or Belgravia. She liked on these occasions to begin with a song of Sterndale-Bennett, partly because of his gay Handelian quality and partly because she liked to think of herself as doing honour to the great teacher, whom she had seen only once, but whose warm and encouraging personality still seemed to fill the Academy after his death. I imagine Mother standing up as straight as Trilby in a du Maurier drawing-room. After a decent interval Miss Reynolds would leave, clutching the small envelope with the tiny cheque which the host, made furtive by delicacy, had slipped into her hand as she left.

After marriage, of course, all this sort of thing would have to stop. But Father, in the twelve years since he left home, had very much improved his position. In the Dickensy back-office he had taken to accounts and double entry with an enthusiasm which was almost hypnotic. How hard he worked through his long days. Nine to seven were just the office hours; but late into the night he continued, as if in preparation for some wondrous but as yet nameless event, some undefined apotheosis—how I understand and link myself to this instinct for enthusiastic preparation, the "for what" never perfectly specified. He would read and re-read, making exact notes from books with such titles as *McKenzie on Investments*, *Gadstock on Estate Management*, with doses of Ferguson's *Complete Violinist*, the cheap edition of Carlyle, and Emily Westmore on *The Styles of Gothic Architecture* stuffed into the spare moments to make up the gaps in his education. Already he had achieved the chartered accountancy certificate which he was later to take up as a Fellow. But still there must be a little delay before he actually proposed to Miss Reynolds. There must be some evidence that he would be able to support her. She knew and she understood, although sometimes the pauses which come in all conversations must have been a little strained, or sad, or anxious.

Then came the piece of fortune. The Lord Brassey for whom James worked had "formed a favourable impression": Father was the object of a recommendation. He was given a post with the well-respected Messrs Tapp and Bird, an accountancy firm as trim and shipshape as their name. He was to be subordinate only to the two partners. It was exactly what Father had been waiting for. On Friday he took the opportunity of a twenty-minute talk with the Captain, in London for a regimental dinner. Next day there was tennis at Allfarthing Lane. I believe the turf of the forty back gardens into which those courts have long since been converted must still retain some essence of the suppressed excite-ment of the particular game played that day. Frank saw Lilla home to her door and said good-bye as usual, but when Lilla came downstairs a moment after Frank had left, she saw flowers on the hall table—two bunches of violets and something else. There was an envelope. On it was written "Miss Reynolds" in the large, good, confident hand which so well expressed Father's desire to be larger, more confident, than he seemed. On this occasion I see (the envelope is before me) he even emphasised that mood to the extent of the extra flourish of the long "s" in the double "s" of "Miss."

Inside the envelope, which with the contents and the remains of the violets was never for very long very far from my mother's reach till the day of her death, was the following note:

1887

Dear Miss Reynolds,
 I should very much like to have an opportunity of speaking to you alone for a few minutes this evening.
 I will come in again at about half past eight, and hope that you will then be able to grant me this favour.
Yours very sincerely,
F. C. POTTER

Father and Mother were married in 1889, and for the first years of their marriage all was happiness. The sun shone from the start. Both my father's parents were dead, but there was compensation in the fact that his share of the Rawlings money was wonderfully helpful. Then came a surprise. Mr Tapp, senior in the firm, died unexpectedly, and to Father's delight Mr Bird took him in as junior partner. Bird and Potter on the portals: Bird and Potter on the office door—and Father worked desperately hard to be worthy of all the honour being showered on him.

These long days and long Saturdays in the office were hard on Mother. As time went on she longed for more tennis-parties and Court Lodge visits, hoped to try out her bicycle, to get a glimpse of real country (the meadows between Wandsworth and Clapham were getting fewer and farther between), felt a little starved of music, needed an escort to the new novelty of the Promenade Concert. But when my sister was born it was the end of Mother's unaccustomed loneliness, and the album bursts out afresh into groups of admiring relations, with the new baby, cheerily supporting twice its own weight in clothes, stuck unable to move in the centre. Bird and Potter were beginning to flourish; and if Nightingale Lane had lost its last nightingale in the general carving up of its gardens, why not begin to think of moving outside S.W. altogether—to one of those houses by Wimbledon Common, even?

The move was to come, but it was in the wrong direction. In the mid-nineties the family luck had turned. Matty, Mother's favourite sister, was consumptive. The treatment of this disease seems not to have advanced, at that time, beyond the kind of therapy given to Keats. Mother devoted the saddest year of her life to nursing her sister. Then came the death of her father, the beloved Josh. Finally, the family failing asserted itself in an unusually bizarre form. Father was advised to improve his investments. A serious and solid broker, an old friend of the firm, knew how to do it. Father read the stock-prices with more than usual concentration, to find every morning that he was on the average five points poorer. With merciful speed the end came. Every penny of his private income had gone. The blow was made explicable but scarcely more bearable when it was learned that Father's revered and honoured friend was clean off his head when he gave the financial advice and had since been retired into an asylum.

Father was forty-four when I was born and weighed down by cares. Perhaps that is why I never at first fully appreciated him—he was, to begin with, too quiet, too serious, not positive enough for a child. But my sister does remember very clearly Father as he was before I came to add to his expenses. "He was my hero—handsome, debonair, vigorous, taking part in everything, picnics, gaieties." He was so gentle—yet the centre of all the social gatherings. "Every day he went to town in shiny top-hat, morning coat, his clothes always seemed new. . . . On holidays he had a wonderful pale-grey suit and a trilby. I remember exploring Folkestone Warren with him, searching for ammonites with a geological hammer. I rode over the wet sand on his shoulders, and suddenly teasing him I accidentally knocked his new trilby into a big shallow pool and it began to float slowly away. I was on the verge of tears, but he laughed—kissed me. . . . He was always like that."

There are pictures of that unshapely, flat-faced, deeply unphotogenic first house, where Muriel was born. It had quite a decent garden. But the new desirable residence in which we grew up together (to set the scene for my own childhood) was in no way an improvement. After the disaster it had to be more economical. It was in the same road but smaller and semi-detached. Though it took me decades to realise the fact, No. 36 was really a brute of a house, though perhaps not at all worse than the rest of the ten thousand houses which were eating up the open land over this part of London at the time. Indeed, it was exactly like them. Every house on this curve of our road was precisely the same. The same iron railings; the same front garden with box hedge and five dusty irises; the same-shaped two rooms on every floor, with a tiny "study" at the first half-landing and a tinier "maid's bedroom" at the second. At the back, the ground-floor drawing-rooms opened on to verandahs identically covered with thick green glass to mitigate the rays of the sun. This was of some conceivable use when these backed east, as they did from Nos. 1 to 18; but when they backed north (Nos. 20–36) this protection from non-existent sun created a kind of greenhouse of cold, preserving a perpetual dampness and a chill mould which percolated into the drawing-room and attacked the very roots of the piano itself, so that there was an invalid atmosphere even about Beethoven.

A great word of the 'nineties was "jerry-built." No. 36 was jerry-built to its finger-nails. It was not only that every water-pipe was exposed to the first attack of frost and that the hot-water system worked effectively only at the moment when the gong sounded for Sunday luncheon; it was the audible transparency of the building material. The Bains who lived next door on the attached side were exposed to every evolution and convolution of Potter music. When Jack, the half-breed Irish terrier with a long, heavy tail, stood in the middle of the drawing-room floor and wagged his tail with his special slow, vigorous rhythm, each china piece on each little table shuddered in unison. Full chords on the piano (and both Father and myself were fond of the noble effects involved with these) caused each glass ornament, bought by my parents in Venice on their honeymoon, to ring and vibrate in sympathy, their outlines grown fuzzy. The tiles in the hall worked loose, so that each year one or two more were missing. The brass door-knocker was a shade too light and a shade too mean, and the knob on which it struck was made of some kind of coloured tin, so that even the postman's bold double-knock was muted to a plink-plink. The walls were so cardboard-thin that it was impossible not to know exactly in which room everybody was.

Scarcely a perfect house for a lying-in. Nevertheless, on the first of February 1900 I was successfully born; and thus, because I turned out to be a boy, was happily involved in the first and only universally acclaimed achievement of my life.

CHAPTER TWO

Bad Day with the G.P.D.S.T.

EVERY morning for five years I used to walk across the familiar grass, cutting across paths and between gorse bushes towards the windmill. The little round island, in the middle of the pond I passed twice a day, had been painted by Turner. Hereabouts, Erasmus Darwin might have walked—perhaps *The Loves of the Plants* were inspired by the ancestors of those same buttercups and chervils. Behind the trees now, but visible in winter, were the Wren houses. If we crossed that railing we might see the seat where Zachary Macaulay sat.

We might, but I didn't. Some detours were the rule on these walks of mine across Clapham Common, but then I had far more important associations to interest me. Even if it meant being a shade late for school, for instance, I could never leave out a certain wooden post, just where Nightingale Lane first meets the Common, the base of which was continually revitalised by the regular Common dogs, and on Sundays by the more distant dogs as well, who came from as far as Stockwell or Streatham to run barking round the pond. I admired dogs intensely from a distance. I secretly longed to possess one, but could never say so because I had been told it was "not really kind to have a dog in London." Yet how easily these Common dogs threw off their melancholy. At this spot I would be certain to find at least one, his bladder never so empty that he could not squeeze out, with a cheerfully expansive stare over his left shoulder, one last golden drop to mark the visit.

After the dogs, I might take a rightish path and look at the place where we had been playing Kind Person Leading Blind Person. There was the rough side of the elm-tree into which, by sixty per cent accident and forty per cent the hypnotic effect of crime for the sake of crime, I had led my sister when her eyes were tight shut. But on this particular summer morning of 1906 I made certain alterations to my route. I had already lingered to charge my batteries with the sight and smell of the tar being spread on the road outside No. 36. Now I had to walk under the brick wall which shut off the greenhouses of "Tea-leaf Grange," as we always called it—one of the seen-better-days houses with big gardens on the margin of the Common. My approach to the Grange wall was along the shallow, dry ditch. There was a good reason for this. In Nightingale Lane I had been walking carefully in the middle of the cobbled gutter, except on the actual drains, round which I shunted with special small-looking steps which were actually fifty feet long. The gutter itself was several hundred yards wide, being the main waterway of the Panama Canal, now under construction. The drains were the locks, and although I was glad to see that these were in working order, the canal itself was not yet, of course, completed. Bands of workmen were still clustered on it, forced labourers dying like flies. The ones who were not dying like flies were especially working on the last remaining bastion between this point and the Pacific, now just visible from where I was standing. Northward now to this final obstacle. Slow but sure. On my left it loomed— to the ordinary eye the decrepit wall of Tea-leaf Grange. I reckoned that if every day, going and coming, I stuck my forefinger between the bricks under one bit of dried mortar and prized it off, the whole thing, aided by a last charge of dynamite, would fall with a shattering roar. Here came the wall. Smells changed from soft to sleepy, from sunny elm leaf to baked wall. I probed and pulled. It was nice, like picking a scab. The Panama Canal was that much nearer completion.

The scene changed. A moment ago I had been riddled with malaria and exhausted by a long day's work in the semi-tropical sun. Now, on the road across the Common, I was pacing the deck. Putting my sailor hat on the back of my head and changing it round (because "H.M.S. *Indomitable*" was at the back) I trod the deck of what must have been pretty well the largest battleship in the world. A vast battery of eleven-inch guns bristled on the foredeck.

But there already, just over the tops of the trees, I could see School, and I felt rather sick. In another five steps I was frightened by the intensity of this sick feeling. I doubted if I should ever eat again. I also felt hot and stuffy.

It suddenly came over me that the end of the walk was near, and that I should probably be having a Bad Day. This was my useful private technical term for things going wrong. I knew nothing of Fate, I merely recognised the absolute fact that on some days things went mildly right; on others everything went steadily wrong.

Usually on school mornings I made a point of rattling off a request to God in my six-second morning prayers. "Please make it a good day today." This morning, I realised with a shock, I had omitted this precaution. "Please Golemavgooday. Jeeshcry, Amen." I had not said this.

I moved sharply across the path. A beaming old woman looked as if she was going to say something to me, "Are you off to school?" probably. This would make me feel sick again. My sailor suit was thin cotton; I loved it: but Mother had made me put a vest on. "The sun's quite cool, you know, darling." Oh, no, please, Mother. But Uncle Jim, who wore a light overcoat even in mid-June, came in on her side. "Even admirals wear a vest under their uniform." Well this might be true. It might not. If I actually *was* sick, it would be possible just to go back home and say, "Mummy, I feel rather funny" or "I was sick." But unless genuine, this way out would for certain bring the retribution of five Bad Days running. No way out of a Bad. I now felt better. No good, of course, praying for a good day now. God's time for listening to prayers was 7.30–8.0 a.m. sharp.

Mother had called after me, "Mind you play the piano nicely." What was the point of that? I just bent my head down.

Then, "Have you got your music?"

"Yes."

"Let me see."

No. I wouldn't. I didn't want her to see inside my satchel—for a reason shortly to be explained.

I dragged my feet sharply to imitate a steam engine and swung my satchel round to imitate a piston. I was having doubts, that morning, about myself and music in general. Today I had to play something at the concert, before the School. Mid-term—the farthest possible point between two holidays. It wasn't the piece, "In a Hammock"—that was utterly putrid or potty—in fact, an annoying thing, it was much too easy for me. Just up and down the scale while Miss Pearl played chords in the bass. A duet. What annoyed me was that I was sure to be the first in the programme and sent up because (this was perfectly obvious) I was supposed to be the world record youngest piano player and therefore "looked sweet."

Another thing was that I was going off music a bit, and for a good reason. In the Easter holidays Mother had taken me to see Mrs Tom Gash, at Worthing. Easter at Worthing was one of the major pleasures of life, and visits to Mrs Gash were part of it. She was the Anne Thorpe photograph in Father's album, and although Mrs Gash was old, she was most beautifully dressed and still perfectly pretty, with a little, straight, white nose and a quiet, but helpless sort of laugh, which made me laugh too. She had an amazing parrot—the only one I had ever seen. She had, also good but less interesting, a pretty daughter who had a son called Stephen.

The parrot, who was believed to have been born in 1799, could sing "I'm quite crazy—love of you," if Mrs Gash gave him the notes. Mother took me along partly, I think, to talk about me to her, and about my newly discovered instinctive knowledge of Pratt's laws of harmony (I could "sing seconds" in a growling sort of way) and of course the way I played the piano.

"He's got such a wonderfully delicate touch."

Well, by a bit of luck, Mrs Gash said that though she hadn't got a piano herself, her daughter, Mrs Thomas, had one where *her* boy, Mrs Gash's grandson, could play, and he's got quite a nice touch too. I remember not liking the sound of this. In the end we had a sort of little audition. My piece was Grieg's "Watchman's Song." I was looking forward to playing this to Mrs Gash, since I greatly admired her and liked the Grieg. Mother had said, "It will give her pleasure" and I was excited at giving her the pleasure. I brought the music in a satchel, the inside of which was dirty or sticky. After being practised the whole of last term, the music did look messy and had a diagonal piece of purple paper stuck on the front to mend a tear.

"Hadn't I better turn over?" Mrs Gash said, but I said no, it was only a page and a half long. I didn't want people too close to me, anyhow. Mother put me off a little at the start. She had a whisper like a shout.

"Now don't take it too fast, darling."

I made more mistakes than usual. I usually enjoyed playing Grieg pieces. But all the natural vigour of the paper had been so beaten out of it that it would scarcely stand up. I did have to make the one turn-over, and this, combined with a certain limpness due to the sea air, seemed to remove the last trace of fibre in the paper, which folded up into a soft roll. Stephen, the grandson, was one of these boys with very good manners, and he held it up for me. Mrs Thomas was too beautiful to look at, but I half glanced towards her when I was playing the last line, which had a rallentando which I started exceptionally early and then drew out and made longer than I ever had before, with nearly three seconds between each of the last four chords.

The Thomas family, she herself perhaps, had been in some way actually on the stage and that made me timid of them. Stephen Thomas was at least a year older than me, and *what a pity*, Mother whispered to me at some point later, because I was the only possible recipient of her confidence, *they let his hair grow so long*. Well, when I had finished, Mrs Gash clapped her hands, but nobody said much. Stephen then sat down at the piano and looked disconcerted, or sad, I thought.

32

Father and Mother,
newly married.

Studio
portrait.

My favourite
"Auntie Herbert,"
my father's sister,
mother of Geoffrey
and Leonard,
aged 21.

Anne Thorpe, later
Mrs. Gash.

"Play the Chopin," his mother said, leaning forward so that her fair hair became the centre of light in the room.

"I think I'd better try the Beethoven," Stephen said. "I'm afraid it won't be very accurate" (with a distant smile at me).

I was wriggling about to get my old handkerchief out of my pocket to rub my nose; but it was covered with the remains of a nose-bleed. Then Stephen Thomas started doing the slow movement of the *Pathétique*. I had never heard of this, and when he began I was thunderstruck. There were great pauses and skilful chordy sort of tunes—a completely grown-up piece. He then actually did the first page of the fast part which followed—it must have been the fastest in the world. He must be a genius, I thought.

Immediately we'd got outside I started jabbering, "But Mummy—but Mummy—wasn't it marvellous?" However, I saw from one or two of Mother's remarks that she thought it was all a sort of trick, that this was a show-off piece, and it was a pity he kept the pedal down all the time. But I could see Mother felt offended by it, and this made me feel that I, too, had been put in the background. Would Mrs Gash ever admire me again?

Afterwards, when Stephen Thomas and I were playing on the beach, and lobbing stones at each other, I, by practically a hundred per cent accident lobbed one a bit harder, and it hit him on the forehead and left a patch of blood which seemed to me enormous. I shed tears, but he did not (nor did it seem to limit the unswerving success of his future career in the theatre and the arts, though my eyes still wander, with a touch of dread, towards the place on his forehead where there once was blood).

All this put me off music that summer. Anyhow I had changed my plans for my career. This term I was going to be an Artist-great-man. My drawing "Father's Walking Stick and Mother's Umbrella," full of little bits of shading, had been approved, in spite of skin-diseasy-looking india-rubber marks. It was to be hung up on show in the corridor, with one and a half red stars on it. Denys Roberts had drawn a picture of fairies, which showed he was "only a tiny little tiddly toddler," as Monica Hill said. Today my sailor's uniform and my long black stockings would underline the fact that I was older than Denys, who was going to sing "Frère Jacques" in the concert, and would probably wear short white socks, like Jacky Downs. I took a look in my satchel. There it was, the thing I had not wanted my mother to see—all safe. The little figure of a sailor. "Joseph" I called him. He wore a miniature sailor's suit, and a tiny cap with "H.M.S. *Indomitable*" on it like mine. One of my men—one of my crew. This, with my police whistle round my neck on the end of a lanyard, should show, if I produced them at the right moment, that I certainly wasn't a sort of half-baby, like Denys.

I had to make another little detour, this time to avoid three really big boys standing in a group—the long-trousers brigade, with severe grown-up faces, all wearing caps and therefore worlds above me—the bright blue caps plus white circle of Dean Todd's Preparatory School. Sometimes these Todd's boys shouted after us. Their faces were unsmiling and scornful. I was glad to drop in behind lanky old Noel Chiltern for the last two hundred yards into school. Although he was in the Upper II and nearly ten, probably leaving shortly, he was friendly.

Clapham High School (through the gates of which I was going to run) was a fine new example of G.P.D.S.T. (Girls' Public Day-School Trust). It was built in up-to-date red brick. The classrooms were sunny and airy. The entrance hall and main assembly rooms were generously floored and walled with expensive-looking wood, the mistresses were Froebel-trained, young, kind and charming; the atmosphere was light and bright and happy, and the junior school, my part of it, which took boys up to ten, was equipped on the best lines of the newest German education for the very young, with music, and movement, and all the good kind of emphasis on manual work which is now a commonplace, but which then (Froebel having only died about fifty years before) was modern, stimulating and part of the movement.

But for me, at that moment, the problem was not to run, on the way to Prayers. This is the difficulty, especially if one is so light that the slightest breeze will blow one like a leaf. But today, not show-offy at all, please. Not start giggling matches with Rosie Howlett. Not run in the corridors, and even if there was nobody in sight whatever, no sliding, although the corridors were so new and skiddy, smelling always of floor polish, a sweet-baked smell, mixed with a wake-you-up scent of fire-proof preparation. No sliding today. And another thing. Watch out for Mrs Woodhouse. Except for Lord Brassey appearing round a door in Father's office, Mrs Woodhouse was the only person in the world I was frightened of. She was very small and walked quickly and silently somewhat bent up, looking as if she was going to pounce, like a picture of Queen Victoria. Very occasionally people who had done something really wrong were sent to her. I had heard of cases when girls who had been almost inconceivably good had been sent to her also. It was possible, if I was good the whole morning, for about a hundred hours probably, I might be sent to her just for that.

At the moment Mrs Woodhouse was reading daily prayers. The School, 560 of them, were standing in the Assembly Hall. I couldn't see her, because my face was up against a great volume of skirts, the big 1907 skirts, with a vestigial hint of the bustle, which the older girls wore at that period. The only figure I could see was a gigantic plaster cast of the Venus de Milo which towered above everybody. But I did not associate this shape, which I regarded as a distortion peculiar to sculpture, with the female figure. This was natural because the young mistresses and the older girls at that time wore enormous blouses filled out with flounces, underneath which their waists suddenly became small in a peculiar, sloping-forward way. The Sixth Form girls, I noticed, made it a point of honour to wear belts too big for them into which they had to pierce a new hole to show that their waist was smaller than the smallest stock size. I took great interest in this. As the sides of the Venus de Milo were more or less straight all the way down, I thought this was the shape of statues, not women.

To the bracing tune of the Overture from *Rosamunde*, well known at No. 36 and therefore something I hummed loudly without changing my expression (No Talking was the rule, but not

No Humming), I joined the tail-end of the exit crocodile with an exact and sober walk rather as if I was on a tightrope, to show I was good, and took two sideways glances at Mrs Woodhouse, to see if she was especially watching me, out of the 560.

Period One today Botany, I thought, taken by Miss Dexter. I wished it was going to be Miss Pegler, my form-mistress, whom I sometimes decided I was going to marry one day. She was out of sight—and took none of my Wednesday classes anyhow. She had beautiful piled-up hair and the biggest blouse in the world, like a wedding-cake and the colour of coffee icing, with tier after tier of lace. Miss Dexter was old as a witch and wore a dreary sort of shawl; but to be good I was going to listen and look so hard she would notice me. Off we went as usual. Monica Hill was given a basket of fir-cones. She was a "good" pupil, useful and brisk. She took them round the class to put one on each desk with a neat little click. Manual study. I had known the Froebel word "manual" for months, and didn't like it. I didn't like Monica or her thin, greasy pigtails: she had a rather sneering sort of expression, as if she was going to sneeze, particularly when she talked to me. She gave me the least-good fir-cone, broken in the middle, and with one end mashed up—perhaps by a squirrel or a crossbill. I got up at once to say, "Please, Miss Dexter, Monica has given me a dirty fir-cone"—but I remembered my plan and sat down again without saying anything. We'd had fir-cones before and I hated them; but didn't absolutely loathe them, as I did acorns.

"You all know what that is don't you?"

Miss Dexter, like most of the more mistressy mistresses, had a "beautiful" voice. "Perfect intonation"—so much so that it was said that when she spoke words like "beautiful" or "soldier" you practically knew how they were spelt.

"I expect you want to know how it is made? And what this object is for?"

The cone was even more vapid than last-week's pollen. High and dry on my desk, it emphasised the indoorness, the sit-stillness everywhere. Already my legs were tickling and tingling to run. But I was going to listen exactly to what Miss Dexter said, al-

36

though her back was turned to us. She was writing on the blackboard what she spoke, making the words thereby doubly difficult to take in.

"The cone is a *fruit*" (she underlined fruit and she spoke the word as if it was made of jelly—a substance which, curiously, I disliked). "And each *scale* covers two tiny winged *seeds*. Now look."

She said it so slowly that there was time to think of six things between each phrase. I looked at the back of her neck, which was propped up by the whalebone supports to her lace collar. Very soft white skin bulged and flopped a little over the top of it, skin which looked untouched by wind or sun, like the pulp of fruit beneath its rind. I wrote it down. "Fruit . . . seed." If only she did not speak so clearly. Now—horrors—she was drawing the tiny winged seeds in brown chalk, to make them look different from something or other.

But I must listen. I copied her big picture of the fir-cone well. This was easy for a future great artist. If I drew hard, it shut out unrestful daydreams of real country, of acorns stamped down in the mess and mush by the pig-house at Bryn Cottage, or the springy mattress of cones below the Weymouth pines—near Sandbanks—something I wouldn't see for years, till next August.

The bell for eleven-o'clock break was ringing. "Now dismiss quietly, children." The running which had been bottled up in us for forty-five minutes was already leaking out of my feet. Now to stand in queue for elevenses, everybody making small continual jumps, the hair on top of the little girls' heads leaping a little higher than they did. Glass of milk—gone. Fine, soft, halfpenny bun, tasting of oven, perfect, crammed into my mouth whole. Then gym-shoes—and all weight was taken out of my feet and I was running, and we were all running, or rather skimming, over the netball court, across hard asphalt; yet I did not feel it. There was Rosie, hair rich brown and curly: let me get my fingers in it, pull her back, while she was running—she never minded, wouldn't start whining like fat old Patricia: she liked it, pulling my collar till I was throttled. There was the new boy Denys, unpleasantly young and small—it was said he was only five—his legs going fastest of all . . . Corinne—I did like her smock, with the roses embroidered in one corner. She was pretty. The shouts were all in my ear—yet they seemed far away and peaceful at the same time. Now I was chuffing, a steam engine: whistle and turn right for the sandpit, past the swing where Norman King broke his leg last term, compound fracture . . . compound fracture—*pound*-fracture —*pound* fracture—it made the noise of an engine steaming up hill.

"Children."

I stopped.

"Any volunteers today?"

It was Miss Dexter, in charge of gardening.

"Stephen Potter—you can have the broom all to yourself if you like. The path's very messy."

I had forgotten—Bad Day. Corinne and Rosie ran on and on away from me round the corner. Already they were as small as leaves, in the distance, while I stood on the stupid path. Clear and tiny came the screams from the sandpit. As a revenge, I did five minutes sweeping in useless jabs.

The last period that morning I liked—Geography. Also there was something Good I had forgotten. In my desk I still had my birthday set of crayons in ten colours: I took them out and arranged them in order, from bright to dull. The mistress was Miss Flynn, who was always smiling happily and exposing a lot of square-looking teeth, which were bone-dry, she exposed them to the air such a lot, by smiling. On her shoulder were pinned two fine smelly carnations. The subject was Australia, which I liked. After you'd drawn the sketch map of Australia, you buttoned it up, polished it off, tied it into place, added the punctuation mark, balanced it on the scales, by putting in Tasmania in the bottom right-hand corner—*bang*. No one else had coloured chalk. I marked the Great Barrier Reef in green, for seaweed. I was busy—and every spare moment I was at work on one of my geographical long-term plans as well. If I rubbed my pencil up and down between the ridges made by the grain of the wood on the top of my desk, I had discovered that the tiny trough would deepen. After a week it was nearly a quarter of an inch deep. In time, obviously, I would get about a mile underground. In more time still, though this would need work over a very prolonged period, probably using Panama Canal forced labour dying like flies, I would get through to Australia. In between grooving, I was working well at the map. Now more grooving.

Suddenly there was a shadow through the window of the door—dark, something cold. The door opened quietly: teacher and pupils stiffened into a position of "taking no notice." My face and ears went red. I knew that Mrs Woodhouse was walking quietly to my desk.

"That desk is school property," she said. I turned my face sharply down, away, rigid. "Valuable school property." Then she dived out of the room again. No punishment, of course: merely a widening pool of reproach in her wake. I had spoilt the desk—and it cost millions of pounds. For the remaining ten minutes of the class I sat quite still, head down.

Hours and hours later three o'clock was near, and it was time for the school concert. A few mothers, towers of hat, had been wandering stiffly round the grounds since lunch. It was not a full-scale affair; but Bad-Day-itis had made me nervous after all. In the after-lunch break I had had a practice on the platform. It took twenty-two steps to walk round the grand piano. I was to play with Miss Pearl. I was sorry it was not Miss Dobrée, because Miss Pearl did not smell so nice; but she let me climb up and put my head inside the piano while she played some notes.

So I was to start the concert. Why not Denys Roberts? He was the really young one. I caught sight of my sister in the audience, and she gave me a friendly smile. I knew this was decent of her, as she was already in Upper Fifth. One or two of her friends smiled too, and the result of this was to make me walk up on the platform with unsuitable stumping gait, to show I was not afraid, even trying to be funny, it must have seemed—my everlasting bad habit when shy, or feeling things against me. As long as I could dispel the little-boy suggestion. I adjusted the lanyard of my

39

whistle so that it showed. Sitting on the platform at the piano, the stool was ridiculously high: my feet were far from the ground. Miss Pearl smelt of disinfectant. The piece was much too potty for me, I felt. Mostly slow octaves, while Miss Pearl did rather more difficult things in the bass. To show it was easy I smiled at the audience. They smiled back. "Attend to the music, dear," Miss Pearl whispered. I did, but to show that this was not enough to absorb me, I kicked my right leg in time for the last few bars. All over. And clapping! I had done it. They would say "Well done." There were some of my teachers in the aisle. I almost ran off the platform; and then I really did run down the aisle. Forgetting everything in my relief, I came to a stop in a long slide, which seemed as if it was never going to stop. I had not meant it.

"Not in front of the audience, dear."

I don't know who said it, but instead of applauding me, they were reproving me. Baby-ish show-off—and I knew it. My sister smiled, but she seemed to be very faintly shaking her head. I made a face at Rosie Howlett, because my eyes started to sting. She made a perfunctory face back. I had not done well. Where was Miss Pegler? She would understand. I suddenly felt really wretched. I sat at the back with the rest of the kindergarten, on the floor. None of the mistresses spoke to me—I might have been buried underground: and Miss Pegler wasn't there.

Soon we were being signalled for, and I knew what it was—the form picture. I had forgotten—the midsummer term photograph; and I had been looking forward to it. Perhaps everything would be all right. There were chairs on the grass—and there of course was Miss Pegler. I ran up to her as hard as I could go.

Suddenly I was running *back*, even faster, to the cloak-room. I had forgotten Joseph, the sailor, left in the satchel, and brought to school specially for this. Everybody was in position, but with a push and clamber I was up on the chair, standing next Miss Pegler.

"Are you sure you want to have him in the photograph?"

What did she mean?

"Well, then, stand behind Kathleen, and don't push, not even in the slightest." Did she think, too, that I had been stupid in

I first achieve the central position, willingly accepted by Muriel, on my mother's knee. I had not then been put in place by my cousins Geoffrey (top), and Leonard, to whom I was later to pay such admiring tribute. Auntie Herbert on the left. Taken in the garden of which I write in Chapter Four.

The awkward incident of the school photograph. Miss Pegler is on the right. The girl in the dark dress is Corinne Griffiths.

the concert? "I'm not pushing" I said in a threatening voice. The photograph was over, and suddenly they were all looking at me. Monica was pointing at me.

"Why, he's got a dolly," she was saying, in her fearful voice, like tin.

"It's NOT."

"It's a DOLL."

"It's not—it's a sailor—the largest toy sailor in the world. It's one of my crew."

"*It's a doll.*" Some of the others took it up. But I was running and crying at the same time. "It's not—not—not." Nobody heard. I got my satchel out of the cloak-room and put Joseph carefully in the bottom. And then I began to run steadily, not crying any more, across the Common, down Nightingale Lane, for home. Now I was really hot, sweating. There were pools of sweat under my eyes. I felt funny. Home, I stuck my whole hand on to the door-bell, leaning long on it; then I reached high so that I could just flick up the bottom of the door-knocker to make it fall feebly on its tinny base. Minnie came.

"Where's Mother?"

"She'll be back in a minute. Why—look at you!"

I walked slowly up to my bedroom, with heavily limping action. I jumped on the bed, head in the pillow for a moment while a wave of sickening thoughts swarmed over me. I would have to go back and see them all tomorrow.

But was I *well* enough? Was I not really ill? One thing I had learned—a good trick: to feel my own pulse. It was fast, all right—very. Different indeed from the "One nasturtium, two nasturtium, three," etc., of normal. Ping-ping-ping. Now I certainly felt sick. In fact, perhaps I was really ill. Supposing I never went back again? Wasn't Freda Tusser prayed for, I thought, when she swallowed an orange-pip? I ate four oranges on Monday. Freda Tusser had appendicitis and died, and when it was announced in Assembly Room people cried. How awful Corinne would feel, if I died. Or my sister—it would pretty well kill her, I should think, much worse than for Corinne.

In the bathroom I felt sick again. I bent over the basin and did a tremendous sort of spit and cough. You could say it was being sick—though perhaps there was a stoppage like Freda had and I couldn't even be sick properly. Mother didn't seem to care what was happening to me, taking no trouble to hurry home to see me. Well, that sounded like the hall door.

"Why, darling boy, you're home early, aren't you? How did you do at the concert?"

So she had come.

"Why, what's the matter?"

It was all right, I said; but my voice must have sounded pretty weak.

"What are you doing?"

"I feel—I feel a little bit funny." Instantly Mother's hand was on my forehead. "Why, you do feel a little bit hot." She took my wrist. "I've just been sort of sick," I said. Scarlet fever. Diphtheria. Lockjaw. I was half-conscious of some such words turning through Mother's brain. I was anxious too. "Would you like to lie down on the bed a minute and let me take your temperature?" She put her finger to her chin. Now where had she put the thermometer? . . . It looked as if things were going to be all right.

I lay back. I knew exactly how it would go. Almost certainly I would sleep that night in her room while Father went to mine. First class. It would be the bilious-attack sequence. Next day would be bed of course. The nervy business of the visit of Dr Oram would have to be endured. Dr Oram never understood me nearly so well as Mother. Once I received from him an extraordinary shock. It was the last time but one I had had a temperature—99. Suddenly he had said "And don't send your Mother running about for things unless you really want them." Since then, however ill, I had taken off my sick-duck look with him and tried putting on a brusque "I'm all right" tone. Dr Oram sometimes came to us direct from Bolingbroke Hospital. His entrances were heralded by smells in contrasted keys. As he plunged the cold sucker of the stethoscope on my chest, an ooze of chloroform and disinfectant, eau de Cologne and Turkish cigarettes spread round me while he blew his nose like a trumpet. He always made me feel feeble and out of it. It was lovely to be languid again after he had gone. That evening, no doubt, Mother would read to me and I would have my last meal early with her, my favourite oil-lamp enclosing us both in the same circle of light, in absolute and final safety. Next day it would be even nicer. No doctor. I would lie in bed and see Mother get ready to go out to the shops. Perhaps I would see her put on her marvellous hat with fur across it, and then her veil, which made her in my exaggerating vision look so beautiful and dignified that I felt as if I must seem to her a screwed-up tadpole—such beauty must surely only admire something big and strong. Then mother would ask me what I wanted. "*Answers* and *Tit-Bits*, please." When she'd gone I could lie in peace and look forward to her coming back. Time began to float, and I would hear through a waking dream the wheels of the butcher's cart delivering from Viney's, as it rattled over the cobbled crossing of the corner, the spick and span trotting of the horse not slowing down for an instant. That boy drives much too fast, Mother said. Such a delicate noise, brisk and distant. Lovely to lie here—until it began to be rather surprising, surely, that Mother hadn't come back. She would obviously be wanting to hurry back if I was ill. The meat for lunch already delivered? She must have ordered it hours ago. Well, something must have stopped her. Surely she wasn't talking to Mrs Clarke at the corner, for hours and hours? I hopped out of bed to go to the window. Mind you don't get run over, she was always saying to me: mind. Mind. Mind. But does *she* mind? *Not in sight.* A policeman would come to the house. Does Master Stephen live here? Don't think of her and she will come. Don't think. Don't think. And there she was.

That's how it would be.

Mother had come back with the thermometer. "Now don't open your mouth at *all*." I pretended to talk, mouth shut—being cheerful though ill. Of course two days from now Mother would be

43

beginning to get too careful, just when I was feeling strong. Well, even now she was not going to make me wear a scarf in June. She took the thermometer out of my mouth. Mother had done Nursing—understood all about thermometers. You wouldn't think they were glass the way she handled them. Now she was staring at it so long I began to be anxious. Supposing I was 108 degrees, like the man I heard Dr Oram telling Mother about, who had tropical disease. Was it possible? Had I got tropical disease? But Mother was smiling.

"Why, you're normal."

Normal? I was silent a little.

"Do you think I'm all right, then?"

"Have a good early sleep and I'm certain you'll be all right for school tomorrow," she said. There was the remotest touch of firmness in her voice.

"I still feel a tiny bit funny," I said desperately. I could see the faces looking over the top of the school wall at me, laughing at me, pointing at me. The boy with the dolly. But I knew there was nothing I could do.

"You didn't do anything wrong at school today, did you, darling?"

"Of course not." But I was running away from her, already arranging in my mind the auguries and sacrifices to placate to-morrow. This was something I had to do all alone. Extra-slow prayers, including one for Minnie's disagreeable invalid sister, Rosa. A resolution not to speak to Monica, not one word: not to look in her direction. Last thing at night I would lick the place on the window-sill where the birds' mess was. I might even suck the blood spot on my dressing-gown as well. After all, two bad days running would be unlikely. I doubt if I had ever had two bad days running in my life.

CHAPTER THREE

Gleams of Hope

"Only one bad day running"—but the fact is that in those days there was hardly an unhappy two hours.

Looking back now there doesn't seem to be any obvious cause for this generally radiant state of affairs. Health perfect of course—and now fifty years later there is a voice which occasionally points out that there is no "of course" about it. Was it partly my sister? She was always on my side when support was needed; but these occasions were rare. Perhaps the gap in our ages—six and a half years—was a help. Parental attitudes to us were different—well defined, so that there was not much chance of jealousy between us.

My advent had been built up for her in a way which is classical and good.

She had been promised a pet in February.

What sort of pet? She remembers it like this.

"All I knew about it was that it would be a surprise and rather better than a dog or a cat. Well, the first day of February came. It was really snowing, and that made it nice. Also Auntie Ethel looked as if she had a secret. The funny thing is that I really knew by then; but I was determined to be surprised. Downstairs at breakfast I saw a new person altogether come in with a tray—a nurse in uniform. I knew for certain then. But as I was still small, all I had to do to hide my smiles was to lean forward and put my face against the tablecloth—press it hard against the edge of the table."

One of the first visitors was the inquisitive Mrs Olwen-Jones, whose long nose took an unexpected inquiring turn near the tip. She would be followed by Mr O.-J. who was so cowed by his wife that he used to wipe his feet on his doormat not only when he came into the front door but when he went out of it as well. Muriel, feeling possessive, nagged at Mrs O.-J. to get a first comment on the new baby, and was mystified when she got a disagreeable glance instead.

"Whose nose is going to be put out of joint now?"

Muriel didn't understand and merely thought it was some reference to Mrs O.-J.'s own memorable profile; but when it was explained to her she only laughed. "You were partly mine anyhow," was her thought. "And I took it for granted you would be Mother's boy just as I was Father's girl."

I was certainly "Mother's boy" just as Mother was boy's Mother. I remember being chilled when I first heard the phrase used pejoratively. Perfect parental kindness was probably the chief cause of these happy times, because it was a fact of life like the sky or breakfast. Before long I was to examine with tingling interest the Mr Dombeys and the Mr Murdstones being cruel to juvenile Dickens heroes and heroines; but I didn't really believe in such things until by a sort of coincidence-shaped-by-fate I discovered the factual reality of such things in the life of the first friend, outside the family, I was ever to make. I took my blessing for granted —even with impatience.

To balance this I should say that I took the ugliness and inconvenience of No. 36 for granted also. In fact I never thought of it as a bad house. On the contrary, it was a house of adventure. True, one got tired of it; but there were a hundred ways of putting that right. Kneel on the top of the upright piano and that damp little drawing-room became practically unrecognisable. I never fully explored the possibilities in the Old Bicycle section of the cellar, where Father kept worn-out and discarded bicycle-tyres. The staircase well was twenty different things, depending on what Muriel and I did to it. The stairs were a fine test for soldiers climbing in full marching order. If Muriel could be got to lower a basket from the top landing by a piece of blind-cord, we were in the Surrey Docks on a busy day, though when I had loaded the basket for the return journey, the bacon rinds hidden in knitting-wool were intended to be surreptitiously delivered to the Prisoner of Chillon, starving in the box-room.

Nor did I ever thoroughly explore Father's little study on the half-landing. Father's strength was that he did not throw things away. Improvident, Father would think, to shove over the bulwark a faded blue diary marked "Cash-book, 1883." Reckless to burn old whist-markers recording the upward graph of games won versus the Reynolds brothers in 1895. Odd numbers of *Vanity Fair* and the *Sphere* can always be useful for reference. The complete *Daily Telegraph* in which the Jabez Balfour swindle was first revealed might be most interesting reading in forty years—might be worth something even, a little: and so of course would sixteen of the fortnightly parts of *The History of the South African War*, by A. Conan Doyle, tied up in a bunch with the wallet containing the less-good negatives from the photos of the Isle of Wight trip, parts of which might be well worth printing, and a thin pack of concert programmes (marked "with Lilla") for the year 1890. About once a quarter Father would have a tremendous clear-out, at the end of which there was always more than there had been before, and more to look at. Then at Christmas this room was the scene of an amazing transformation. Traditionally Uncle Josh then slept in my bedroom—with the joyful result that I was moved to the couch in the study. From this prone position the whole room was transformed. In the morning dark of December, shapes were distorted. For a moment I did not understand where I was. In fact, so far as I was concerned No. 36 was a place of romance. There was nothing wrong with it whatever.

If the Potter family had ever been regular week-end-away people it might have been different. Uncle Josh, the socially expert, was the only relation to break into this field. It was to be many, many years before I saw the inside of a really comfortable country house. Had it been otherwise, the faults of No. 36 might have been more obvious. One is reminded how "Edwardian" describes the well-to-do people only. With the exception of Mother's hats, and the cut of Jim's jackets, there was nothing recognisably Edwardian

47

about No. 36. We sometimes saw luxurious London houses, like Lord Brassey's mansion in Park Lane, which incredibly had its own private lift. It seemed enormous, but now its delicate aristocratic line would be dwarfed by the hotel buildings. Here (or to the window of Uncle Josh's bank, which overlooked Trafalgar Square) we were taken to see royal processions—King Edward's funeral, King George's coronation. Our sense of superiority was heightened by the fact that some of the crowd below us had taken up their places sixteen hours earlier. I was in a splendid position to keep a beady eye on the Red Cross men dealing with casualties —slightly crushed children, ordinary cases of collapse and very occasionally an epileptic fit.

The chief glimpses of Edwardian feasting I got in those days were the tins of mixed and broken sandwiches, a treat for me, even when they were a little dry. These were left over from Mother's bridge-party of the night before. Edwardian social life for me was connected mostly with St Luke's Church and the Vicarage, the boundaries of which began just beyond our back garden.

A special day like Harvest Festival, a function not obviously connected with Wandsworth Common, was entered into enthusiastically by the two Miss Martlocks and Emily Gracechurch, who got twenty of the biggest marrows and cauliflowers from Gode's, the greengrocer, and put them between the feet of the stone angels signifying Commerce and Labour and draped them round the steps of the pulpit to give the effect of Plenty. These were days, minor Christmas Days, when we called at some of the biggest houses I ever entered, like Mrs Hine's. Once a year Canon Clarke would give a children's party, sending out invitations:

Games and Tricks
From Three to Six.

Canon Clarke was a huge figure of pale-faced geniality, a sort of temperance Falstaff, with spacious Victorian side-whiskers, and a waistcoat as wide as a sail rigged with chains for gold crosses, a spectacle-case and a fat watch which he would pull out clankingly as a signal for guests to go. He was certainly kind and lovable, though it was a surprising fact, never admitted or mentioned by anybody, that his sermons (now he was older) were a little boring and watery. He was a famous man to our family because he was the editor and founder of a placid, overwhelmingly harmless and successful paper for young persons called *Chatterbox*. He was eighty at the time I remember him, but lived many years longer.

Perhaps then the explanation of the enjoyment is that the pleasures came at well-separated intervals. In other words, there was a slow meting out, with long periods in between, which nevertheless had their own quiet glitter of looking-forward. I have known a few children who had all the things I missed—the big rambling house, the real garden, the dogs and ponies, the cars and the sailing; but I'm not sure that these unrationed treats have made them more happy. Take the theatre, which was meted out to me at the rate of about four plays a year. Not only was there no daily T.V. "drama" to blunt the edge of the excitement. Any comparison between theatre and cinema, even, would then have been to the overwhelming disadvantage of the latter. Although in 1910 a whole big page of the *Era* might be devoted to Film Notes, the cinema to us then was a sort of peep show, a Saturday-evening comic journey, a joke. 1910 was the year of Chaplin's first visit to America; and although it was to be four years before we saw Keystone Chaplin, there were the Keystone cops and the educated comedies of the sad-faced acidulous Max Linder. "Comedy, Drama, Travel" was the Holy Trinity engraved over the poky little entrances to the moving-picture houses. But "Drama" was to us always the biggest comic of the lot. The children now laugh at the occasional museum excerpts from these pieces and sometimes regard them as reflections of the dramatic taste of my childhood, making me want to answer back that this was an epoch which was still tingling with the impact of Oscar Wilde, a period able to grapple with the best plays of Shaw and Pinero, of Galsworthy, of Granville-Barker. Film "Drama" was always a family joke, and the captions became our watchwords. "Making his entrance unobserved—a shady Oriental doctor," "Three years

D

49

pass slowly for Grizelda." The cinematograph (including Kine-
macolor at the Scala) increased the glamour of the rare theatre
visits by comparison.

Other pleasures were rationed in the same way. There was no
large-scale commercialisation of children's books, for instance, no
Walt Disney Inc. atmosphere. True the "funny papers" were
made with old-fashioned machinery, full of phrases like "Biff Bang
WALLOP" and "chortled he." But the books were meant for
keeping. It was the golden age of children's classics. The over-
sweetening and loss of freshness did not come till after the first
War. Some were loyal to Kenneth Grahame; a rival clan to E.
Nesbit. Moreover, these works were new then: even young children were conscious of publication dates. *Just So Stories*, read
and re-read to me by Muriel till I knew the verse part of it by
heart, had been published in 1902. *Peter Rabbit* appeared in the
same year, but soon each year there was a completely new Beatrix
Potter to give an extra edge to Christmas. Father's finances would
just stretch to a subscription to *Punch*, but not to boy's magazines
for me. I was dependent on my cousins Geoffrey and Leonard for
a sight of the *Captain*. I made a dive for it on my visits and was
just able to keep up with the wonderful new school stories by
somebody whose very name sounded as if it might belong to a
popular boy in the First Eleven—P. G. Wodehouse. I read *Psmith*
in concentrated rushes. The *Boy's Own Paper* had to be delayed
till Christmas, when Mrs Hine, who lived in one of the few last
big houses in Nightingale Lane, gave me the bound annual
volume, every page of which I read (finishing about mid-February)
including every word of that endless serial "From the Slums to
the Quarter-deck: the Story of a Lad of Grit."

Reading was the chief run-of-the-week Nice Thing, with music
and games and railway-lines a close second. The music Nice
Thing was basically the acquisition of a new tune. You heard it
for five, ten, forty times and it was suddenly inside you. It might
be *The Policeman's Holiday* or "Drink to me only"; "The Lady of
my Heart has caught me talking to Another" out of *Patience*, a
psalm-tune by Turle, a Handel gavotte played by Mother, or the

Chopin Prelude out of the *Sixth Pianoforte Tutor*. The fact that you had to repeat it twenty times before you "got" it made the getting twice as pleasurable.

The chief reading pleasure is the first—the huge trick of learning how to do it. There are periods of pain, of inward belief that this tiresome progress will never be finished. I found these difficult to bear, and tried all sorts of ways of pretending I could read fluently—opening books, looking serious and turning my head from left to right. The thing becomes a great horse pill, sticking in the throat interminably. But when words to begin to slide in, the event is surprisingly sudden and complete.

Before that happens, the great art is to get clamps on to people who will do your reading for you. Father was Chief Reader in those days. The best moment of the week was the arrival of the weekly comic *Puck*, one penny, not a mere halfpenny comic like *Chips*, but *Puck*, which had just started to have two pages in actual colour, the colours never quite fitting the lines—a fact which used to distress me when it was bad enough to diminish the reality of my favourite characters. Sometimes I'd start waiting at four-thirty, though *Puck* wasn't due to arrive till five; and before the interminable half-hour was over I would have had to go upstairs to look at my new celluloid dolphin. And then there was *Puck*, lying on the doormat, new and stinking splendidly of cheap printer's ink.

"Father!"

The legs of grown-ups seem to push through treacle just when there is most need to hurry. Soon I was on his knee in his study, and there amid the smells of cigarettes lighted, cigarettes recently grown cold and stubs gone dry with age, he would work through every page of it for me. Saved for the last were the Adventures of Professor Radium, the inventor, who discovered ways of peeling bananas by electrical x-rays, or going to Australia by underground slide constructed with the help of mechanical moles. To make quite sure that neither of us would let our eyes leap ahead to look at the last pictures before we had read the first, Father would fold the paper up very small, so that we could only look at each "frame" separately and in the right order.

How marvellous to be read to. Father seemed to enjoy it as much as I did—in fact, because I enjoyed their less eager, more indifferent voices, I preferred the reading of Jim or Ethel or Mother —Mother reading *Brer Rabbit*, never completely comprehended by me, and therefore, though fascinating, to be placed below the rank of first favourites. Was the "Tar Baby" a real thing, or wasn't it a real thing?

Now I can hear Aunt Ethel, her voice amused but a little sharp because she was waiting to go down to bathe. We are in Blackberry Dell at the top of one of the little gullies leading down to the sea below Ballard Down. How *funny* Auntie Ethel was, reading this chapter. " 'Not the same thing a bit!' said the Hatter. 'Why, you might just as well say that "I see what I eat" is the same as "I eat what I see!" ' " How far away from nasty things I was; from that horrid bird that whistled outside my window at No. 36 in the frightening early morning light; from my pillow at Mrs Bess's lodging, which I hated because it smelt of cat. Here the sun was warm and sleepy. I could smell blackberries. Aunt was pausing. "Go *on*."

"He won't understand this," she was saying to herself. Her unwillingness increased my desire for it.

"Anyhow *go on*," I said.

Books are more real than life at this stage. The idea that they were written, that there is an author, is an intrusion. I refused to believe that *Through the Looking Glass* was only a dream, as the framework tiresomely implies. I skipped by instinct Lewis Carroll's poem at the end which suggests the whole thing is make-up. "By Beatrix Potter" suggested a label not a person. True, I was soon saying that "Ballantyne was a billion times better than Henty": yet if I thought of Ballantyne it was as one of his own heroes (it is usually an "I" telling the story): but I did not, and still do not, want to know a single fact about his life, or of the life of the authors of *Owd Bob*, *Black Beauty*, *White Fang*, *Little Women* and *Good Wives*, or *The Family at Misrule*. The first book which I ever thought of as being written by somebody was *Gulliver's*

Travels. I disliked *Robinson Crusoe*, which was more goody-goody, if possible, than *Tom Brown's School Days*, besides suffering from long descriptions, particularly long descriptions of making things work, a power which has been so long in me unnourished that the act of changing a spare wheel, or a record on the simplest automatic gramophone, leaves metal surfaces scratched and smeared with my blood.

By contrast I loved *Gulliver's Travels*, which I read in an edition illustrated with brilliantly apt little woodcuts. There was a life of Swift at the beginning, and since that was illustrated in the same way I read it as one of the stories and thus understood for the first time the conception of a person writing a book. Soon after this Muriel told me a first fact about Kipling, already revered by me as a name. We were reading, or she was reading, the song in the middle of the *Just So Stories*:

> For far, Oh, very far behind,
> So far she cannot call to him,
> Comes Tegumai alone to find
> The daughter that was all to him,

"When she was still very young," Muriel said in her grave voice, "Kipling's own daughter died. Just a few years ago. He wrote this story after she died."

This was the beginning of my discovery that an author was a real man. The song about Merrow Down, now seemed to me disastrous, yet somehow overwhelming in a sweet way, making my eyes burn many times with tears, which were not less painful because they never quite became liquid. It seemed to make reading a more serious business altogether. In fact never again was a book to be a decent secret place of my own. Whether I liked it or not, the author was going to be always with me.

Ways of moving were another part of life the pleasures of which were increased by being released to me slowly, and singly. The delight of a new way of travelling is that it reveals a new through-the-looking-glass sight of familiar ground. Shopping with Mother had many good moments connected with the mosaic floor and sawdust and dogs of my private low-level world in shops like Sainsbury's; yet there were boring patches connected with the steady slowness of Mother's pace always straight down familiar, worn-out old Ramsden Road. But when I was allowed to bring my iron hoop (wooden ones no good) every bit of road seemed re-created, especially the detail of curves and carriage entrances, and the different textures of pavements. *Slow* hooping was my particularity—I considered that I held the record for this. An extraordinary sense of balance was innate in myself I fancied— slow but never falling. A special touch on the slow hoop could make it ring deeply within itself like a gong, particularly on the hard level of the right-hand pavement of Sudbrooke Road. Sometimes the hoop was linked in my mind with the life facts I was discovering at that moment. For instance, slowly revolving it would be the world and on its rim not people, of course, but millions and millions of microbes of different nationalities. It was a long time before the hoop was ousted by roller-skates. *Then* of course the whole road system between Clapham and Wandsworth Common was transformed more completely than ever. Shopping was one continuous treat. The route had to be altered from Ramsden Road to the parallel Endlesham Road because on the right-hand side there was no intersection at the bottom of the hill. Then on its flagstones, beautifully smooth and seemingly specially created for this purpose, I could get speed up for a swoop down and a rush up the other side. During the height of the roller-skate period I hardly ever took them off even in the house—it was even possible to get slight movement in the hall, though it brought the tiles out of their sockets.

There was Dr Milne who owned a car in our road—I remember something towering, open and fawn-coloured. Very occasionally he took me with him to his garage. But these excitements were too rare to hope for; and the ordinary transport pleasures soon to hand were sufficient for anyone. Going up to London to shop with Mother, for instance, meant not only the complex experiences of the Army and Navy Stores, which always included at the very least a long stare at the train section of the Toy Department, a long smell in the Leather Goods, a long stew in the splendidly fearful odours of the menageries and a melting visit to the Sweet Department to buy Pyramid Creams—a sweet so delicious that I had to try not to think of it on ordinary days; it meant also a drive up in the Victoria tram. Electric trams had the dignity of newness then —there were still horse trams on view. Our tram was apparently drawn along by invisible hands or, as I thought, sucked along by some force emerging from the slot between the lines. Anyhow, it was possible by getting in front of the little queue and running full tilt down the middle of the compartment to get the seat just behind the driver, and to observe him carefully all the way up, to see the air-stream flowing up under his great overcoat and stiffening it out like a bell, to see how the wind and cold seemed to make his cheeks permanently rocky and red and cheerful. It was the carlessness of those days which quadrupled the effect of the first bicycle. This, of course, brought huge new areas, the Crystal Palace and the golf course on Wimbledon Common even—completely foreign parts— well within range. With two spanners, three speeds and a new oil-lamp, this new B.S.A. was the best present I ever had. It cost eleven guineas, and seemed in no way less marvellous to me than my first car twenty years later.

Visits to the museums and the Zoo were sufficiently spaced out to be considerable treats. In the Natural History Museum, my favourite, Father used to play, in early days, a trick, in which my collaboration was necessary. He would lead me up to the life-sized model of the whale or the reconstruction of the *Diplodocus carnegii* with my eyes shut, on my honour, so that I could get the full shock, the moment of fear that perhaps I would not be able to orientate, to recognise, to tell the difference between front and back. The Diplodocus sent me off on a long, lax, unscientific enthusiasm for prehistoric animals. They were a great theme for funny drawings at school. I still have a grudge against George Morrow for using his authority as a *Punch* artist to perpetuate in his drawings the fallacy that palæolithic man and the giant reptiles were contemporaneous. The results of such dis-educational behaviour take years to undo.

There were iron models of extinct Saurians in the grounds of
the Crystal Palace. This visit was rare, but one of the more
sharply interesting partly because of the element of ghostliness and
fear. In the grounds I had to savour the shock of the Pano-
rama and enjoy the dread of the water-chute. The great grubby
building itself was ghostly partly because it was so enormous.
Max Beerbohm used to say that he always pulled down the blind
of his railway carriage passing Penge Station, so as not to be able
to see the monster. How willingly now one would stop the train,
Penalty £5, for one more glimpse of those great glass haunches.
Inside everything was unreal. The iron statues and ornaments,
the giant ferns and agaves, the empty side-chapels deserted except
for some statue group being energetic all by itself, the confused
rumbling echo, like the working of the sea in an unexplored
cavern, the peeling paint, the general emptiness and vagueness
made it seem as if it were perpetually the last day of the season.
Even when we were children it suggested in some way the finish
of something. When we were all much older, and the burning
down of the Palace coincided almost precisely with the Abdication,
we knew we were right.

The carlessness of my father's generation also certainly increased the pleasure of the seaside holiday. The edge of our appetite for the sea was never taken off by casual day-trips to the
South Coast. The act of booking seats in a train and emerging into
the New Place made the experience more complete. Above all, the
carlessness of the coast generally helped to keep the edges of the
seaside from becoming domesticated and to preserve even in
August a decent element of country loneliness.

Our ration for seaside holidays was generous—a fortnight at
Easter and a month in August. Father and Mother and later
Muriel early showed what I, the youngest and the most conserva-
tive, thought to be a mistaken tendency to experiment in choice of
place. There were two years in the western wilds, for instance—
both mistakes I thought—one at Teignmouth and one in the unheard-of place of Bude. There was one extraordinary year when as
if in pursuit of the hidden secrets of the North-east Passage, my

family chose to pioneer as far north as Whitby. Whitby then was divided into Residents and Visitors on one side, and a mysterious section called Poor People on the other. This poor section was a notable experience for me. It was interesting to see children with bare feet, and legs which were dirty right up to the knee. I could not help lingering by the extraordinary smell which came from the drains and the corners of the road, never forgetting, according to Mother's instructions for action in the presence of bad smells, to spit largely whenever I noticed one. It was in the days long before the era of free milk, and vitamins were only on the verge of discovery: in consequence, to my mingled dismay and pleasure, in this Poor People area, a quarter of the adults were bandy-legged, and the knees of half the little children were so wide apart that their legs formed almost a perfect circular O. Mother was full of sympathy for the poor angels, but said that these bow-legs were due to parents who allowed their children to walk too early. Anyhow, it was clear to me that it was the Poor People's fault.

But on the whole Mother and I managed to keep these divagations within bounds, and in the end Worthing at Easter, and some place in the Swanage area in the summer, became the fixed rule. The special interest of Worthing was that it contributed my sole experience of hotel life. This would in itself have been enough to fill the last month of the spring term at G.P.D.S.T. with pleasant anticipation. The Marine Parade Hotel was a tall, narrow, Regency building with no disadvantages whatever except a w.c. which was so unbelievably lofty that its ceiling extended beyond the reach of any known broom and was therefore packed with generations of cobwebs, so that I had to keep my head bowed not to look at them. What it did have was a dining-room with menus, four and even five courses (although the fish portion was so small that Mother always gave me hers as well to make up) and a male waiter, who called Father "Sir" (in a mumbling way) and whose waistcoat was so complicatedly stained with the browns and greens of the different versions of the two main Marine Parade soups, that I stared at it whenever it came level with my nose, though with a withdrawn impersonal expression so that the stare wouldn't be noticed.

Thirdly, there was a room marked "Billiard Room." This place was also marked "Smoking Room" over the door, and it did contain an actual billiard-table, about one-third size I should say, with cushions which somehow made the ball thump or hop on contact. But the whole room was filled with the savour of cigar-butts, chalk, billiard cloth—the exact unvarying smell of billiard room which has thrilled me ever since. If the weather had been too fine I used to long for rain so that Father and I could play uninterrupted.

I loved Worthing. It was where Mrs Gash lived, it had the long, flat sea-wall along the top of which I could walk, it had Luff's, the little home-made sweet-shop at Broadwater where we used to make our yearly visit by hired carriage, it had the Unfinished Hotel, one huge towering solitary wall of which stood all alone to the west of the parade—monument to the Jabez Balfour bankruptcy episode which had shocked the balance-sheet side of Father's mind so profoundly. On our last morning I always walked the full length of the parade saying good-bye personally to each lamp-post, each iron chain post and each breakwater, waving a general farewell, also, to those fine fresh pebbles over which, a fortnight before, I had run so happily down to the edge of the sea. The sadness of those last days seemed to reveal the melancholy of Worthing. Worthing was fairly unfashionable in those days; but now that no seaside place in England has any pretensions to exclusiveness, perhaps the quietness of its Regency back-streets and Victorian frontages will bring it back to favour once more.

For the summer holidays we finally dug ourselves into the Isle of Purbeck—which generally meant somewhere in Swanage or near it. There were rival holiday factions among our neighbours. The Ventnor people listened coolly to talk by Scarborough people, and Scarborough thought little of St Ives. For years to come, when we were planning the long vacation on some snowy day in February, everybody, Muriel and Father especially, made strong moves to imitate Uncle Josh's enterprise and go to Knocke in Belgium or somewhere in Normandy; but Mother and I were only

half serious, because we both knew it would be England and probably Swanage in the end. I remember later the cold douche of the
discovery, in my last year at school, that Swanage was to be considered rather trippery and ordinary. I remember having to admit
to myself that the name "Swanage" did have a batter-pudding
sound. To that rather sniffy boy Flap I used to say we were going
to the "Corfe Castle area". Flap always spent his August in the
Highlands—something to do with shooting. "Swanage sounds
like Relations," Flap said, thereby getting the two favourite in-
gredients in my holidays with both barrels. Years later I was made
indignant all over again (dumbly till now) by Paul Nash's essay on
Swanage. He lived and painted there, yet he was offendingly
superior about the "ridiculousness"—describing Swanage, I think,
as the graveyard of the local stonemasons who made good, the
mausoleum of the great Mowlem and the great Burt. These two
fortune-makers had died long since, but they do still perhaps
dominate with the purposeless little Mowlem Institute, the stone
clock-tower on the sea with no clock in it and stuck on nothing in
particular, or the superb aesthetic floater and historical anachron-
ism, I might add, of the Purbeck marble column surmounted by
realistic cannon balls and erected to commemorate the sea victory
of King Alfred over the Danes.

There was always one good but brief family row during the
holidays: usually brought on by two wet days running, all food
and no exercise. But apart from that we enjoyed every hour of
these Augusts.

They began with a ceremonial walk on the first day. Had there
been any alterations or "improvements"? Hardly ever, thank
goodness. The same shops and the same old friends inside them,
as we went the usual round to get the sensible walking-stick, to
groan while Father bought an absurdly floppy sun-hat or jeer
when he went to the chemist to buy some "Indigestion Mixchah"
(for third-day stomach trouble in this dangerously new climate and
foreign latitude). We would keep an eye out for those fine Swanage
fixtures, Dr Pierce and Mr Jackson of the golf club (never to alter
—never, for forty years, to age). Of for that essential and

admired holiday family the M.-J.s: or the Bevan boys, who un-
fairly actually lived in Swanage, or rather in the bay, of which,
swimming or sailing, they were the lords, always annoyingly three
shades more deeply browned and bleached than the most diligently
healthy visitor. Best sight of all to look for was the *Bournemouth
Queen* or the *Monarch*, paddle-steaming stoutly out to Old Harry
Rocks for the five-thousandth time, but still with the pride and
polish of a maiden voyage.

After a week or so we were old seaside hands, and felt ourselves
boss of the whole place. Our four part version of "Sing a Merry
Madrigal" was in full working order: and for lighter music,
marching back from the Scarlet Dominoes at the Mowlem Institute, we would sing the new "Alexander's Ragtime Band," besides older songs brought up to date.

> Let's all go down the Strand
> (have a banana)
> Let's all go down the Strand
> I'll be Peary you be Dr Cook
> I'll tell Shackleton to sling his blooming hook.

Is it true that I inhabited a rather different Swanage in those
days? Instead of the stiff little emporiums and cinemas of Station
Road there were fisherman's cottages and tiny shops roofed and
walled in the kind of Dorset stone which seems to grow freshly out
of the ground. On the front Powell's, now the big photographers,
was then only a tiny kiosk just under the lee of the Mowlem and
served not only by Powell himself, his white beard turned yellow
by the fumes of acid, but also by the two Miss Powells, their arms
stained with hypo up to the elbows, but kind and helpful even after
having spent half the night developing the entire Swanage photographic output of the day before. This generally included a reel
from my No. o Brownie, to see the results of which I waited outside the shop fifteen minutes before it opened, shivery with anticipation.

In those days, anyhow, the stone gifts of Mowlem and the em-
bellishments of Burt all seemed to fit into the cosiness of the little
town, with its curve of sea, safe and sunny, the soft waves clucking

among the wooden roots of the pier. On the Peveril Point side of the curve, the south side, the walk was up the hill towards more stone—near the quarries in fact. There was no touch of grimness about these shallow mines. The stone was warm and lively. It was many years before Natural History was to give me a new eye with which to enjoy this coast all over again; but I recognised the content of crushed shell which gave this stone such a light and animal texture. The walk would be up past the quarries, past the REST AND BE THANKFUL seats into the area of the "Castle," a sort of battlemented stone tea-shop, to see the pick of the Burt showpieces. Essential to visit once a holiday (we usually kept this for a rainy day) was the Purbeck stone Great Globe, the map of the world chiselled on its surface. Though rather wretched with little rivulets of running water at a wet moment (the Globe got smaller and smaller as we got older and older) the yearly sight of this thing was always a pleasure and a shock. Near by there was the stone map of the South Coast, with direction arrows pointing not only to the Isle of Wight (out of sight behind the headland) but also to the romantic unknown—to France the unexplored. Dieppe . . . Cape Finisterre. Let into the airy cliff above was Burt's stone plaque, to remind us that even these glorious bounties would not last for ever:

THE SOLEMN TEMPLES, THE GREAT GLOBE ITSELF.

I enjoyed the reference to the modern marvel before us, and the delicate allusion to the fact that even the most permanent seeming works of man, not forgetting those set up here on Durlston cliffs, might one day disappear.

YEA, ALL WHICH IT INHERIT SHALL DISSOLVE.

Father, reading it out, would lift his voice, but although this lifting had the curious effect of making his voice even less audible (it may have been the wind and the rain as well), I began to know and appreciate the lines, and to respect Father's grave expression.

A splendid walk to do on a rainy day; and if it was really a rough day we would take it half a mile farther, along the cliff path high above the sea, pay sixpence at a little wicket gate to an old man as weather-worn as the hawthorn and juniper trees and like them permanently bent eastward by the west wind, and then climb down the slippery tunnel to the Tilly Whim caves, where the Purbeck stone is torn back and the tenacious Portland foundations beneath them make a platform for the sea to saw and suck at. One last fling from the unquenchable Burt (LOOK ROUND AND READ GREAT NATURE'S OPEN BOOK on a smooth wall of the oolitic limestone) and then, on really long-walk days, we were away to the complete wildness of the coast beyond, the gentle wildness of Dancing Ledge, the tragic gloom of Chapman's Pool, the stinking seaweed, heavy with flies, or even, when we were much older, the remoteness of Kimmeridge Bay, and Arish Mell Gap.

On another day, a sunny day, the walk might belong to a different world altogether. Old Swanage, Mowlem and Burt wouldn't be in it. It would begin on the Ballard side, on the sandy part of the beach: and this was Parsons territory. All the bathing tents here had "J. Parsons" stamped on their front flap, the raft was a Parsons raft, the café with its lending library of fifty novels was Parsons, and I believed that the waves and the grains of sand were somehow Parsons as well. In the centre of it all the man himself would be standing, in those days. I admired him more than anyone else in Swanage, more even than Mr Jackson, the Hon Sec. of the Golf Club, and Father himself was nervous of Mr Jackson. I admired Parsons not because of his height and great girth, which were remarkable, nor even because of the fine salt-beef colour of his face, nor the majestic gaze at the horizon, his small eyes looking far over my head, the calm stare of the man who has changed the face and fortunes of his own folkland. What fixed my attention were his feet, always bare beneath his tucked-up trousers, and looking as if they had been exposed to the weathering of sand and salt water for centuries, so that even his big toenail was worn down to a vestige, a silvery semicircle about the size and shape of half a threepenny bit.

For the walk, the Parsons sand must be left behind. We would shuffle up the shallow cliff on a path between the warm brambles, pulling a bit of bracken to whisk away the flies, then along the foot of Ballard for the climb up Nine Barrow Down—and there once again is complete wildness: not the feral sea-coast battlements of the cliff-side this time but the small wildness of a chalk hill. Below to the right stretches the darkness of Egdon Heath to add to the loneliness, with perhaps one spiral of dust in the distant middle of it, as evidence of one road somewhere, and one horse and cart. Then suddenly over the Western end of the down, the ruined towers of Corfe Castle, their outlines dazed by the evening sky behind them. Like the baseless fabric of this vision? The words were buried away far too deep for me to think of them. Soon there was the important business of scones with cream in the tea-garden of the Banks's Arms Hotel.

Date of such a walk might have been 1910 or 1911. These were particularly good years. August 1910, especially, was packed with extraordinary incident. I knew a big treat and surprise were blowing up for the end of July, and sure enough Mother and I went down to Swanage four days ahead of the others: and I had the unheard-of privilege of staying alone with her, and in a hotel—the Victoria. Surprise: she was going to rent a little house for us. Incredible—we were to have a house in the country (to be sub-let during the rest of the year). "The Rest" was like No. 36 in style: in size and shape it was a No. 36 bisected down the middle and one of the halves thrown away. But the railway line was at the bottom of the garden, and if I stood by a certain gate and leaned over, the four-down-trains-a-day would swirl by within four feet of my nose, and the lines would be bouncing beneath the weight of the wheels.

1911 was the most wonderful hot summer on record. Next year in the Royal Academy (to which we all went every year) there was a picture of trees round a pretty lake on a hot day called "The Halcyon Days of 1911"—which seemed to me, when "halcyon" was explained, to establish in an extraordinarily satisfactory way the fact that last year's fine weather really had been fine, and that I had enjoyed it.

There were ups and downs, of course; nor was I invariably

allowed to rule the roost. About 1910 I experienced a disappointment. A failure of loyalty.

Mother had relented on the subject of dogs. Her fears that it would mean work for Minnie, that the garden wasn't big enough, that the dog would grow despondent, were all unjustified. As soon as she bought it the dog was an instant success at No. 36, and had taken charge, though in a genial way. It was only I, the official owner, who felt a slight sense of disappointment. The dog, called Jack, was bought for three and six from the greengrocer. It was an Irish terrier of sorts, a large lively puppy with a long tail. We knew nothing about dogs at No. 36. We were inclined to think that the dog's tail should not be so long, though I believed it to be some variety which naturally had this. We had heard of cutting, but Muriel and I had agreed that this would be cruel. I remember sitting in the drawing room that evening, alone with Jack the first time. I was at the table, the dog was lying alertly by the fire, head on paws, gloomy eyes on me. I felt at a loss. Near the age of ten most things I wanted I prayed for. I remember saying words to the effect "Please God let Jack like, honour and obey me."

The prayer was never granted. I stood up, no doubt too suddenly. The dog gave a high annoyed bark. I approached him, hand held out vaguely.

"Good old dog," I said. He growled.

"You are my dog," I said clearly and slowly. The dog gave three high barks; there was even a suspicion of a howl.

"Quiet, Jack," I said more firmly. Not too early to start training, disciplining, I thought. After ten minutes of this Minnie came in, saw the puppy, and bent down ecstatically.

"Oh the sweet little boy-boy . . . the treasure, the sweet boy."

She sat on her haunches, crowing at him. The dog wagged its tail roughly, licked her ear and knocked her cap off.

"Din-dins," she said, and Jack got up and trotted out after her. That was to be the pattern of my relationship with Jack.

The annual visit to Luff's, Broadwater, Worthing.

Early
reading.

My uncle Herbert as I last saw him.

CHAPTER FOUR

Jim and Auntie Herbert

BEING happy is not knowing whether you are happy or not—
never thinking about it, as indeed I never did at this time. Once
you admit there is something missing——

I was not going to admit it. Certainly not yet. A complete
August by the sea once a year ought to be good enough for anybody; but, all the same, by child-measurement the interval from
one August to another is rather a long one—more like forty months
than eleven. Besides, "seaside" was something different from what
we were beginning to want most. Buried in the centre of the new
cheap suburbia, yet before the age of the new cheap cars, what we
longed for was country. It was years before I myself, always in a
London school, knew the country look of a fine June (and there
were plenty of them then) or the absolute difference between early
and late July. When Father bought No. 36 the shores of the country were much nearer. Clapham Common and Wandsworth Common must still have had strong touches of their nineteenth-century wildness. Nightingale Lane and Burntwood Lane were still
half worthy of their names. My sister, whose country-hunger was
more clearly defined than mine, used to aim her walks at a big
field near Wandsworth Common full of marguerites and campions.
She tried to imagine that a disused plot in nearby Sudbrooke Road
was a meadow not a rubbish heap, until one day the discovery of a
dead cat destroyed the rural fiction for ever. By 1908, for me, everything in sight was tasteless anti-country. No road with a wild grass
verge to it: no blackberry bushes in the autumn; no clinging vir-
gin grass to roll in, no good manly mud to splash through, no distances. Battened down under sensible mackintoshes or watertight
roofs as we were, there was no real rain, just as there was no real

sun. Above all, there was no smell of the country, to change with each hour of the day.

Worst of all would be a fine Sunday. Let us take one round about May 7. The fact that I would almost certainly have to go to church would turn the fresh sunshine into yesterday's Lyle's Golden Syrup on an unwashed-up plate. How could I make myself once again get through this "hour and twenty minutes" (a full four hours by my time scale)?

"You'll wear your nice suit, won't you darling?"

As I thought, of course. Everybody going to church. Well, let's make the best of it. How about this idea, for instance? I might *get good*—no temporary feeling but something which was to last for ages. I would make myself think of the words of the prayers, "for the poor . . . for the sick," although, unpleasantly for me, after a heavy Sunday breakfast in the heat, this last phrase was associated in my mind solely with the image of people actually being sick.

The possibility of being made good by a church service was a reality to me. On Sundays in August we used to march from Swanage to Langton Maltravers—two and a half miles—to hear the rector, Mr Coulter, conduct the service. The simplicity of his manner, the cogency and brevity of his sermon, his impressive way, after a pause, of closing the Bible at the end of the sermon—all made me believe in the goodness of the Christian religion. Mr Coulter could certainly give me a general feeling that I was perfectly good, although this was sometimes hard to distinguish from being perfectly well. Anyhow, on the downhill march back to Swanage, walking back with the Watkins and the Smiths, our feet felt as if they were an inch or two off the ground.

But new St Luke's, two minutes' slow march round the corner, was different from Langton, and after five minutes of the service I knew my thoughts would wander all the same. Mr Salmuson's voice when he intoned seemed to be inside and outside my head at the same time. Was I perfectly well, it sometimes made me think? Having known the words of the opening prayers by heart long before I could understand them ("That we may hereafter live a godly, righteous and sober life") I found it difficult to mean the meaning;

and indeed, all those items which belonged to the first third of
the service were clouded by the thought that this was only the first
third. It is true, however, that the psalms came now and I enjoyed
singing them, liking the race-between-hurdles system of fitting
different-length verses to the same tune; and the sweet-sop taste of
the nineteenth-century ones (played by me on the piano interminably all through one holiday) made me feel religious. The *Te
Deum* one must admit was worn-out old cabbage stumps again.
Very occasionally we had the *Benedicite* instead, a splendid change.
The remarkable words of it referred to those best of old friends, the
things I knew only out of books:

> O ye Wells, bless ye the Lord . . .
> O ye Whales, and all that move in the Water.

All this made me exchange pleased glances with anybody in our
pew who would look at me.

The Potter family in church had a good pew, next the aisle
three rows from the front. We all felt some pride in each other.
I was certainly proud of Father on these occasions, quite at home
in his churchwarden's frock-coat—so much more comely and at
ease than in his seaside clothes. He had a charmingly sincere way
of handing the plate, a modest straight back when he stood on the
chancel steps for the offertory hymn. When, to top this, the hymn
was the one of Father's own composition, my face was slightly red
with pleasure. I looked neither to right nor to left.

I could make myself listen to the lessons; but after the second
one came the ding-dong dirge of "I Believe." Gloom settled on
the church, and if the sun was slanting temptingly through a door
I must keep my mind off it. Distractions were hard to come by
in St Luke's. There were no gloomy corners, no chance of
ghosts, no cold and dripping tombs. There was stained glass, of
course, 1902, through which it is true very occasionally a ray of sun
might alight on my head to make me feel that Jesus was chalking
up my goodness and my enthusiastic way of saying prayers. It was
a red-brick church, with pleasing decorations in mosaic.

There was, however, always a change of one interesting thing.

Mrs Bentham-Cook might bring her daughter Sheila, who though twenty years old was shorter than me and had something wrong with her. Sheila might start making a long gurgling *"Arrr"* sound in the sermon, or possibly even a sharp *"Rrrak."* On one splendid Sunday she was led out, making this *"Arrr"* sound followed by *"Rrrak"* right down the centre aisle. What I might call a medium-weight distraction might already have come if the Magnificat was sung to the music of Bunnett in F, instead of an ordinary psalm tune. Although this, of course, was meant as a show-piece for the choir, Mr Arrowsmith, the chemist, who sat a little behind us, would sometimes (alone of the congregation) join in adding a tenor part developed on an instinctive method of his own. If nudged by Mother, Father might feel he ought to look round at him frowningly as a sort of protest. As a compromise, Father turned round, but instead of frowning would look pleasant. We might have the Litany, which was almost interesting by the very in-incredibility of its length. Also it was read by old Mr Cave from a most unusual position. He knelt in the centre of the main aisle about ten feet in front of my nose, so that I could examine his boot soles millimetre by millimetre.

Again it was just possible that, in the absence of Mr Clarke, Mr Cave would do the sermon. Mr Cave must have been the oldest curate in south-west London. His regular job was part-time visiting preacher at Wandsworth Prison. The interest here was that his sermon was incomprehensible not only to me but to everybody else. Mother used to giggle a little. Mr Cave half moaned and sang as he spoke, and then suddenly would say clearly at the top of his voice: "It is the *heart* . . ."

Best thing of all which might go wrong was that the new organ, put in cheaply by two men from Fademan's the plumbers, working at a cut rate (after hours only), was liable to "cipher." This interesting technical word meant that one rather high note on a piercing reed-stop sounded continuously as soon as the motor was switched on. The organist, Mr Drummond, became expert in con-structing a sequence of voluntaries based on this permanent note.

Much more likely, all would go with deadly smoothness. Even

the final release into the sun would be full of discomforts. No possible chance of running in my uncomfortable church clothes. Father and Mother would stand—actually stand—talking to friends, while mad electric currents shot through my legs. Hats would be lifted twice as high on Sundays, taking twice the time, while my feet itched with a stinging rash. Next would come a walk of deadly slowness across the grass of Clapham Common, which smelt of stale dog. For the afternoon it would just be the back garden of No. 36. True, a year or two ago I had discovered two ways of breaking the tasteless familiarity of this small square. One was to spend the whole afternoon walking round the top of the outside wall, which for a time did change the perspective and angles completely, besides giving me a view of wild-looking trees in the Garth and the de Paiva's big garden beyond. The other was digging. By going really deep it was possible to see ground which not only I but nobody else had ever seen before. And if I got down below four feet I came to a cold-Christmas-pudding layer of caked gravel. Sour smells buried for hundreds of thousands of years swam up into my face as if a gas-tap had been turned on; and though, of course, I knew nothing about the geology of gravel-beds and the evolution of the Thames Valley, it did cut beneath the platitude of geranium-and-nasturtium, and showed me it was possible to pioneer even at No. 36.

Instead of the little chimes, which made our holiday churches so inviting, the St Luke's bell was single, severe and metallic. On this particular Sunday, which was full of depressing sunlight, it did occur to me that I might just cut church altogether. The eight o'clock bell had sounded more flat and uninspiring than usual, a single note with all the fruit squeezed out of it, leaving only the rind.

"I don't want to go to church this morning." I was perfectly free to say it. I had once done this before. I could have a good oil with my new oil-can. Oil Father's bicycle, oil my roller skates, oil the points on my railway, oil my sword, so that it would easily and silently slide into its scabbard. I could oil the front door so that it would be useful work. But I knew that I would hear the sound of the eleven o'clock service from across the garden.

When your fathers tempted me, proved me and saw my works.

My favourite part of the service. One could not quite hear the music of the organ, only a vague thumping from the bass notes as if people were moving furniture. From outside the church looked surprisingly small and pathetic. Poor Mother. She must be wishing I was there. I felt half sorry even for the church, without me. Even the *Te Deum* would sound thin and sad. The fine day would be spoilt however I got out of it.

There was however one way out, with honour: one last chance. This could be the escape. Supposing—I hadn't planned this, it suddenly came to me—supposing by some heavenly miracle Jim wanted to go to Warlingham.

My Uncle James (for some reason I had always called him Jim, and for a joke they let me continue) lived with us in the second floor back. I began hanging round Mother. "I don't suppose," I started; then with a rush: "I don't suppose Jim would be wanting to go to Warlingham today?"

"But I thought we were all going to church together this morning."

Mother was disappointed: I felt myself that no good would come of Avoiding the Nasty. But Mother spoke again.

"You can always ask him, darling."

I was upstairs standing outside Jim's door. I stopped and listened. Music! He was whistling to himself between his teeth—while he brushed his hair, I guessed. Always a good sign I knew. Jim looked pleased to see me, but he always did. He asked me to sit down a minute. He was always wonderfully polite. It went with his smallness and neatness and boniness. The top button of his jacket seemed fastened extraordinarily high on his little pigeon chest. "Had you any special idea?" he asked me. I said I was wondering whether he didn't want to go to Warlingham today? I made an assing-about joke. Didn't he think Leonard, my cousin, would blub tremendously if he didn't see me? "There is consider-

70

able chill in the air," Jim said. Even in my happiness I could not help feeling scornful of that high, stiff collar on this hot day. What would Huck Finn have thought? But now Jim was teasing, because his back was to the window when he said, "And do you see those threatening rain-clouds?" (peering at the gas lamp in the corner); but I was already afloat, knowing it would be all right. Soon we were walking, Jim's short little legs keeping pace with my near-run to the L.B. & S.C.R. Wandsworth Common Station. First pleasure, steam train. Next, passing Balham Station, where there had been a fire and where half the woodwork was blackened cinders. I took in the smell of this richly, standing up against the window. Then, in a few miles I had managed to get the window for the event which celebrated the opening of the occasion—for the moment when suddenly the drumming of the train through the long cutting fell away and there before my eyes was the pool of empti-ness, the change in blood and nature—the disused chalk-pit on the Warlingham line. Here it began—the country.

The chalk-pit had gone. A fleeting shade—the first great nice thing was over. But soon I would be stepping out into a supply of more nice things than I could cope with. I sat down again and looked at Jim. I knew he wanted to pull the window up again. He looked quite tiny in his corner. Sometimes, in the morning, I used to listen outside his bedroom door. *"Oh . . . oh* dear," I used to hear him saying to himself. His shelves were covered with pill-boxes—he was always very careful about his health. Sometimes he would give a very prolonged but perfectly delicate soft and man-nerly belching hiccup. As soon as he got back from work in the evening he would walk softly to his cupboard in the corner of the dining-room, pour himself out a small whisky, fill up the glass with a roar from the Seltzer syphon and take little bites at a thin arrowroot biscuit. Father, Mother and Jim all took their drink with a sad, distasteful expression, as if it was medicine. Coming in-to the room twenty minutes later, I would know Jim had been there because of the delicate transfusion over the room of the smells of whisky and (just as strong to my nose) of bitten arrowroot biscuit.

But the train was slowing down. That wonderful sensation of

carving into the platform! I was out and standing still in the sun.
Everything was made small and quiet by the sun. The lumpy,
wooden planks, the carriage doors beginning to bang already, the
way the guard didn't bother to blow his whistle but just gave a
wave—it all made the station seem like a homely family party, all
part of the country. So was the long hill we had to climb, up to
Bryn Cottage. I hadn't seen a hill for weeks. And here was Leonard, my cousin, on his bicycle come down to meet us. "Such a
charming, nice-mannered boy," Mother was always saying, but he
was something a thousand times better than that to me. He was
very tall and very old, about twelve, with tremendous hands which
could grip both of mine in one so that I couldn't get away. Look at
him now, coasting down the hill on one pedal and (marvellous
trick) it was his right foot on the pedal. He stopped the bicycle
suddenly with terrific brakes and a sort of telemark and a whirl of
dust. Of course I did not greet him. He might not have liked it. I
would be aloof, hard-boiled. "Watcher mate," he said (after talking to Jim) in the splendid imitation of Cockney he always used at
this time. "Watcher" kept making me laugh all the way up the hill.
I forgot Jim.

Up the hill and past the house on towards Butterfly Walk. We
would meet the others coming back from church. We did not ever
really get to Butterfly Walk. Unfortunately we always met them
too soon; but there was a sense of Butterfly Walk in the offing.
Uncle Herbert and "Auntie Herbert," as I called her, and Geoffrey.
Geoffrey was even older than Leonard; even more handsome. He
was tremendously clipped and firm and exact in his speech. His
eyes were large and commanding. Both boys were high up in their
school O.T.C., and both were exceptionally good at imitating the
voices of sergeant-majors. It couldn't have been better.

Soon we were back at the house (modern, gabled) for a pre-
lunch check-up on the garden. This was so big that you could not
really see the bottom from the top. I had to run all round it at
least twice. It was a real garden with rough places and bushes and
a little wood, besides the big lawn and the official flower beds.
There was Bluebell Dell and a steep slope at the bottom.

First of all, a test thing. Geoffrey and Leonard would want me to try their latest prototype of the home-made four-wheeled cart, with front wheels steerable by string. I was the only one of them small enough to get in, and they wanted to experiment to see whether it would get down the path of the steep slope without falling into the ditch at the side. I knew this was coming. It was the only shadow over the visit. I was bad at the steering. But as long as I got through it without getting hurt hard enough to cry, all would be well.

They always learnt new technical facts from this trial run, and while they started taking things to pieces I could wander off alone and experience again that perfect feeling of floating, of everything all right, of everything friendly, which I had when I got out on the station platform. It would come again best if I stood near the chicken-run. In those days the true sound, to me, of deepest country, i.e., the deepest I knew, was that soft yet penetrating small bray, which at ordinary moments, the quiet times between the hysteria when they were fed, came from the hens. Years later, when my standards of wildness were more advanced, a hen would be the last thing I would choose. I might care to speak of the light twittering of dotterel, alone in the great reindeer-moss plateau on top of the Cairngorms. But this mad little hen-sound was just as perfect wildness to me, mixed with the feeling of lying on my back in tall, uncut grass, and staring at the clouds.

Then Auntie Herbert's voice—"Lunch is ready, boys." Then Leonard being very funny, beating the gong as if it was a big drum in a band. Then Uncle Herbert repeating the call, which annoyed Geoffrey and produced a clear and cutting "All *right*." How strong and jutting Geoffrey's chin was. My own was rather soft, tailing away.

Mountains of food for lunch of course. We boys did all the talking. No Uncle Josh to stage-manage the show and keep us all attentive. Jim was always shy of noise and sat rather bent up over his plate. Uncle Herbert was nervily benign, behind iron-rimmed spectacles. If anyone dropped a fork, or splashed gravy, he would explode into a little ineffective, "Oh, good gracious," or a mechanical

73

"Mind—mind." This seemed to bend Geoffrey back like a spring. He would twang back into position with an "All *right*, Father." Auntie Herbert of course was perfect in all the row—perfect comfortableness, perfect common sense, capacious kindness and perfect humour. Any kind of maleness always amused her. Geoffrey carved—but if those capable hands were sometimes a little too strong and the knife gritted on the plate, a "Take care, take care" would burst from my uncle against his will. It would be like a whiplash to Geoffrey. Both boys were in the centre of the age when it is difficult not to be irritated with one's father at meal-times. A fierce "All *right*" from Geoffrey. But my aunt just laughed at them.

Of course Uncle Herbert was living at home then. Perhaps he felt the boys a bit on top of him. Perhaps they didn't quite appreciate his notebooks. When I had finished eating I had a nice long stare at his face. "Of course he is a little bit *plain*," Mother used to say, indicating strongly that whatever faults Father might have, everybody agreed he was handsome. As a matter of fact, I was pretty fond of the looks of Uncle Herbert. He had a tremendous country suit which not only smelt pleasant, but was so thick in its tweediness that his coat almost stood up by itself when he took it off to work in the garden. It was a nineteenth-century face I suppose—one which I was often to see again in the photographs, taken in the seventies, of the fathers of eminent Edwardians and reproduced in their autobiographies. The elements were a pair of humdrum spectacles, a big red nose and a big round beard so solid and exact in outline that it looked false. Like Josh, he had been in banking; but unlike Josh, he had never been able to enjoy his time there. His tastes and hobbies were country. The very day, the exact hour, that his pensionable age arrived (his sixtieth birthday) he signed every meticulous last letter and closed every ledger with solemn precision, but with burning excitement. So came Bryn Cottage, Upper Warlingham, which for him meant not only the country but also a chance to be alone with the two objects of his greatest love—his notebooks and his wife.

Of course I was aware that after lunch Uncle Herbert would take me up to his study and show me his notebooks. My attitude to these notebooks might be described as multivalent. First of all, what did my heroes, his sons Geoffrey and Leonard, think about them? Not sure. Obviously in a way they were what my school friends would have called a little bit potty. They were notes he had made, perhaps, about a small mound, in the field above Butterfly Walk. Or a sign of a Roman Road, or the mark of the foundations of a Tithe Barn.

Uncle hauled down two big books from the shelf, so heavy that they fell with a thump on the desk and the little study was full of dust lifting up in the sunlight. Today he was saying something about a "soffit"—nice word—and he showed me a little water-colour sketch of a beam with carved marks on it. If I could open his paint-box I liked it better. He had a magnifying-glass in his hand which he kept gripping and ungripping with a convulsive movement of his enormous bony fingers while he was explaining to me. Perhaps the chief exhibit would be something which he had written in print in the *Warlingham Parish Magazine*—not actually print, for the Mag. was reproduced by jellygraph. I liked staring at his hand gripping the magnifying-glass. There was something thrilling to me about this grip, and no wonder. At a time when I did not know the difference between a chaffinch and a starling I knew the name of the shrike or butcher-bird because of this hand. The shrike is a carnivorous bird and impales its meat on the spines of the blackthorn to mature for eating. Uncle Herbert, making one of his spasmodic impatient clearings at the bottom of the garden, had scratched his hand deeply on one of these thorns, and the hand had festered and corrupted so violently that the surgeon had cut off two of his fingers. This was a great event for me, and sitting by him at his desk I had a splendid close-up of this monstrous three-fingeredness, this huge bony claw, and the seams in the skin where the amputation had taken place. If Uncle saw me staring at his hand he would slightly withdraw it. He would keep it bent back under his sleeve. "It looks so horrible," he once said in one of his convulsive mutters. "Hateful—horrible." I think he felt it must be unattractive to my aunt—as if she loved him for the perfection of his physical qualities.

75

Then he pulled out a note about "a scratch dial on an East jamb near Caterham . . ."

"I think I'll go to the loft now, Uncle."

He put the notebooks back in place, slowly, one by one. It was all right for me to go. "Letting me play with the boys in the loft" was a rule of these Sundays. The boys suffered it well. Auntie knew it was the thing I loved most. Jim knew that the wish that I *should* play with them had been expressly implanted in his ear, with a noisy whisper, before we left home. "Those boys have at least been taught to use a saw," Mother would say. Frank was quite hopeless at such things. "Wouldn't it be wonderful if you could make something, a sort of little shelf for yourself? A special place for your *Captain?*" I never had the *Captain*, and anyhow what would be the point of simply cutting through a plank? But in fact Mother was always afraid that I would never be really good at using my hands, and that I might saw through a finger. Leonard's hands were so capable and mobile, made equally for strong grips and delicate adjustments. I was inclined to keep my short fingers held out straight, as if they were the rays of a fan, or, less organised even than that, as if they had been cut out of dough, for pastry. Mother was torn between a vision of pride in a wall of bookcases made by me, and a fear that generalised septicaemia might follow a cut.

As I was climbing the ladder up into the loft I could already hear it. I sat on a sackful of sawdust and listened. "Play it again," I said. "Certainly," said Leonard, "if the audience will raise one finger to indicate which he requires." He bowed low. How funny he was. Of course this was the most wonderful of all their possessions, though familiarity had made me take it for granted. A phonograph, with three records and an enormous mouthpiece. The records were cylinders: we usually had one of them on most of the time we were in the loft. "I will have Wan U Swee," I said. Never having seen the title written, I thought it was something Chinese. Each of the cylinders started with a roar, then a scratch, then a rumble, then a voice like a parrot saying "Edison Bell Record." No. 1 was Harry Lauder singing "I Love a Lassie," which

76

I rather hated. No. 2 was the comic one with the good tune we could all sing: "Parp, *parp*: parp parp," the overture to *Tannhäuser*, and Leonard was funny after it was over and did a very good imitation of the whole thing, including trumpets and the violin arpeggios which come in during the last half-minute. No. 3 was Wan U Swee. It was different again. It was something I could never quite hear and never quite get out of my head, and yet it purveyed a most clear and definite effect of excitement and strangeness which increased every time I went to Bryn Cottage, so that in the end, though I could never whistle it, I seemed yet to hear the sound on the way to Warlingham about the time I got to the empty chalk-pit past Croydon. It was years before I knew what this music was.

The *Wand of Youth* is one of Elgar's programme pieces. The second suite begins with a March, grave and awkward, like a man on stilts. Then suddenly Elgar inserts a different tempo, slithery and delicate, and the key changes to major. Perhaps it was the pleasure of this change—the delight which a snake must feel when it sheds its skin—which gave me the feeling of excitement. This was how I began to think of it. There was the door into Bryn Cottage garden, and inside the garden there was the door into the loft, and inside the loft the door into this music.

Soon Geoffrey was showing me his new big vice made of steel, and the ordered nest of his tools, not broken, like ours at No. 36, and with parts missing and left around so that they could never be found, but all in special racks, the different bits for the drill arranged like organ-pipes in order of size. It was all too hopeless. They were patient, but I doubt if I was allowed to touch one of these things for ten seconds before Geoffrey snatched it away and said "Not like that." The Bryn Cottage Express, too, gave me as much uneasiness as pleasure. This was the model railway—and in the Bryn Cottage loft there was a permanent track of it laid down. Their gauge was No. 1: mine, at No. 36, was o. Their engines came from Bassett-Lowke, mine from the toyshop in the Clapham High Road. Though I might affect a loyalty for o gauge, the advantages of the Bryn Cottage express dashed my spirits, particularly as the sun was low enough now to be climbing well up the ceiling and digging into the cobwebs half-way up the walls of the loft, which meant that the marvellous day was nearly over except for watching Uncle Herbert feed the chickens, with lots of fussy exclamations from Uncle at the one independent-minded hen who always managed to escape. "Dratted little beast, don't *do* that, don't *do* that." His voice sounded as if he was wringing his hands. I called out good-bye, but he didn't hear me.

I tried to keep up conversation with Jim, my benefactor, on the way back; but in fact we were both silent. On the reverse journey the chalk-pit was something I tried not to notice—the final drawing down of the curtain on the good day. It was difficult to know what to do when I got back. To go and look at my trains would be quite wrong—feeble. Play about a little on the piano perhaps. Have another try at Captain Marryat—but every book and picture-book in the house seemed extra stale. Try and avoid Mother's "Well, how did you enjoy it, darling?" because I couldn't and wouldn't say one word about it. Wanting to bury myself in bed: wanting to get away from everything, and every person. Not even saying goodnight to Jim, forgetting to thank him for the treat—forgetting to notice him, because he sat still in his armchair, with his book.

Heaven knows how long it takes to see these fixed figures as changing people, with a past and a future. My sister was quicker than I at seeing relations as if they were real persons. Uncle Jim —the quiet and diffident one; but my sister points out that not only was there a time, before I was born, when he was gay and lively; before that again he was the clever, gifted and favoured one also. Jim the perfect young personal private secretary with his exact manners, his diffident presence, his deftness, his languages— besides the romantic fact that he was employed by a famous man, frequently mentioned in the newspapers. When Lord Brassey's *Naval Annual* made its annual appearance, Uncle Jim was mentioned in the introduction. At home he was the smart one of the family, the happy dandy with the wide grey tie and pearl tie-pin and presentation cuff-links, and a great name for telling funny stories and singing comic songs.

I myself never saw Jim like this at all, because the great blow of fate caught him soon after I was born. I never heard the comic songs except for one, the tune of which he used often to whistle between his teeth. Very occasionally we heard the words of the refrain.

> He really was a very pecu
> Oh yes pecu
> A most pecu
> He really was a very pecu
> A most peculiar man.

Of course I identified him completely with the "peculiar man," whistling this tune between his teeth when he was cheerful, or sitting in his armchair staring at the fire and making no sound and very little movement when he wasn't. I "knew"—that is to say I had been told but had never comprehended—the story of the tragedy. Once the go-ahead Jim, the lucky Jim even of the 'eighties and 'nineties, had actually got engaged, although he was Jim, the shy of women. It was after Father had proposed to my mother. With Father as cover so to speak, Father protectively to windward, Jim braved the critical eyes of Court Lodge and proposed to the next most pretty sister, Lucy. Charming quartet. Double wedding? Far from it. The engagement was on, off, on until, when Jim was in his early forties, the two got married suddenly, in a burst. . . . An ideally happy couple with a pretty, sunny little house. . . . Six years of perfection—until one day Lucy was taken off to hospital for a sudden, serious operation. In two days she was lying there dead—and Jim just stood at the foot of the bed, holding my mother's hand so tight that she could hardly bear it, and repeating as if he was explaining to himself, to Mother, and stating it to the whole world "Lilla, that is Lucy . . . Lilla that is Lucy" until his voice got louder and louder, and Father and Mother had to take him away and bring him home.

Muriel remembers the funeral, and "the horrible sight of grown-up people crying," and "everybody dressed up in black for years and years." It was mixed up in her mind, she says, "with mourning for the death of the old Queen, and the South African War glooming on and on." After the funeral Jim came home to No. 36 for the night. Of course Mother wouldn't let him go back to the empty house. You must stay here a little, she said. The little became twenty-nine years.

In early days, particularly, uncles and aunts were treats, so far as I was concerned. To have an uncle permanently on tap was a piece of luck. Dark days meant nothing to me, and if I ever thought of Jim at all, it never occurred to me that there was anything to be sorry for him about. On the contrary, I was always trying to get him moving. I used to stump up the stairs one at a time calling out "Jim, Jim" at the top of my voice, and there he was, sitting still!

"Jim, you're late for tea."

"Oh dear, so sorry," Jim would say in his tentative voice.

"Jim's coming," I shouted, thumping back down the stairs, "The Avenue," by Hobbema, swaying slightly, the oil-lamp standard in the hall buzzing with vibration, a tile from the mosaic on the hall floor somehow shooting out of place. In the hall I looked back to make sure, through the banisters; and there, of course, were the black legs of Uncle Jim, as silent as an insect's, delicately descending in my wake.

Jim's stay with us was temporary—permanently temporary. That helped to make it bearable for Mother. She did occasionally complain a little to me, much later, half stopping herself in mid-sentence. He helped to make the budget balance, and that was partly the point. It would make it easier to send me to a proper school. He still had his bit of the Rawlings money. He was generous with tips. And he elaborated the art of being out of the way. He had a kind of acknowledged territory in our dining-room–sitting-room on the left of the fireplace—his own armchair, one size smaller and one degree less comfortable than Father's; and he used to sit pleasantly and completely cut off from the general family swirl, while he read his favourite novelists—Turgenev, Balzac, Flaubert. The fact that he read Turgenev and French

My Sister Muriel

Aged 3.

Aged 6,
as I first knew her.

Aged 17.

Uncle Josh
(Josh II),
being Josh.

Uncle Josh, playing
the name part in
Don—one of his
favourite characters.

novels in French was certainly an extra insulation, one more invisible curtain. We got in the habit of talking through him, past him; of playing games almost on top of him and yet never violating the territory.

There were one or two unspoken arguments, undeclared feuds. Half the shelves on Jim's side contained Jim's books. The shelves on both sides had been finished off, by the ineffable Fademan's, with a varnish which never dried, in twenty years, so that all the books stuck slightly. The outside ones, particularly, needed a tearing wrench before they were freed (the noise of unsticking is always associated in my mind with reading *Chambers's Encyclopaedia*). But Jim thought a different kind of stick-proof finish was Father's responsibility (he was only there temporarily, anyhow). Father thought Jim might have helped. So it was never done.

Of course I hated the fact that his presence sometimes put a slight stopper on our noise. The piano in the next room must have sounded terribly loud in his ear. My Beethoven quick movements must have tried him; but I believe my Wagner period coincided with the merciful beginnings of his deafness. I myself wonder, now, how he stood it. Years later, in my creeping-out-of-the-chrysalis stage, I was as strong-minded in my criticism of people who "gave way" to tragedy as Mr Dombey himself. Myself ignorant of what tragedy meant, I even thought of asking Jim firmly why he didn't *break Fate*, lay the ghost, start a new life. As poor Jim was by this time seventy and decidedly deaf, I am glad he was spared that particular lecture.

His retirement at the age of sixty-five increased the pressure. It was difficult for him not to be rather more about the house. His presence began to get more seriously on Mother's nerves. He made a buoyant effort to find little things to do; he tried to suggest that there were important reasons why he should be out to lunch, so that he would be out of the way. He developed a new trick of *hovering* (the secretary bird, we used to call him) standing still in the hall not quite sure (though it had been clear to him a moment before) why he was there. Between Jim and Mother a measurable degree of hostility—of course mostly unconscious—began to develop. It was interesting. I sympathised with Mother, and I admired the technique of Jim's hostility—which he pursued without the remotest alteration of his perfect politeness and determination to keep in the background. It might simply be the way he didn't ask Mother to pass the sugar, but sat courteous and immobile, looking comfortably hopeful that it would somehow be passed all the same. It might be in the use he made of being deaf.

"Good morning, Jim."

Mother would say it in her clearest voice as he sat down to breakfast, with a "surely he can hear that" glance sideways at me, which of course Jim saw. Counter-move—Jim does an exaggerated lean forward and carefully cups his ear, putting it almost under Mother's nose. As he got deafer we all fell into the habit, an outrageous one, of carrying on conversations just below the threshold of his hearing. He had plenty of the necessary wit to take occasional revenges for this. Mother might say for instance:

"Stephen was always so gentle, as a baby."

Perhaps Jim had made a slight reference to noise—

"Just a touch . . . an occasional delicatissimo on the piano perhaps?"

"Stephen has a particularly good touch, when he wants." Mother's voice grew firm. "And the funny thing is that he was the gentle one, as a baby. Not Muriel. I came home one day and found the nurse in tears. Muriel had bitten her." Jim was reproved, yet he leant forward to pursue the subject.

"Was that recently?" he said.

"Jim, *dear*!" Mother laughed; but Jim had scored.

The last phase of Jim might be mentioned here, though it came much later. It was a surprising one. He began to play his life out of key, or perhaps it was the old Jim turning up once more, after all.

He suddenly became rather positive, and rather jolly. It began by his prefacing his seven-o'clock whisky with a visit to the Salter's Arms in Nightingale Lane. This was known. He was seen coming out of it. By the temperate standard of my family this pretty well amounted to "drinking."

Sometimes Jim would come home in a mood which can only be described as a determination to score off somebody. If a dull, duty guest was present when he came in, he would put on an expression of exaggerated concern when he was introduced (he seemed to demand an introduction) and say, "When precisely did you say you unfortunately had to leave?"

More than once from the crow's nest of his lofty bedroom I would hear him singing his song, very gently, but still definitely audible:

> He really was a very pecu
> A most pecu . . .

Once I glanced in through the half-open door to take a look. He was leaning zestfully out of the window, staring at the blackbird on the sooty top of our holm-oak. On a warm May evening this bird would exude clear song like a pricked blister. Jim, level with the blackbird's eye, looked: the blackbird looked at Jim in the black, bird-like swallow coat he always wore, neat, agile. He seemed to be hugging to himself an amusing secret these days—a secret special to the age of seventy-three.

A few months later I had a shock. Opening the front door one night, I found Jim lying on the steps. He looked so tiny—a little dark shadow—I thought someone had dropped a coat. Then I hovered, frightened. We helped him up, found he was able to speak, was very apologetic and seemed to think it the occasion for concealed smiles. We were never able to discover whether it was a stroke, an ordinary stumble, or whether this was the sole recorded occasion when he came home in a state which might be truthfully described as a little bit unsteady.

As soon as he had passed his mid-seventies, the renaissance of Jim became even more unmistakable. There began a regular summer migration to the south coast, to Worthing. Here he made pleasant new friendships with, for instance, the proprietress of the Balmoral Court Hotel, who had a pretty daughter of forty-two whom we called "Jim's girl-friend." It was certain that the small hotel atmosphere, where the residents are much jollier than is usually supposed, was relatively more receptive of Jim's new mood, now that my parents were not quite so uncritical, and none of us at No. 36 were so young, nor therefore was No. 36 always so exuberantly cheerful, as before.

There is a snap of Jim walking very dapperly along the Marine Parade and wearing his straw hat at an angle which had a touch, once more, of the Lupin dash. Indeed, the silhouette of Jim, as executed by Balthazar Watkins, the artist who had a little kiosk for this purpose at the end of the pier, might conceivably, since his body was still as thin as a paper-knife, have been the Jim of the 'eighties.

Jim was away a lot now, and the sense of general relief at home was palpable, although (for our sake, never hers) Mother was deeply worried about the Will and was already getting angry about it before she knew what it was.

"It really is not fair that he should take one penny of what he was going to leave to Muriel . . . really when one thinks . . . exactly what kind of a woman *is* this 'proprietress'? . . . when we've looked after him . . . all these years . . . years . . . years . . ."

Meanwhile Uncle Jim was buying another new suit, having his moustache clipped to an even brisker, neater shape, and planning a small dental adjustment appropriate to a new set of lower teeth. Unfortunately the shock of this tiny operation killed him. "To think he should have died at Worthing," said Mother, her anxiety redoubled.

Father read out his Will to the small band of us who came to the funeral. Jim hadn't got very much to leave—we all knew that. But each and everybody concerned got exactly what was right, exactly what was expected. The Jim tactfulness and the Jim good manners had remained perfect to the end. So that was that. No weeping and wailing. The business of missing him, of thinking about him, came later, and slowly.

I had seen quite a lot of Jim one way or the other; but to my very great regret his sister "Auntie Herbert" and the Bryn Cottage contingent passed, with one exception, out of my life. The images of

Geoffrey and Leonard were long fixed and indeed growing in my mind as heroes. After the Agricultural College at Wye, Geoffrey's parents helped to buy him a farm: visits to this, though much rarer than to Bryn Cottage (now gone for ever), provided me with my first close sight of country. Still "seeing" more with my nose than with my eyes, I was presented with the splendiferous scents of cowpat on buttercup-grass, the heavy odours of cattle-cake, of horse-manure, of Geoffrey's horse (sweaty because Geoffrey, looking fine in the saddle, loved to use it to trot round his acres), of barns and cobwebs and sawdust, and best and smelliest of the lot, in the centre of one of the barns, a wreathing, writhing oil-engine with a big loose flap-a-jack driving belt. Leonard was in the Army from pretty well the start of '14–18 and became more glorious to me than anyone had been before, not only because of his dangerous fighting but also because, through his mechanical talent, he was in at the beginning of the thing called "Tanks" before any of us knew quite what Tanks meant, much less what they looked like. I remember Leonard drawing a picture of one especially for me before photographs had been published. Bryn Cottage had come to an end, but (like Geoffrey) I had begun to come under the spell of Uncle Herbert's notebooks, and on the farm at West Hoathly I did a lot of snooping around with him for clues and vestiges of the old barn before the farm was there, and of the "berwick," the barley farmhouse, there before that.

The remaining fingers of Uncle Herbert's right hand had grown even more compensatingly powerful, and Uncle Herbert had grown even more self-conscious about their nobbly ugliness and tried harder than ever to keep his hand hidden—afraid that my aunt would find it repulsive, because he had always felt that in looks he was far from worthy of her, and that his luck in being loved by her, now he was seventy-two, could scarcely hold much longer.

It was in fact about this time that Auntie Herbert disappeared. This perfect, gentle, understanding person, who made everything all right by laughing at us, I loved then second only to my own mother. But she did something wrong to me—that is how I thought of it—she began edging out, crossing herself off my list, as it were. She was in fact ill—really ill—and so became someone whose feelings had to be considered. She had played piano duets with me formerly; but now because of her cancer her left arm was out of use. So she invented a way by which she would play the left hand with her right hand, while I played the top with my right. This one-hand-each method (two right hands) was to become for me in the future a favourite way of reading music, particularly classical music, fugues of course most of all.

My piece for that particular term was the Death of Ase—"Ase's Tod," from the *Peer Gynt Suite*. I was always getting her to do this with me, of course, and telling her how to pronounce the title in Norwegian. The great joke, tremendous giggle-point, was that in Norwegian it sounded like "Orse's Dirt." I remember Mother sailing in here with one of her monumental pieces of tactless tactfulness, putting her finger on her lips to stop me talking about Ase's death, since in her good judgment Auntie Herbert, the prognosis of her illness being what it then was, hadn't got long to go either. All this gave Auntie much amusement, but it made her sad as well, realising the shadow she cast. I couldn't be quite easy with her. I stared at her back between her shoulder-blades, imagining that this going-to-die was in some way visible and frightening; or I just felt utterly miserable that she was going away for ever.

She died: Uncle Herbert remained. They had moved to Worthing, where there was a new galaxy of churches for Uncle Herbert to explore, and on the Downs plenty of neolithic flints for him to sketch for his notebook. "Most interesting, most *int*eresting," he would say, over and over again, his voice going high in his throat and his spectacles flashing with his love of it. It was he who pointed out to me the significance of the pilaster strip on Sompting Church. When he joined up with our holiday in Dorset he explained the meaning of the regular terraced shadows on the hill above Chapman's Pool, or came home with the news that Arne Church contained an original altar slab. He once let me go out digging with the Sussex Archaeological Society, and I ate an enormous cress tea afterwards, the biggest of my life. I was always perfectly prepared then to dig for nothing whatever; but to dig in the hope of finding something—a piece of reindeer horn or a shaped flint! He made such things better than interesting. They were somehow urgent. He had the power to say, "Look!"; and now that his wife was dead he was taking on more research than ever; the long line of notebooks grew longer.

About a year after my aunt died I went down to stay with Uncle Herbert at Worthing. I think it was the last time I saw him. Soon he was getting out his notebooks, his microscope, some new neolithic artifacts, a peculiar sea-shell and a photograph he had taken of Sompting Church wall, the sun raking it so that the weathering was exaggerated. It was nice to be sitting there again with these special things clear and exact on the table-cloth under the light. The edge of the flint sparkled, but its heart was as black as ever, like petrified darkness. I enjoyed handling it. It was made for gripping.

"Tell me first about that one," I said. "Tell me exactly what it is and where you found it." But the lesson this time wasn't going to be about flints. He took it up in his convulsive fingers and put it down again. Up again and then down again, in his old three-pronged claw. He always hemmed and hawed a bit before he got going—usually, I used to think, because of suppressed excitement, plus being old. This time he wasn't looking at the flint though—his eyes were screwed up. When he did speak I didn't know whether he was talking to me or himself or what.

"They all mean nothing," he said. "They are nothing at all. Now that she is not here any more." It was a shock. I answered—something—but I stared pretty coolly at his face, then at the flint, then back to his face again, as if to remind myself. This is the neolithic object. That is grief.

CHAPTER FIVE

Soft Hand—Firm Hand

UNCLES like Josh (in contrast to uncles like Jim) are in a powerful position. Uncles in general do not live in the house. Father did, and everybody who lived in No. 36 was inclined to be on top of everybody else.

My first and clearest memories of early days with Father are connected with the bathroom, not times to savour affectionately in retrospect. Of the material improvements of my later life, I value bathrooms most of all. I mean specifically having more than one of them. We then only had one very small one for family and staff (Minnie). It was a quarter filled by a Victorian chest of drawers, for Father used it as his dressing-room; and there was, of course, no hint of running water in the bedrooms, only huge jugs, half-full of dusty cold water, to be supplemented by small tin cans of hot. This meant that the bathroom was a centre of tensions and thwarted rights. It was an understood thing—or at any rate understood by Mother, *not* accepted by Father—that Father and I should be allowed to use it at the same time. Theoretically it should have been me first, as I left the house first, for school. But as I lay in bed trying to get up, again and again came the irritating and depressing sound from along the passage telling me that I had missed the boat.

Father was intensely self-conscious about functional necessities, and unfortunately for him the lavatory was so acoustically lively, and the wood and plaster of the house so thin, that the noise of pulling the plug sounded like a strangled cataract.

Once in the bathroom, Father would close the door with an exultant bang, except that it wasn't quite a bang but a muffled thump, because on a hook inside the door were three or four of

Father's partially retired, battle-scarred, rather horrible dressing-gowns, which he put here out to grass, as if they were favourite hunters.

When I tapped on the door Father would call out nervily, "Who is it?" as if it could be anybody else but me. Why not leave the door unlocked? The reason was, of course, that he was perpetually careful of the preservation from even the male gaze of his naked body, particularly, of course, of the male parts. I would have to tap on the door, then wait till Father (whose body was in fact perfectly personable) had got out and swathed himself in bath towels. Then in the armour of one of these diseased old dressing-gowns, so much less pleasant to look at than his white back, Father was himself again, and my impatience would partly give way to admiration at seeing him in command of his cut-throat razor, which he liked to manipulate with an unwonted excess of manly determination. Father would shut and half curtain the window, in case Mrs Clarke (the vicar's wife who lived opposite) should catch a glimpse of his naked forearm. On hot July mornings I could not bear this, so would wait outside to double in as soon as he left so as to thrust open the window for a positively explosive escape of heat and steam.

Father was a great "practice-in-the-bathroom" man. One day he would be repeating Italian phrases for his business visit to Milan next autumn, using the bold declamatory voice he kept for foreign languages ("*A che ora parrrte?*"). Another time he would be rehearsing the dictation of a letter, looking at himself in the glass very probably. "It is surely unfortunate that his client should have chosen this moment to reveal. . . ." Or maybe if it was a day in July, the finals day at Sudbrooke Road Lawn Tennis Club might be approaching, and Father as President would have to be thinking about his speech at the prize-giving. Through the door and the dressing-gowns it came: "I think we all feel . . . no . . . I think we would all agree that Mr Werrex has done wonders with the new heavy roller, and I think everybody agrees . . . no, feels . . . that the courts are in apple-pie order. I think we would all agree that Mr. Werrex . . ."

I admired Father for being asked to make this speech; but I had a feeling I would not completely enjoy it when the time came.

There he would be standing in a little group by the pavilion. Certain to be a breeze slightly flicking up the lock of his hair, and blowing his voice away from the patient little audience towards the Swiss rolls and the paste sandwiches. His light voice had no carrying power whatever, although he stood on tiptoe to emphasise the phrases he was most anxious to make tell, such as "Inner Man." Every two minutes a horse van would clatter by. While it was passing Father would stand silent, head down, and lift one hand in an amused deprecating gesture, as if to say no oratory on earth could fight against this sort of handicap.

We would all be quite proud of him, but although Father "spoke so beautifully," language was not one of his gifts. He also "read aloud beautifully"; but I much preferred Jim, whose voice was thin and reserved.

Another of Father's root beliefs was that he had inherited his own father's gift for telling stories. In fact, he had no idea of it; or perhaps it was that the subject matter was wrong, and reflected his father's source-book of plots, a thick volume called *The Parents' Assistant*. If, as often, he was going through one of these on a walk, whenever a horse trotted by the gentle voice was drowned; but it didn't matter, because I wasn't listening anyhow. He thought it would amuse me—me already deep in Red Indians or Jules Verne—to tell me stories about a character called "Farmer Giles." Even I, even at that age, knew that such a name, and a story beginning "Once upon a time Farmer Giles got up early in the morning to feed the horses and give water to the cattle," was bad story-technique: and I perfected a mode of seeming to listen with thoughts more excitingly fixed, for instance, on the latest news of the Race to the South Pole.

When I first became fully aware of Father . . . he stands out so much less clearly than my crisply-fashioned aunts and uncles and seems at first to hover dimly on the edge of the crater of mother-love in which I was still somewhat buried. No wonder he occasionally seemed relatively colourless to me in those days.

He looked not very different from his pictures in the Reynolds family album—slightly built with pleading honest brown eyes, tenderly handsome, courteous, gallant—the exact image, perpetually, of the perfect son-in-law. In the wedding pictures he still has the small soft side-whiskers—side-burns—of the 'eighties with his little moustache. But in my young days he was podgier round the waist, more fiftyish—he looked in person rather like a restrained version of Lloyd George. One of his very few personal ·vanities was his looks, or doubts about his looks. He used to stare nobly at himself in the glass and pull his moustache, which had been allowed to grow too big. Later his moustache soaked up so much cigarette-smoke that by the time he was sixty it had turned rusty. It was stuck on his upper lip like a big disorderly rosette more than half obscuring the mobility of his mouth. "Shoulders back, dear," his mother may have said to him: and at sixty (and indeed at seventy-eight) he would constantly, at surprising moments, twitch back his shoulder-blades, making his watch-chain jingle.

These moments often coincided with somebody saying something solemn. Whatever it was—whether it was about the seriousness of a railway accident, or the Germans preparing for war, or the necessity for buying a book on it if you wanted to understand Auction Bridge, or the mention of some man who had lost his life in the *Titanic*—Father would thrust back his shoulders, look down to see that his stomach was well in, and put on an expression of earnest gravity which included the slightest hint of Land of Hope and Glory.

I would not say either that Father's profession had much glamour for a boy. He was a chartered accountant. "*My* father's a chartered accountant," I would say to school friends, but it didn't sound too strong. It was easy sometimes to admire, occasionally to be interested. Father seemed to work a nine-hour day, and then came home with heavily bound account books to frown at his £ *s. d.* jigsaw, correcting in red ink, charting courses, circumventing dangers, writing with a combination of boldness, exact finish, and a wonderful power of *clearing up*, which I realise now were the opposite or reverse side of the domestic character which I saw. It was a treat to be allowed to go to Father's office. First there was the one in Great George Street near Petty France, then a row of Georgian houses, now big Government buildings. In his little room I saw my first electric fire and my first telephone (the number was Westminster 2).

Later there was the bigger office where father spent most of his life in a room in which everything was furred with dust. I regarded this felt of dust as a fine attribute of grown-up-hood and man's work. Out of the big windows was a view of two hundred and fifty backsides of two hundred and fifty similar offices towering round the courtyard where grew nothing green and down to which only a dusty and grey light could reach. I gazed out with a little chill sometimes because this was supposed to be the scene of my future life too, a fact haunting the whole of my teens, though I could never allow my parents to suspect this feeling nor fully admit it even to myself.

I admired the massiveness of the ledgers; and the names on the back were fixed majestically in my mind, never to be joked about, like names in the Old Testament. JOHN WATKINS TRUST. SOUTH-END WATERWORKS COMPANY. EARL DE LA WARR. Statements of accounts, particularly those involving the estates of wealthy men, concealed the plots, retold in the abstract style of mathematics, of stories sometimes dull, sometimes dramatic. But of course not one tiny scrap of information of a remotely personal nature concerning any of his clients would ever escape from the lips of my father. Even his stories about Farmer Giles were carefully set in Somerset, one of the few counties in which none of his clients resided even occasionally. Sometimes, like a shock of doom, one of these Olympians would appear before me in person. The fact that his name was already familiar to me on the back of a ledger would give his figure Michel Angelo proportions.

Father used sometimes to introduce me. "This is my son, Stephen," he would say. He would then look at me with some pride, while I looked shifty. I had not been taught the old, safe, clear, "How do you do, sir." Confronted with Lord Brassey, a name associated with a whole shelf-full of ledgers, I stood unable to move or speak before this stocky and genially red-faced figure; then I suddenly dodged round the corner.

Some aspects of this Victoria Street office I could like. One was the valued old faithfuls, Father's clerks, who called him "sir" and after whom he shouted in a commanding voice "Drake!" or "Spong!"—a voice we never heard at home. Another feature suggested that Father might have been three per cent to blame for his financial disaster of the 'nineties. He indulged a taste for very small speculations. Persuasive young men would walk into the office and successfully prove to Father it was worth his while putting fifty pounds into a new kind of dye for linoleum, or a patent tin-opener, or a bottle-top, or even an anchor for small yachts. Examples or miniature replicas of these objects were on show round the office; the anchor was in the passage in a glass case. None of them was ever much good. In the main I had to admit to myself that the office was a dull one compared with Uncle Josh's bank, or my vision of the Government Department of Auntie Ethel, whom I imagined, because she was "in the War Office," to be surrounded by drums and breech-blocks and eleven-inch guns.

The intensities of Father's hard work and early struggles, the will-power which made him continue his self-education—these heroisms never percolated through to me. It never occurred to me then, nor became more than dimly clear later, that a corresponding period of work and "getting on" might be expected of me. "Father's at the office" was just an uninteresting safe fact of life like "Minnie's in the kitchen." I was vaguely aware that he hadn't got as much money as Margery de Paiva's father, because our garden was thirty-eight foot long not three hundred yards. Father was coming home tonight. Good, but——

What was that Mother was saying to Minnie?

"Is Uncle Josh coming to dinner tonight, Mother?"

How can I explain the thrill of pleasure if the answer was yes? All I knew was that of that very fine array of uncles and aunts I had inherited, he was the best, the finest in the world. That he was the best (to name one of a million things) at pretending to be a tiger and crawling after people upstairs. Done perfectly, one must even now admit, with a most unbearably comic face and snapping jaws. Also he was so vigorous; and to hear his fine clear voice in the hall put the whole house in order. I would never call "Mother" (if frightened in bed) when he was in the house—I should have died of shame. But there was no need to call, because his voice seemed to sound inside my bedroom.

"Step!"

"Yes, Uncle Josh?" The manliness of his nickname for me called for a crisp reply.

"Will you listen with all your ears and both eyebrows at once?" Oh mixture of the comic spirit and wit combined!

"If you are interested in the mere dross, mere dirt, . . ."

"Absolutely certainly, Uncle Josh."

"Mere filthy lucre—*Watch my hands* . . ." Then he would snap his mouth shut, glare and make a fine magician's pass, and there would be two new half-crowns, straight out of one of those little canvas bags at Drummond's Bank, under my plate. (Later, upstairs, I would take them out and give them a good feel, sniff their bouquet, and give them a suck as well, in order to multiply sound by taste.)

It was all done with such finish and clarity. Clearness was certainly part of it. His good thin suits were definite and pressed. Then (I had never before seen this fine trick) he would twitch up his trousers to keep the crease as he sat down, displaying unwrinkled socks over a tremendous leg, and perhaps a sock-suspender. All these novelties seemed to me unattainably manly. His watch and his sovereign-case clipped and clapped shut as cleanly as his wonderful long cigarette-case. He was a counterpoise of exact fittings-into-place.

It may be that children like clearness in grown-ups more than anything else. I know I was irritated by the opposite. There were certain times, notably meal-times, when my nerves were pulled tight simply because there was nothing definite and I felt the dead

94

weight of the absolute harmlessness of the proceedings; the in-
nocuousness of the pauses pressed hard. "No, thank you," somebody might say. "No beetroot for me." If only one piece of plaster,
just a small piece, would fall off the ceiling.

Instead, came Uncle Jim's characteristic slip-slap-slop, very
quiet, when he was eating gravy; or Mother's flicking away, with
her fingers, of non-existent crumbs. But if Uncle Josh was there
it was as if the footlights were turned on, the overture begun. It
was an occasion. If I was staring at him for a cue, he would pretend to tuck his napkin into the top of his collar and look guilty,
to make me laugh with him—but privately. If Father was looking
wise and thoughtful because he didn't know what to say, Josh
would draw him in by asking him "if he would advise Rose to sell
her Prudentials." And perhaps the real purpose of the remark
would be to give Mother a chance to say, "I got quite a nice little
dividend the other day"—a fact already perfectly well known to
Uncle Josh, but the pleasure she had in this would make everybody
talk.

Then near the end of the meal Josh would get the sort of silence
he loved and would start on a story. This story-telling gave me
absolute happiness. Yet there was anguish in it. Uncle Josh
would start:

"Of course, army discipline in the old days . . ."

Maddening little habit of my beloved mother's—as soon as
someone started to tell a story, she would get up and put coals on
the fire. Then Uncle Jim, bent up over his plate, a little deaf and
timidly obstreperous, would try to get attention by not hearing or
pretending not to hear. Josh began again:

"Army discipline then . . ."

"Silly pin what?" said Uncle Jim. He was always questioning
the divine right of Josh.

"Dis-cip-line." Uncle Josh would sing it out comically like an
order and make a comic courteous gesture with his hand to indicate "if I may speak."

Seeing my eyes on him in burning attention, Josh would talk as
if to me alone.

"When your grandfather was a private in the Coldstream Guards."

As if we didn't know all *that*. No matter.

"Buck House Guard was as strict a parade as any in the Army—in the world. The Buck House polish started five days before."

(Then a lot of military details I once knew by heart.)

"By the time they had put the last scrap of polish on their boot soles . . ."

"Boot *soles*?" somebody had to say; so, of course, I did.

"Each one had to be carried downstairs so as not to crack the leather polish."

"*Carried?*"

"Yes, Step. You would have seen your grandfather carried downstairs in a dust-sheet."

"What," said Uncle Jim, boldly sceptical, "was the object of the sheet?"

I knew the story of course, so I started to plunge in with, "Why, it was because of the dust."

"If I may just finish" (jokingly majestical) "it was so that the pipe-clay on the lappet" (I can't remember the real details) "should not rub on to the red of the jacket or the gold epaulette-band."

Occasionally Uncle Jim might make a rebellious interjection.

"Wasn't it rather difficult to present arms in a sheet?" This simply made me feel awkward *for him* and made Josh stare round at everybody with a half-hidden dimpling smile, as if to say, "Old James is in one of his cranky moods."

The most absorbing stories would be rather confidential. Quite often they would be about somebody doing wrong. I remember one about the Rillo Road Lawn Tennis Club, a case which thrillingly got into the papers, where the headline was "Home Office Clerk." A member was suspected of stealing from the changing room. He was detected by an exciting system of tapes, tied to coats, and dangling through holes bored in the wall. When he was challenged he "turned dead white." Three or four of these stories ended with someone turning dead white. Uncle Josh always said these words with a relishing trap-door snap shut of his mouth, though everybody, including himself, was a very gentle person and supposed to be terribly sorry about it, and I personally, for instance, said "God bless Home Office Clerk" every night in my prayers for a week. But I was struck by the way he liked saying the words "dead white."

Then there were other things to add to the marvel. Unlike any of us, the outermost bounds of whose normal outside life were limited by the tram journey from Clapham Common to Victoria, he had a life elsewhere. He had this wonderful profession, above all, of being in a bank. I knew nothing about the small and rather touching boy who'd cut his schooling short to earn a living at sixteen. Now he was half-way up in Drummond's and, moreover, lived there, at 49 Charing Cross, which really meant he lived at the wonderful address of Trafalgar Square, perpetually confronting the lions and the Nelson column, the frequent traffic and fire-engines. Not only had he this wonderful job, but he was brave, because last thing, at the abnormally late hour of midnight (which he must therefore have sat up for every evening) he went round the vaults with a night watchman, he wearing a bowler hat as protection against a sudden attack from behind, and the watchman with a truncheon.

One other link bound us two together. The Little Father of the juniors of Court Lodge, keeping order in the rabble, could not resist keeping me in order as well.

"*Step—your mother wants a cushion, I think.*" Crack, it would come out with a clarity to make one tingle. Was I fidgeting at the end of the meal?

"Your mother's not finished, great seigneur"—and I suddenly became glued to the chair, having intended to slide off it, to stalk Jack the dog round the table and prod him with the soft end of a candle. It made me wince: I looked stuffy—Bossy Uncle, Bossy Uncle.

But unconsciously I liked it, because I most certainly needed it, with things almost too easy for me at home, my mother being completely maternal, too protective, my father (how unspeakably grateful I became for this later on) about as disciplinarian as Mr Pickwick, one of those rare characters who, when he was at home at any rate, was so far from wanting to hold the floor like Josh, that he regarded any general kind of conversation which brought him in as a jolly kind of good luck. Where does the Bible say "Be not a lion in thy house?" How excellently Father interpreted that text. All the same, it needed an Uncle Josh to give me the necessary cold douches.

"You'll never get on if you don't speak distinctly: use your consonants.

"Look, Step, never have nails looking like that." No offence— no offence indeed. It all fitted in with the manliness, the general stage management, and above all the clarity of Uncle Josh.

It was in the middle of the war that Josh approached the prime of his days. Although fortyish, he had managed to get a commission in the R.A.S.C., to work at the base camp at Rouen, and become the second Captain Reynolds. He looked very fine in a great horse-girth of a Sam Browne which somehow crammed his big figure up into a fine chest.

Later there were to be other glories. He bought that marvellous rarity, a bull-nosed Morris; and he sometimes took me for drives for the sake of drives. And he used this car for "week-ends with the Balgarnies at Winchfield," where of course I was never taken, but just the phrase gave me pleasure and daydreams and made me admire him more.

I suppose the most important thing of all was that Uncle knew the arts and was genuinely connected with artists. There was one Great War Sunday, when he took me with him to dig trenches with a lot of middle-aged gentlemen, a detachment of Sunday volunteers which included Shepperson and F. H. Townsend. "Artists" meant exactly that to me. The drawings of the different *Punch* artists were so familiar to me that I could and did imitate their signatures (particularly the long S. of Shepperson) blindfold. Shepperson affected, in his drawings of well-brought-up *Punch* children, compositions with a lot of black shadow, and I privately thought that these graceful sketches were about as far as art could go.

Then there was music. Josh had inherited his father's fine word-of-command voice, and could somehow sing with it. True it was often used rather unsuitably for gentle love songs, including remarkably modern songs like "Pale Hands I Loved," or Seymour Hicks musical comedy successes like "Betty the Beauty of Bath"; but he also had the staggering gift, which to me then and ever since seemed impossible, of singing comic songs; and forty repetitions would not have tired me of, say, the "Marriage Song of the African Chief":

> And when she got there, she found on the floor,
> The bones of the wives he had married before.

His face was distorted in a horrible glare when he sang this, and it gave me a laugh which included a spinal shudder.

Biggest of all the Josh marvels was his connection with the stage. It was not just that he was a personal friend of Mr Brookfield, the dramatic critic of an actual London newspaper, the *Referee*—not just that he took me to plays like *The Only Way* and *Seven Days' Leave*, in good seats near the stage so that into my youthful nose were blown the huge refreshing smells of the Lyceum and the different bouquets of the Haymarket. It was not even that first "going round after" experience, when, curtain down on the *Flag Lieutenant* at the Kennington Theatre, I was taken to see, in a magnificently smelly dressing-room, the actual actor whom eighteen minutes before I had seen being stabbed in the forehead by the Bashi Bazouk. There was this man with a bloody bandage still on his head and yet modest and calm as if he was a normal human being—and shaking hands with me.

The London theatre of those days indulged in one weakness, by the accident of theatrical history, which was particularly attractive to boys. It was still expert in the mechanical dodge and trick scenery. The big stages of the Coliseum, the Lyceum and Drury Lane were fitted with batteries of trap-doors, revolving scenery, storm and even sand-storm effects, and the miraculous and dangerous "star traps," from which the genie shot in a cloud of smoke. Soon the cinema was to do these conjuring tricks much better—so much better that (in the cinema especially) they lost their thrill. But when I went to my first theatre it was the Hippodrome, in 1905 less than a year old. I could enjoy with everybody else the aquatic spectacle, could see the arena, unbelievably gushing water, turn into a lake. It was *The Flood*. The dam had burst and the villain was struggling in the water. But when, on the stage in the Wild West scene, the giant redwood tree was struck by lightning and fell across the stage crushing the redskin as he waited, with bow taut, to pierce the heart of the pioneer's beautiful wife, it was too much. My cries drowned the storm. I was taken straight home to No. 36.

A little later came the great series of Drury Lane pantomimes, surely the most elaborate of the century. The music was conducted by Jimmy Glover, and needless to say only Josh had the knowledge and nerve to speak of this personage with such familiarity. There, in *Jack and the Beanstalk*, I could see the bean-plant grow with my own eyes, till its stem was as thick as an oak and its head must be far away through the roof of the theatre. There Stanley Lupino contrived his marvellous leap, from the top of the step of the giant's staircase, sixteen feet high, to applause from the whole audience. There, in the *Sleeping Beauty*, waking up just before the most elaborate transformation scene in the Drury Lane cycle, were Lupino and George Graves, Graves the perpetually irritable, especially when as on this occasion he was coming to life in agonies of rheumatism, having stood as a sentinel upright in armour for a hundred years. Loads of dust fell from their shoulders. Large birds flew out of nests hidden in the century-long beards, and the rusty armour creaked and scrunched deliciously.

Sometimes the pleasures of the theatre were almost too great. Once Uncle Josh took me to see James Welch in *When Knights Were Bold*. There were no ordinary seats left so he took a small box, high up, like a house in a tree, and next to the stage also, so that the trap-doors and dream effects were right under my eye. The combination of this princely seat and the extreme funniness of the play stuck in my gullet. I laughed hopelessly, recklessly: my throat was bursting. I was never again to laugh at a play so much. I lingered after it was over. The box was being tidied up for the evening performance. It was ours no longer. The theatre had gone dead. But for the impossibility of doing such a thing in the presence of Josh, I would have wept.

Often, though not so much with Uncle Josh, I dreaded the hour or two after the theatre. After the matinee "tea at Gatti's" was the regular thing.

"What did you enjoy most, Stephen?"

Someone would be certain to say it, leaning forward and smiling before I had spoken, while we sat round a little sweatily, still hot and excited. Then the pause, while we waited for service. "Ah?" Father would call, unobtrusively. Then "Wait-ress" in his gentle, his almost inaudible command, his faint tenor shout, somehow combining, with his irritation, a respect for even the most un-helpful members of the female sex.

"What did you think of the actress who played the pert girl?" said Mother to Muriel.

"I liked her," said Muriel.

"A very beautiful young woman," said Father with the same courtly tone he used for the waitress.

"What was your comment?" said Jim.

How feeble and unclear we were in contrast to those calm beings on the stage, their expressions so definite, the actor flesh of their faces so firm. Don't let's speak of it. Why talk of it?

It is difficult now to remember or understand the height and dignity of the status of actors in those days. They were near the apex of their standing in society, and neither this nor their popular standing had yet been dimmed by the light of the film stars, nor by the general lowering of the rank of the acting pro-fession which followed film star publicity technique. Even the names . . . Violet Vanbrugh, Henry Ainley, Basil Gill, Arthur Bourchier, Cyril Maude, Charles Wyndham, Sholto Dennistoun,

Aubrey Fitzgerald, had a regal ring about them. To speak to such people or to know them, would have been inconceivable in my world. I felt an almost religious respect for the stage, so that thirty years later, when working with actors was part of my everyday life, I was still rather nervous of them, at first contact, and even now wonder whether it is possible for anybody to slide straight into an absolutely ordinary remark with an actor—whether there does not have to be some minute token ceremony of beginning, or entrance.

No wonder Josh's chief glamour, for me, was the fact that he himself had often crossed the footlights. Wyndham's and the Bancroft were two first-class amateur dramatic clubs going in for good plays and intelligent productions; and the new Galsworthy at the Haymarket or the new Pinero at the St James's would find its way into these highly skilled amateur societies a year or two later. Josh, as Sir Peter Teazle, was acting with a cast which some-times reached the fringes of professional performance. It was a world in which acting was important but which took second place, on the stage, to an elaborate demonstration of dignity and manners. Gradually Josh became more and more absorbed in the plays of Barrie (he later made a special study of *Dear Brutus* which became to him the essence of everything moving, everything true, everything dramatic, and everything essential to the sensitive understanding of life; and he was to spend much of his time in the early 'thirties producing it—for amateurs it's true, but, to his happiness, for a fee—a professional at last).

My only doubts about Josh were connected, strangely, with his acting. I would never admit this to anybody else, but at first I did not admire him on the stage. He was somehow diminished. He became quite little. He was audible enough—deafeningly so. He suited the gesture to the word, but it was somehow mixed up with the Guards; the word had a military ring: the gesture was something of a semaphore signal. Up, down, left, right, it came. His arms looked as if they were stuck on, and moved by wires. But he worked hard at his predominating passion. After the war he matured into a character actor of genuine force.

The "seeing through him" stage, which had to come, was a long way off yet, for me; but I became interested to notice that my sister, six years older than me, seemed already restive. "You're *dotty*," as I used to say to her whenever she changed, even if it was from Dornford Yates to Compton Mackenzie.

But this sacred rightness of uncles was being examined by wide-open blue eyes when Muriel was on vacation from Oxford. Josh's intellectual background of Kipling and Barrie, which I accepted as good and permanent, was beginning to look marshy to Muriel, the scholar of St Hugh's, who was climbing peak Gilbert Murray and even setting foot on the unexplored passes of *Crime and Punishment*. Peak Murray was somehow linked with progressive political thought, such as had never been seen in our family records, though Father read *Chartism* in the 'eighties. "Aha, thou belongest to the Liberal Persuasion," I wrote to her. "Thou shouldst putst such thoughts in the wagger-pagger-bagger." That was my mental and letter style aged fourteen. Why, Mr Wanderson, who lived at No. 28 up the road, was a Liberal, and he was a conscientious objector. But Muriel talked freely about Liberals.

Sometimes, in consequence, an Uncle-Josh-coming-to-dinner night might be half spoiled, though in an exciting way. "Have you heard the latest about Mr Wanderson?" Mother might say, rearranging the crumbs.

Oo! Muriel was looking down at her plate, hard. I became very wide awake.

"No, and I am not sure I want to," Uncle said, extra quietly.

"Well, I met Miss Martlock today . . ."

Good Miss Martlock was very good, very kind, very nice, and a gossip. No one was ever known to go to any service at St Luke's Church, even eight o'clock on Saturday, without Miss Martlock being there. (As I was at this time doing *Macbeth* for matric I called her the temple-haunting Martlock and was perpetually repeating this joke and explaining it.)

Before Josh took hold of a conversation he allowed it to remain aimless.

"It was about the Admiral case—what was his name, Frank?"

"What was that, dear?"

"MISS MARTLOCK'S ADMIRAL?"

"Nasmyth."

"What was that?"

"Nasmyth," my father called out with a little shout no atom stronger than his normal gentle voice. It was not that Mother and Father were growing deaf at this date, but they had a kind of un-spoken pact never to be audible the first time.

"Well, according to Miss Martlock it is just as important to save the life of a German as an Englishman. I mean, of course, dear, that that is what Miss Martlock said Mr Wanderson said about the Nasmyth submarine business."

I just sat quiet, waiting for Uncle Josh to take the thing in hand. He did.

"Well, no doubt they are all very brave men and we can just leave it at that, can't we—without getting the approval of Mr Wanderson, who no doubt in his present agricultural duties is more expert in the judgment of rotten turnips."

This seemed to me tremendous. But I could see my sister was getting ratty.

"How can you, Uncle Josh! How can you!"

Father tried to look solemn, as if he held an opinion. But Muriel was speaking:

"I think Mr Wanderson's beliefs are just as important as anyone else's." Her hands on the table were clenched.

Uncle Josh paused. How good he was at such moments, very quiet. "The gentleman at No. 28 is, I believe, a conscientious objector. Good. He has a right to it. Good." He turned slowly, glanced at Muriel's tense soft hands, and assumed an expression of kindly urbanity. "I have a right, I believe, to conscientiously object to Mr Wanderson!" On some such occasions before, Muriel had left the room, with tears of frustration. She was getting pretty blue in the eyes, I thought, but she stuck to it.

"That's—that's not grammar, Uncle Josh!"

Josh dabbed his mouth carefully with his napkin.

There had not been, lately, the same kind of link between him

104

and Muriel as there had been between him and me. Those more mature young women he admired, Lily Elsie or Marie Löhr, were, he believed, none the worse for knowing nothing whatever of Rupert Brooke, Pass Mods or the Fabian Society.

He started more quietly than ever before.

"No, I suppose it isn't grammatical. And I suppose if a drunken Uhlan came lurching into the room and attacked your mother this very moment you wouldn't do a thing to stop it, but, my dear girl," (almost inaudible with courtliness) "I am quite sure whatever you did it would be grammatical and the best possible English."

Of course it didn't escape me that this was a cut at Muriel's intelligence, which Uncle Josh never quite approved of. He was certainly looking very humorous indeed, just like when he was telling a story about somebody turning dead pale. And the strange thing was that I do remember not being at all on Uncle's side of the argument: I was a little on the side of his performance. I still admired the performance. I guess Muriel must have felt rather isolated. She cut away quickly after dinner.

May my pen rot if I seem to paint Uncle Josh as even a little cruel or pompous. It wasn't that—*it was not that*. Josh was sometimes a certain kind of person. The world could be divided into two classes of people, those who feel, and those who play at feeling; those who speak directly, and those who must first create a small wave of personal emotion to carry them through the conversational crisis on its crest. Josh was one of these small-crisis men. They might be called Emo people. Emo and non-Emo is the division. My sister at this stage in her life could not accept Emos: so her liking for Uncle Josh suffered a temporary eclipse. Emos were all right for me; but, whether that is because I had a different way of looking at people, or because I was purposely delaying my disillusion, or because I half realised that in Josh Emo was an essential part of his character and liked him well enough to accept this—all these were questions I would have to learn to answer later.

CHAPTER SIX

Traumatic Experience at Rillo Road

Long before the Mr Wanderson incident, great changes, as was to be expected, had taken place in my life and general position now that G.P.D.S.T. days were over. There had been Rillo Road Preparatory School, and then of course the big change, bigger than I had a right to expect, to the main school where my education was to be completed.

Rillo Road had not been a success. It had started with a shock which I was never quite able to get over. Up to and including the age of ten, I was the Crown Prince of No. 36. Except for the much-needed briskings-up from Uncle Josh, and his excellent "if I were you, Step" approach, I was the favoured heir. Everything I did was considered slightly remarkable. What I wanted I usually got: and since everybody was fairly kind to everybody else anyhow, everybody was always exceptionally kind to me.

Suddenly this idyllic situation stopped dead; and I did not like it. For half my days, half my time, the world became different.

It happened on my third day at Rillo Road Preparatory. The first two days had been neutral, ordinary. Rillo was a local day school anyhow; and after every morning I bicycled home for a notable midday lunch, extra large, plus special cream cheese, with Mother. There were new school-books for Mother to admire, new football boots to buy, my cap, blue with a white circle, to be handed round, and my descriptions of the masters and the top boys, the monitors, who had special caps with the school coat-of-arms sewn in above the peak.

For the first few days I thought I was going to enjoy Rillo Road, if only because so far I had enjoyed everything else. It was the autumn term, and so I had football boots. I had a bicycle. The school was over on the far side of Wandsworth Common, and this meant two ways of watching trains. The best vantage point (though this entailed a good deal of deft coasting across the Common on the bicycle pedal) was the little footbridge over the lines in the centre. When a main-line train came boring and carving through the cutting, the blast of smoke seemed almost to drive the little bridge into the air. Standing on the centre of the bridge, I was the look-out man on the crow's nest.

On the other hand great engineering works for the new electrification of the line were in progress. The best place to see these in 1910 was from Wandsworth Common Bridge by the station, particularly as the bridge itself was being raised six inches, one side at a time.

During my first week at Rillo nobody spoke to me, particularly. This was natural. I wanted to be liked, and tried to smile at boys and look friendly. I thought I would address one of them. On the way to afternoon school I saw Winstanley, handsome, tall, one of those monitors with the special cap. On my first day I had noticed and admired him. He was watching trains. I can see him now, his bike on the footpath, leaning casually against the parapet that he could watch from the saddle. I thought I would look too.

"Hallo," I said. He did not seem to hear.

"The one-forty-eight main-line is due, isn't it?" I said. In a moment the one-forty-eight came shaking and jigging round the bend, to bury its ferocious speed and bursting smoke beneath us. The pleasure was to stand steady, look calmly, never flinching. But Winstanley remained motionless after the train had gone.

"Shall we be late?" I said. It was nice to be talking to a monitor.

"Late? What for?" He was gazing down the track. "No school this afternoon." There was so little intonation that I did not understand; then he suddenly looked at me.

"Are you *daft*?"

What had I done? What did he mean? Home again I found out the meaning of "daft" and it dismayed me. It was a reproof. No one had told me that Thursdays were half-days. For no reason, he disliked me. Or was it my ill looks? Was I perhaps unpleasantly ugly-looking? Was there something wrong with me? Never in the whole of my life had anybody spoken to me like that before.

The shock was out of proportion. Everything then—making friends included—had to start from being hostile.

Soon, at Rillo, I was beginning to think I was not going to be good at being a schoolboy; that I had no talent for it. I was vaguely aware that other boys are different. Playgrounds give them confidence and they eat the air of class-rooms with cheerful appetite. Not me. Nor was I any better with the lessons. But then one thing I could never learn was a lesson. Even with G.P.D.S.T. (where I knew the teaching was good), there it was: there was the syllabus of the term neatly written out by Miss James in her woundingly clear writing: "Period 3" in black ink, "Botany" in red. Just the sight of that written down, and the certainty that Botany was to be repeated for every Friday of term, made me know beforehand that I should never be able to understand it.

I was not particularly fond of the games, either. I liked the cricket ground, but I liked the halfpenny ice-cream cornet at the shop by the entrance better. In autumn I liked marching off past the October bonfires to the football fields, but I liked my football boots much more and seldom slept with them far from my bed head. The bullying at Rillo was slight, though most of the junior boys were thrown into the furze bushes on the Common twice a week. I knew and even proved that it was true that fighting back was a way to stop this; but on the whole I disliked hitting almost as much as being hit. I generally preferred to bribe myself clear, not without pricks of conscience, by means of the gift of a fourpenny firework. On the complicated system of Danegeld then prevailing, this would buy immunity from bushing for one week.

I can remember a mass of details at my other schools, but Rillo is dim. All through one year we had the text with footnotes of *Henry the Fifth*, and the phrases ding-donged in my head tire-

somely—"'a babbled of green fields" ... "by Chesu he is an ass."
How boring, particularly, was the man Fluellen; how bad the jokes.
There was one natural teacher there, Mr Ashley, said to be "very
delicate." Most of us expected and, of course, wished that he
would fall down dead for the curiosity of this; although he was a
popular master. He was good, for instance, when he told us (after
returning from Spain), how at bull-fights the guts were ripped out
of horses, trailed on the ground and then put back again for next
time.

Mr Low, the headmaster, was a knuckle-rapper, though he was
energetic and kindly. Despite the glass of the thin partitions
dividing the forms he controlled the whole school with his thick
blue pencil. Money must have been very short, but he managed
to arrange those treat days, those special expedition days, which
stick for ever. The Boat Race was a disappointment because
Cambridge never turned up (sunk: 1911).

As a compensation for this disappointment we were taken to
see Ernest Barry sculling over the same course. The style of a
great sculler is perhaps the most satisfying and effective-looking
action of any sport in the world, and this gave me the notion that
rowing was something desirable and admirable. That it was a
great occasion was further built up for me by advance descriptions in the newspapers. In *The Times*:

Sculling. The championship of England. The sculling race from
Putney to Mortlake between Ernest Barry and W. Albany takes place
today at 3 o'clock. The start is by mutual consent. The men just
nod. Two cutters follow the race, in which Tom Green and Tom
Sullivan show Barry and Albany respectively and Dr. R. B. Ethering-
ton-Smith is to act as umpire. Of the two men Barry is the better
known, as he has come prominently before the public by beating
George Cowns and the "record" in 21 m. 12 sec. in 1908 and by his
contest with Arnst on the Zambesi in 1910.

The Portsmouth dockyard visit was a success. H.M.S. *King
George V* and the *Elizabeth* were being completed—the first a
mass of rust—and these were names to become famous in the
war. (Occasionally one of the new "Dreadnoughts" would anchor

off Swanage Bay: and these objects were somehow more thrillingly satisfying to the eye, more gazeworthy even than steam engines.) Also there was Twickenham, for Mr Low's son was the justly celebrated "Tid," England's greatest three-quarter, who could melt his way through the toughest defence by his feinting, flickering run, with twists and turns too rapid for the eye to comprehend.

My reports, of course, were not very good. Then as time went on Mother began to worry about the social status of some of the parents.

"You said that like Waterlow, dear," she used to say in one of her clear little whispers, "accents" being something it wasn't proper to talk about openly. Waterlow was the sad-looking boy with the glaring spectacles and the deeply confidential manner who was my companion on summer half-holidays. We used to bicycle to Bolingbroke Grove, alongside Wandsworth Common. May was the month when all the sterile ranks of No. 36s took a holiday and dressed themselves up in bouquets and buttonholes of white horse-chestnut and dark-pink horse-chestnut and lilac and laburnam and patent-leather copper beeches till everything looked like a real Academy picture called "The Pleasing Burden of May," the title of which I much admired. Waterlow and I coasted along towards Dents Road and Gorst Road, two adjoining streets which met in a U at the bottom of a slope. It was a tremendous test of high-speed bicycling. After whirring past each other with faces grim as racing drivers for twenty minutes, we would reveal our real mission and stand unobtrusively half behind the hedge of No. 16 Dents in order to stare, without appearing to do so, at "Abercorn," No. 33 Gorst, opposite. This was an empty house, apparently. The TO BE SOLD board had been up for ages. Yet was not this itself an unusual fact? The front garden showed signs of having recently been dug. It was no unusual thing for empty houses to conceal a gang of forgers. Then why had the owners left so hurriedly? Was it not precisely that false move which, less than two years before, it must have been, finally led to the discovery of the body of Mrs Crippen?

We watched this place for about a month. We called it "suspicious circumstance." The less anything happened, the more we stared—particularly Waterlow, the lenses of whose spectacles were as thick as small wrist-watches. This went on all one dreamy summer, till when bonfire smells started Waterlow rode away one day singing out "serspicherss circumsterrse" at the top of his voice (in the accent which made Mother feel uneasy) thereby finally giving the game away to the man whose face one sometimes almost saw, watching through the hole in the derelict curtain which half covered the top-storey window.

CHAPTER SEVEN

Bad Report

BUT whether Waterlow's voice was a real threat to my accent or mine to his, it was Father who made the surprising decision to hurry me on to another school, and who chose as that school the famous and historic one of Westminster. Financially it must have been heroic, though it was twenty years before this fact ever occurred to me. There was some saving in the fact that I was one of the day-boys. For this I was everlastingly thankful. "Day-boy" has no pejorative significance at Westminster, although one must not be too ready to explain this laboriously to non-Westminster people, and although, truth to tell, this half attendance did give sometimes a sensation of having only jumped into the icy waters of school life up to the knees, so to speak; and I felt guilt when I thought of the hard beds of the full-timers.

Westminster is a great school; and like all such it has its ups and downs. Two of my sons were happy and successful there in the 'forties. But my days there were on the whole the worst of my life, even though they never deserved a word more grievous than "unpleasant," or "disappointing." That fine, popular, fresh-looking boy Dacre used to say, "Well, personally, I enjoyed every bit of my school life"; but nothing of the slightest interest ever followed this remark (nor, in his case, by chance, did anything particularly interesting happen in his career). In fact, on our rare subsequent meetings he always seemed just that one bit more faded and wistful—in consequence, as it were, of having eaten his meal the wrong way round, having his peaches and port and cigars at the beginning. Willie Field, by contrast, hated life at his Rugby—"really loathed it, was really completely miserable." Afterwards he fitted into life with reasonable ease; but he was never able to pass Rugby

Station, even at eighty miles an hour, without feeling condemned and frightened. For me Public School was simply negative to start with.

On my first day (in the Fourth) I was presented with the vague, the wheezing, the rambling discipline of Mike, its form-master. I could not understand what was going on: and in class I trailed in the uncomprehending rear ever after.

There were good days and bad days, by inexplicable pre-ordination, just as there had been at G.P.D.S.T., but the contrast was even greater. A really good day would, for instance, include a friendly glance from a senior boy. A super day could be produced, I still believed, only by some heavenly reward, possibly by some gabbled form of morning prayer, the wording unchanged over ten years, yet once in a while inexplicably hitting the heavenly jack-pot. On a super day (in early 1915, say) unbelievable things might happen. Marchmont, for instance, senior house monitor and tremendously big and healthy-looking, with splendidly cut hair always in shape, and that easy, indifferent stride (instead of the normal anxious scramble of school), on one occasion went out of his way to speak to me. It was while we were all knocking about with the soccer ball as usual after Hall (luncheon) in Dean's Yard. The ball came to me high out of the air. Usually I would wave a foot feebly, miss and make a little ineffective run. But this time I somehow wedged it tight under my foot, killing the bounce dead in one slight motion. And there was Marchmont, who played right back for the First Eleven, standing beside me. "Well trapped," he said. I looked solemn, my eyes stinging with tears of pleasure. With such a start, experience taught me that every-thing would be happy and friendly for the rest of the day. But experience also taught me that however carefully I told my C. of E. beads next morning (meaning my prayers)—so hard that a vein stood out in my neck, and possibly bowing my head in a sort of collapsed way I had seen Miss Martlock, two rows ahead, affect in church, sinking into herself (it seemed to me from the pew be-hind) whenever the words "Holy Ghost" came into some prayer

H 113

—in spite of all, the next day would be bound to bring a complete reverse.

A typical bad Westminster day (date, say, early '15) would start with the usual inappropriately delicate fluting from the blackbird outside my window. Early morning light; which in No. 36 land always seemed stale, not fresh. Soon Minnie would begin to stick her head round the door, saying in the refined, modest little voice she often used early in the morning (in obedience to some start-of-the-day-resolution):

"It's half-past eight, Mr Stephen."

Minnie was always up and working, from seven in the morning till ten at night. Still stuffed with sleep myself, I resented this. In two minutes a healthy black coil of hair was stuck round the door again, little white cap on the top loop.

"Time to get up, Mr Stephen." Then—I knew it was coming—a little pleasures-of-living line, welling out strong and sudden: "Did you hear-that-blackbird-isn't-he-sweet?" I put the sheet over my head. Of course Minnie was my friend and this was a bit comic, but no kind of smile was possible on a Westminster morning. Anyhow, I would dig myself down once more, as a sort of revenge, in a way. It was at this time during term I was perfecting ways of blotting everything out. Burying myself in the bedclothes was one. Or I would hide myself in a story I was telling myself. No need to shut out the other voices in a room: I could not even hear them. I would be striding in huge riding-boots through the mud of my cousin's farm-yard, in my hand a curved knife as big as a slice of melon, to repair the driving-belt of the oil-engine. Or perhaps the daydream would transfer me to a school story I was reading, in the world of which I existed far more concretely than I did in shadowy old Westminster. "*Cave*, it's the Head," cried Figgis Major; and each boy dived for his desk.

"It's *ten to nine* . . . " This time it came really sharp, followed by a slam of the door. True, I was almost overdoing it this morning. Daily last-momenting had whittled down the time between bed in a road off Nightingale Lane and Westminster Abbey (via Wandsworth Common Station) to a remarkable thirty-four minutes.

Eight-fifty-six: up and speed to the bathroom. Father would be there, in full shaving insignia, two kinds of razor-strop, shaving papers, big shaving-bowl with decades of the refuse of previous shaves to add to the morning's soap-pudding. Goodness how slow he was, I thought. It was momentarily irritating. Quick with my teeth, because I hated the taste of Pickrick toothpowder. Everybody in the family had Pickrick. The idea that I was free to change it to something I liked better was destined not to occur to me for four years. My washing could be done in four splashes in ten inches of geyser water. Hands not being properly washed, uneven nails, tufty, unbrushed hair would somehow help me to hide from the unpleasant day. Smoothed-down hair would have made me feel unprotected, as if I was sickening for something, or going to a party full of old women wearing smelly furs. A degree of grubbiness in my apparel, certainly, was a sort of protection against the chilliness of school behaviour, like Arctic clothes against Greenland.

I disliked the school dress, tails and a top-hat. Their smartness was quickly undermined by me. The thin material of the trousers soon acquired, rubbing against desks and benches in the treadmill, the shine of decay. I put on these clothes touching them as little as possible, as if they were infected.

Downstairs, while Father was still shaving militantly near the roots of his moustache in the bathroom, planning reforms of the morning timetable, I was already, at one minute past nine, grabbing my way through Minnie's pale scrambled eggs on soaking toast, sitting stiff on the edge of my chair to remind myself of the passing minute, head turned sharply to the left to take three looks at the *Daily Mirror*. Glances—very quick. Cartoon first—turn to the W. K. Haselden page. How marvellous he is. But political today. Disappointing. "Witnesses in the Dead Brides case. Prisoner's interruptions." I like murders when I've got into the story, but haven't got into the story of this one yet. "Huns laugh as victims drown." Where? "Valuable Patriotic Picture

Absolutely Free." Might write in. "Richard Chatterton, V.C., A romance of Love and Honour" still going. No—Mother says tosh; but rather ripping lines printed under the title of this Ruby M. Ayres serial:

> A laggard in love and a laggard in war,
> What did they give him his manhood for?

Good. "We must try to Love Germans: says Canon of St Paul's." Should be in prison. No, must be cracked, dotty. Quick look at the new children's thing, Pip, Squeak and Wilfrid. But Minnie was standing behind me, longing to say something. I stiffened. She bent over the paper. "Oh, Wilfrid is so funny this-morning-isn't-he-sweet?" Absolutely no flicker of response from me. Of course Minnie was absolutely on my side. So was everybody on my side, here at home. And in a few minutes I should be across the barrier, in a place where I was nothing whatever, somewhere Minnie could never come. Minnie had better shut up.

Now the real spurt started. Nine-four and I mustn't get entangled with Mother. Out of the house before her anxious face appeared over the banisters to say, "Are you warm enough, darling?" I crash my bike down the front steps, seeming to hear a strained cry from above: "It's quite a *bitter wind* . . ." It trails away. In a moment I am hot with high-speed bicycling. I thought of Ginger Jack, in sweater and scarf, sprinting round the rugger field, training for the match against St Bede's. Thigh-muscles "as hard as wood." Mine must be fairly big, with this tremendous force I was putting into the pedals. In the school story I was reading last term (*The Human Boy*) it said that "the arms of Corky Minimus," when he was stripped for the fight, "looked like cabbage stalks." Already, it seemed to me, I was past that phase. The arm-bending exercises I was even then beginning to try seemed to me to be producing a very faint white thickening, about the size of a robin's egg, in my biceps.

Drive, drive, drive—the power of my thigh-muscles was extraordinary, I thought. The freedom—for I was not yet fully dressed in the hated clothes. By a special arrangement with Mr Cramp,

the person in the station ticket office, I used to leave my top-hat
and tail-coat in a cardboard box there every evening when I got
off the train, to be put on again next morning in my lightning
swoop through the station. My glorious bike, with the three-
speed gear, and the new oil-lamp (which I liked to keep on even
in day-time); handle-bars polished with Silvo! I was absolutely
loyal to the make of B.S.A., which sounded so dependable, with no
fancy advertising, no cardboard cut-outs of silly girls coasting, like
the Triumph posters. Something to do with revolvers, B.S.A.
was. How silently the bike could coast, now, past the Home Shops
pushing their well-known row of smells in my face as I flicked by,
with the stink of the rotting apples in Tebbutt's basement pervad-
ing all. Flash down the hill and then get a great run on the hill up
the other side . . . but wait, slow down a fraction for a possible
show-off. There is Claude Hine, in his new uniform, walking to
catch the nine-twenty-one, obviously. Claude Hine is a hero.
Perhaps he will wave. He tried to join up by giving his age wrongly,
did in fact get in early, and now already he is a full lieutenant. To
have two blobs on the sleeve . . . Of course I know all the rank-
marks perfectly, and many of the ribbons. If I met a lieutenant-
general I could make this clear to him. "Like a Greek god,"
Mother said of Claude, who had delicate features and hair so fair
it looked almost white. The only Greek god I had actually seen
was the ten-foot reproduction of the Venus de Milo in the concert
hall of Clapham High School for Girls. Claude Hine certainly
looked better than that. Thank God I wasn't wearing my odious
top-hat. Should I impress him with my extraordinary speed up-
hill, as I passed him? Or should I slow right down, so that he
could see I had the flags of all the Allies stuck into a band of cork
along my handlebars? I had not got the Japanese flag, because
Japan had so recently joined our cause; but I had fixed a rosette,
in Japanese colours, round the tool-bag at the back of the bicycle
saddle. Somehow Claude didn't see me that day—in typical Bad
Day fashion, though he may of course have seen the Japanese
rosette. I half-waved. Was it cheeky? Had I been cheeky?

That slight slow-up made speed crucial. I had to admire the

way my legs thrust me over the bridge for my top-hat ticket-office, on the far side of the station. Fling the bike in, old coat off, bang on the tail-coat and the top-hat, fur half-coagulated like a rat-skin, and then leap up the staircase to stand dead-centre of the foot-bridge over the line. The overhead electric, platform 2, was due in at nine-eight, but if the electric was a fraction late, since it stopped at Clapham Junction, it was better to get the steam, the nine-ten, platform 4, not just because it was steam, but because, splendid Wandsworth Common rarity, it was main line and so went straight through to Victoria. There we all stood on the bridge, myself now in full Westminster clothes, including the top-hat, which had to be specially made, owing to the extreme length of my head, of which I was self-conscious. The hats on the business men around me seemed by contrast to belong to them. I felt they must regard mine as namby-pamby, and kept up a frown to counteract this impression. We all looked gloomily down the up lines, ready to trot downstairs to platform 2 or 4, just as they had most of them waited already for five years (and might, so far as the future of the time-table was concerned, wait for another forty) all according to whether electric or steam came first.

It was electric, slightly disappointing—and, as often, this meant standing in a full carriage wedged, not able to move much. Also the train was one minute late, which would mean nine-twenty-one at Victoria. Could I make Chapel? And during this ten minutes I ought to be trying to learn ten lines of Latin Rep. On this Bad Day the Buck would be bound to pick on me. "Let us hear Potter's version of *Aeneid*, Book I," he would say. Grasping the rack, I couldn't find the place in the little blue book. I would have to wait for the stop at Clapham Junction. Things were shaping badly. No time to indulge in railway pleasures now, though I can't help enjoying the rap, almost like hitting a drum, as, boring through the Wandsworth Common cutting we flicked under the foot-bridge, swaying along at fifty I should think. Any tinge of pleasure now must make the prospect of the day worse. Even the interweavings and counterweavings of the lines which throng round Clapham Junction must be ignored. Pipe-smoke stung my eyes. I threw my horrible hat in the rack, and managed to lever out *Aeneid*, Book I.

Tunc Venus. Haud equidem tali me dignor honore . . . I knew the first line, anyhow. If Venus is a god she certainly was not so handsome as Claude Hine; indeed, I rather disliked that stuffy little mouth on the statue. But now I really had to stare out of the window as a green Waterloo train, level with us since Clapham Junction, began to sink, first slowly then ever more quickly down below our level, to dive beneath us, rushing suddenly miles away to the east with its load of business faces which a moment before had been vacantly staring, their newspapers within a few feet of our own. Next moment, like a gong, the noise of our train became deep and hollow as we seemingly slowed up and hung above the river before finally floating down the hill, all power switched off, deep into the roots of Victoria Station, and then that last final sound-change as the roof gave echo to make me feel the familiar cold shiver, school.

Now dart for the bus; now to side-step the slow shufflers. Eight minutes could just get me into Chapel; but the bus situation was not good. No. 24 was my main hope. In these good old days of rival lines each route had a different character. The 24 was a fast, courageous little mongrel, with dangerous, rickety top deck open to wind and rain. If I stood up, it was like riding the Roman chariots in *Quo Vadis*. But today I had to make do with a No. 11, a stolid "General," slowest of the lot. And sure enough Victoria Street had thickened up—a small cavalcade of Army and Navy Stores dray-horses were stamping and snorting dead across the main road in an excess of energy. That was that. On a Bad Day missing Chapel was likely to lead to punishment.

I settled back. It would probably mean a penal drill. This dreary custom was typical of Westminster punishments at that time. It was somewhat psychologically shaming; and it involved no pain—a dreary trudge round the school yard. Dippy Walkerton, who was generally supposed to be less than perfect mentally and made the most of this fact, would be certain to be one of the party. He didn't find it psychologically shaming at all. Loathing compulsory games, he knew that penal drill was the one certain way of getting out of them: so there he would be, tramping round the yard with a slight but effective parody of the military walk, somehow slouching with his legs and marching with his body. Still, much as I admired Dippy, I didn't fancy looking ridiculous behind him.

Useless now to try to learn my Latin Rep. Well, it was just an extraordinary tendency of Fortune that I should always be caught unprepared with Rep. Maybe the Buck would pass me over. I would try the trick, sometimes effective, of looking eager as if I *wanted* to be asked to say my lines.

But suddenly No. 11 had sprung into extraordinary life. Was I going to be in time, after all? We really pounded along the last stretch. The gate to Dean's Yard was in sight. I stood on the step, ready to jump off at the first suspicion of a slow-down. Guards on steam trains could, I admitted, step off tranquilly at even higher speeds and stand stock still. I had often studied them. I was content to be the best at buses. Nearly twenty miles an hour, and my expression was relaxed, thinking of something else. Now for a real sprint, straight to the side-entrance of the cloisters. Here was another invention of mine. Near the entrance there is a monument to somebody like Sebastian Coltmarsh:

> Safe in the Redeemer's arms
> He rests, his ashes here below . . .

The ashes were represented by a large urn with no back to it; and behind this false front it was possible to stick my top-hat, my umbrella (part of our uniform) and even three lesson-books as well. I remembered to bring my *Aeneid*, so that I could surreptitiously learn five lines of Book I.

Everybody agrees that one of the great, the really tremendous advantages of Westminster School is that for Chapel it makes use of the full glories of Westminster Abbey, where every day at nine-thirty in the South Transept the school sits for prayers, the intoning of a psalm and the reading of a lesson. One always tried to squeeze whatever drops of interest one could out of such a colourless situation. For me, besides the excitement of last-momentism, there were two. One was to try and thrust myself into a seat which made it possible for me to get one foot, or one kneeling knee, on the tombs either of Charles Dickens or of Tennyson. The other was associated with the extraordinary behaviour of Gow. This was approaching a marked stage. Gow was our Headmaster. I only spoke to him on one occasion during my school career. This was when I sat for the "Challenge" or scholarship entrance examination. He had called me up for a brief *viva*. He stared at me through spectacles thicker than Waterlow's—so thick that I felt as if I was being looked at through opera glasses. The lower half of his face was covered by a large, swooping moustache which had the appearance of being detachable. The whole effect was of being addressed by a dummy. In what seemed to me a ventriloquist's voice a question came from behind this mask. "Can you recite the Apostles' Creed?"

This seemed to me some trick question, designed to upset my balance. "No, I can *not*," I answered with a cagey smile. The top twelve in this examination were awarded scholarships. Out of fifty-six candidates my place was fifty-fifth. Of course I knew "I believe in God the Father," etc, in fact I knew most of the morning service by heart; but who had ever thought of calling it the Apostles' Creed? Gow's one contact with us back-row boys was his recitation of the Latin prayers in the evening and his reading of the Lesson in Abbey in the morning.

The dim light and Gow's weak eyes made it difficult for him to see the page of the Bible in the Abbey that morning. He stood side-face to catch the light. From this angle his almost globular lenses stuck out on stalks like the eyes of a lobster. His voice was toneless; yet he must have prided himself on his reading of the Lesson, or rather his memory of the words. But his memory had recently become less good than he would admit. He only managed to get through the lesson three times out of five. The other two he would slow up and come to a stop.

Now came the great bi-weekly opportunity of Gow's understudy, the Rev. W. S. Witto. Witto, or "Sacred Sam" as he was called, was unofficially the head religious master. His form, about half-way up the school, would be mine in a year or so, and I dreaded it. But I was fascinated by Sam, and liked to observe him meticulously, with long stares. It was reported that he had some hopes of stepping into Gow's shoes; and he certainly walked about cloisters as if he was somehow set apart from the other masters, a fact which he indicated by canting his head slightly upwards, and displaying the beginnings of a watery smile on his lips, an expression which I was never able to identify until years later Muriel took me to see the Peruginos in the Uffizzi, when I remember saying, with a great explosion, "Sacred Sam."

Gow was reading from Luke xxi, and he began to have difficulty in the third verse. "This poor widow hath cast in more than they all . . ." His memory failing him, his eyes unseeing, he stopped short, glared at Sacred, and then sat down; whereupon Sacred rose slowly, walked deliberately to the lectern as if he was in a procession all by himself and finished the Lesson. The brilliant thing was that Sam got a definite dig at Gow on each of these occasions, because although of course he could have seen to read it, he really did seem to know these bits of the Bible by heart, and showed that this was so by tilting up his chin so that his friar-like profile could catch the unearthly light from the windows. His voice, unlike Gow's, was a delicate tenor, so quiet in timbre that it never reached beyond the second row of any audience he was addressing.

Half concealing my Rep. book from the wandering eye of any master, I took cover under the slight interest aroused and learnt five lines of *Aeneid*. In the scramble out afterwards I made my detour unseen to retrieve my belongings. Things were going better. Unnoticed, and with hat behind me, I made for the side passage of Ashburnham House (my House) which although officially prohibited to people like me was usually fairly safe.

However, there, in the middle of it, and advancing towards me, was the space-filling form of Marchmont. Marchmont as Head of House was a great heroic figure. How different, I thought again, from all of us. He never scuttered along a passage: he was unhurried, and his step was firm. He had big, dark eyebrows, and his rich hair smelled of vanilla. His face was a healthy red and white, and had no spots on it. His eyebrows were big and dark. Very occasionally he would give me some just perceptible greeting, perhaps the faintest suggestion of a smile round the eyes only. All agreed, in serious moments, that he was extraordinarily decent, and I once heard an Old Boy say from the depths of the solemnity of his new-found oldness that Marchmont was a very good influence on the House. But at this moment he gave me no greeting whatever. After passing me, however, he stopped. "You were in Chapel, I see," he said, "but it's not an awfully good thing, is it? To come in at the last possible moment?"

"No . . . I'm most awfully sorry."

"And one other point, look—the Abbey's not really the place to do a last-minute swatting up of your home work. It's not awfully good for the School, is it really? And I suppose really it's not awfully good for the House."

Typical start of such a day. A tick-off from that thick, gleaming hair, those fine, fresh cheeks looking as if he had just been running round the playing-fields. Very probably his face never went through the spot phase nor the wax phase—the paleness London seemed to inflict on most of us. And I had done something which wasn't nice to speak about. All possible chance of anything going right for me that day drained away in a second.

Incredible, I thought, how people like Marchmont seemed to be somehow in charge of the situation from almost the start of their school life, while people like me bobbed up and down in their wakes. Stunned, I saw him a moment later in the "Under"— the junior locker room—walking through a mob of us towards the notice-board, touching gently, in order to move him aside, the shoulder of little Penwit, who bounced back a yard as if he had been stung by boiling water when he saw who it was, so that at once there was a moat of space round Marchmont, as with a calm gesture he pinned up a list of names ("The following will appear in House Trials") then swung round and made steadily for the door, gazing straight ahead, his expression grave and troubled. Fizz and

I used to mutter that this serious expression of Marchmont's was put on and swank, because he was not only Head of House but also a double pink and Secretary of Deb. Soc. besides being associated with a list of eminent Marchmont Old Westminsters a yard long, painted with hundreds of initials on the walls of Up School. It took me three years to realise, thinking back on Marchmont, that in a way his mind probably was not so set on impressing Fizz and me as I then thought. Two of his five brothers had already been killed in the War; by the time next term started he would be miles away in a training battalion; within twenty-two months of that dignified walk through the Under, he would probably be trying to crawl forward in some hopeless and ineffectual raid on some Flanders salient, and his name would a few months later be read out by old Gow at the beginning of Friday evening prayers. But the immediate fact of life being that he had just admonished me, I returned again to the thought that he was a bit of a swank, and I very much doubted whether I would ever speak to anybody, any other boy, that day.

But the sight of Fizz and Elsie in the mob round the notice-board made me change my mind. Marchmont was by this time walking up the exquisite Wren staircase of lovely Ashburnham, a route which only monitors were allowed to use, and which I at that time had never heard of, wasn't to see for twelve terms and was only to use once, fifteen years after leaving school. The absence of Marchmont revived me. Elsie I rather liked, not less because I was able to feel superior to anyone who, having long, sandy lashes and curly red hair, was inclined to be a House pet. Fizz was a little white-skinned rabbit with small, dry, upper teeth which fanned out irregularly over his lower lip and were made no better by an inefficient metal plate sliding up and down like a shutter when he laughed, which he did nervously and continuously, bubbles forming round the edges of the tin of his plate.

"Wanted in the Upper," I intoned into their ears, meaning that my news was that I should be had up before the House Monitors, though I was pretty certain Marchmont would let it go.

"Why?"

My face wore a sarcastic smile of indifference. All three of us, though no longer new boys, were part of the ruck in this lowest section of the House. All the same, there was a chain of command even among the serfs, and I regarded myself in a kind of way as partly the boss of Fizz and Elsie. Both of them—day-boys like me, of course—lived typically on the Victoria line, and it was surely a sign of feebleness and lack of independence in them that they both caught a train which got in nine minutes before mine and left them, therefore, with far too much time for getting into Chapel.

"Pi-jaw from Marchmont," I explained with a hand at my brow in despair. It meant nothing to me, they should know.

"Squeaky squawker?" said Elsie, referring to my last-minute Chapel entrance. "That's nothing to do with the Upper."

"At least two seconds to spare. No: I mustn't do prep. in Chapel! New rule. 'Bad for the spirit of the House.'"

"O God our help in ages past," Fizz intoned, looking solemn and giggling at the same time.

"Did you answer back?" said Elsie, beginning to giggle too, for no reason.

"Not a word," I said, imitating being dignified.

"I bet that made him feel rotten."

"He's probably shaking like a jelly."

Taking a double brandy . . . wetting his pants . . . listen, everybody, that's Marchy-parchy's teeth chattering. . . . As the wit increased so did the giggles, especially as we were walking up the steep concrete stairs to the Buck's for the first lesson. Fizz dragged his ruler along the iron railing to imitate Marchmont's teeth chattering. The pattern of the day was fixed. It was to be me the leader of the underdogs: so I must not show undue anxiety about work—indeed, I must show a desperado indifference to bad marks.

Yet, secretly, I would so much rather have been among the good ones, among the promising. "You've still got John Sargeaunt with you," Mr Erskine Clarke, our vicar at home, reminded me earnestly.

"J.S.?" I said. "Yes, he's a terrific chap."

The true teacher, known even beyond the school. The man of the wonderful touch with boys. I boasted about him. And of course I'd scarcely spoken to him, nor he to me, in my life. His form was top of the school—the History Seventh.

It seemed to me there was little chance of my shining with any of the masters I actually met. There was little Mr Liddell, always kind; but he was a home friend, a blessing to be taken for granted. The rest I never got near. It was masters on one side of the fence and me the other. Yet I was so often on the verge of being interested. I would be suddenly surprised into a realisation that the words in my Livy text-book, for instance, were well placed and economically chosen, and for a moment the Latin would break through the doodles and ink-blots. I even began to get satisfaction from the compressed effect of Horace and liked words peeled down to their pith. Making Latin verses was a good game, and I could enjoy the rhythm. Even Willett, whose bad view of me was fixed and irrevocable, on one occasion, which I never forget, said that I sight-read a piece of Greek verse well. And a marvellous thing had happened to me in Buck's two days before the Marchmont incident. The order in which one sat in form followed the order as it was left at the end of the day before—a constantly shifting position, therefore. The first boy to know the answer correctly as the question went down the lines ("next . . . next . . . next") moved above the first boy to be asked the question. Wonderful leaps could be made: great straddling advances. I had been stuck near the bottom of the class for a week, and only two days ago Fishy Wicks, sitting number one, had read out "fulget Oriona tellus," and I knew this instantly for a ludicrous deformity, shouted out the splendid word "Oriona" (according to the custom with false quantities) and flew weightlessly to the top of the class.

My place in form that morning was still quite high, but I knew so well what would happen. Not being called on for Latin Rep., I would be sure to be called on in the construe—Ovid, in whom I found no spark of interest. In Livy, besides the story being not totally boring, there was always a chance of soldiers dying of thirst or men deflowering somebody's youth. In Horace only last week there had been that extraordinary bit about the woman with tooth-marks on her neck. The curious thing I thought to myself is that last night, following my Orion triumph, I had really intended to work up the Ovid, really prepare it for once, so that there would be no worry. As long as one knew the meanings of the words. . .

In the circle of the oil-lamp, doing my prep. at No. 36, I had been sitting at the table. At my elbow were the H. G. Wells short stories. New idea—read one H.G.W. as a reward, when you have *finished* Latin Prep. But the stories are really short. I would read the shortest I could find, as a foretaste. I began the one about the butterfly specialists and the rare specimen which couldn't be caught. In the grip of Wells, the outside world disappeared. The tiny remarks of Mother, the deprecatory coughs of Uncle Jim from his corner, were completely unheard. At the end of the story I was still in Wells. It seemed to me that I could see the butterfly on the tablecloth beside me. I felt giddy for a moment and then realised where I was. I went over to the biscuit-tin. Supposing I saw the butterfly there? What should I do? I felt I had to read one more story, to break the spell of the last. I hadn't looked at the Ovid. It wasn't my fault. I really had become swimmy. In fact, I had to get myself some orange-juice and a ginger biscuit. It was surprising Mother hadn't noticed anything. It could be said I wasn't well.

I knew how it would be in Form that morning, and it was. I would begin stumbling with the translation as soon as I got to my feet. Stelling and Van Else would begin chipping in with the correct translation instantly. They were waiting for it, tongues hanging out and positively dripping, always on the side of the master, with their serious, shut-up faces. Masters' favourites. Losing my position at every mistake, I had to face the long, ignominious shuffle down from desk to desk. Indeed, in order to retrieve something out of the mess, even if it was only a giggle from Fizz and Hilton II, I had picked up my pens and books before I started, with the gesture of one who prepares for a long journey, so as to build up my reputation as a don't-care-a-damner. After all, everybody was pleased at a complete smash. The Buck didn't care one way or the other.

"'Crinibus passis' is particularly inaccurate in every respect this morning."

This was his Latin nickname for me because my hair was "in all directions," as if I was distracted (through no fault of mine, I thought to myself, but a typical handicap inflicted by fate, one patch of my hair near the front growing backwards, against the grain, so that brushing it down would simply make it stand vertical). The Buck looked on us all with amused tolerance which, it seemed to me, made him the nearest approach to a decent master we ever got. He examined inky marks as if they were the spoor of some animal, but he did not revile us. He himself, of course, was always dressed with exact elegance, including a carefully placed, large and expensive tie-pin, which seemed to hold him stiffly in place, rather like the pin through a butterfly specimen, I thought that day, with the Wells story still in my head.

I had no idea what "Buck" meant, of course, till I heard B.-T. say that it was really a word for our "knut" (like Basil Hallam's "I'm Gilbert the Filbert the Colonel of the Knuts") and that it dated from Regency times. B.-T. said this was about the Buck's period, and although I only knew vaguely when this was, never having got, in History, beyond the Armada, it confirmed my feeling that the Buck was fantastically old.

The masters really were old. The reason for this (absence of the young ones in the '14–18 war) did not strike me till years after. Certainly soon after I left there was a great exodus. Mike I know went. Mike took the lowest form of all; and he used to stride up and down, with bristling moustache, in a constant state of wheezy ferocity, completely abstracted from the scene—an old, failed, master whom nobody took any notice of. "*Attention, bêtises*" was his constant cry, while really trying to make *himself* concentrate, to shock himself awake from the gentle dream in which we were all dissolved together. He was quite fond of children in a dazed sort of way. He often drifted into French, which was a second language to him, though he never taught us any, nor was he allowed to take any higher form, since conversation French was never mentioned at Westminster. Etheredge and "Death" were our French teachers. Etheredge would hop round the class with abstracted fierceness, occasionally tapping one of us on the knuckle with a thick blue pencil. "*Jument? . . . Jument? . . . Jument?*"—he would dance from boy to boy till he got the meaning. He was as impersonal as a dynamo. The atmosphere could not have been more different from Mike's. There really was a touch of electricity about it. No one ever dreamed of being inattentive with Etheredge. He had no loose ends, no meaningless mannerisms, like Sandy, who used to finger his pink bald patch as if he was eviscerating a boil. Etheredge was exact, as boys require. There was no attempt to make the language interesting; but the whole thing was a sort of challenging game, backwards and forwards like rackets. I used to prepare for his class.

One left Etheredge with some knowledge of how to read French and a decidedly improved French vocabulary; but any attempt, present or future, to speak the language was finally withered out of one by "Death." Death's white cheeks were set in a mould of gloom. His features seemed to be settling more and more towards the bottom of his face as his moustache weighed down more and more implacably on his chin. I once took a peep at him in the Masters' Common Room, and it struck me that he was just as unbending with his colleagues. His class-room was on the ground floor at the back, looking out, through dirty windows, on to the Ashburnham lavatories. Even on a May morning the atmosphere was early November. Death got his nickname from the fact that about the eighth week of every term his Latin class arrived at a passage in Cicero which was the cue for Death's one great "teaching point," as we should call it now. He saw some similarity in the passage to the speech of John Bright in which the celebrated warning against war was uttered:

"The Angel of Death has been abroad throughout the land . . ."

I 129

Dead silence in the class. Salwey II—new boy—suddenly started attending!

". . . you may almost hear the beating of his wings."

This whole passage was really said extraordinarily well by Death, whose Hindenburg appearance suited these sentiments exactly. He was always in a good mood on the day when he delivered this speech, and there's no doubt he looked forward to it.

French is, by contrast with angel-of-death Latin, a language which later I learned to associate with elegance and gaiety, but Death's French lessons were delivered in exactly the same Ciceronian tone of voice. Standing very close to me, so that his chill sank into my throat, he would try to make certain that I distinguished the different pronunciations of "*le*" and "*leur*." "*Le*," he would say with a lightness like the flick of a dinosaur's tail, and then "*leur*" with a tremendous suggestion of a buried glutinous *r*, as if he were spitting up molten lead. This method, which was to make me permanently inhibited in modern languages and potbound with my French for life, was usual in Public Schools of this period.

My other lessons that day included, besides Latin and French, Maths in the afternoon under "Bill." Bill had a passion for using chalk; he was inclined to concentrate on Euclid for the sake of the diagram. Bill's class was usually the "long period," three to five— that sojourn into melancholy when thought and feeling stopped, and the hands of the clock seemed glued to its face. I was to learn later in my life that from the teacher's point of view two-hour periods are treble, not double, the length of one. We knew these old masters by their moustaches. Old Bill's moustache was hard and grey, petrified with age; but it was a baby face, with wide eyes made sadder, no doubt, by the long afternoons. All of us, boys and master, lived for the end of the lesson. Thinking of the cigarette in the Common Room, Bill fondled his gown just where it was most eaten away with cigarette burns. As a reminder of his most recent moment of freedom, a faint but by no means noxious flavour, which I was later to recognise as the aftermath of one pint, drifted from him. In class he never gave an inch, never expanded, never made a joke, exhibiting a personality far different from his natural one. Out of it, as his face showed, he longed to be friendly, popular with men's men, loved by children. Probably long disillusion had taught him that this unbending front was for him the easiest, and indeed the only way, since he was not a natural teacher, of "keeping order." At a hint of insubordination or cheek, this cherub stare could quickly change, the eyes bulging from his head, the whole face straining, hyperthyroidic—quite alarming enough to restore us to torpor. To begin the lesson, Bill sat at his desk, pretending to examine exercise-books, thereby hacking the first, hard seven minutes off the clock-face; then he would suddenly unleash a cloud of chalk, draw a diagram on the board with the speed of a lightning artist and tell us to "turn to Proposition 7, Book IV" in our books, and then go through the proof of it on the blackboard. This was carried out at great speed, as if Bill was showing off to us, and accompanied by a rapid, choking, half-strangled "explanation" impossible to follow. The chalk writing, with its signs and abbreviations, was very like that of a doctor's prescription, and of course illegible to us, just as his words, which were pressed out of him in a series of puffy squeaks, were half inaudible. Even had they been clear, their speed was far too great for us to be able to understand. Bill was always waiting for the perfect pupil who would comprehend him as readily as he had understood, in his last year at Cambridge, Professor Styles. But because he had long given up hope of such a pupil, after the first performance was over he would provide a second performance in which he spoke equally fast, equally unintelligibly, but with measurable angry pauses between each step in the argument and a high "D'you *see*?" After fifteen minutes of this, Bill very carefully wiped the illegible chalk marks, modelled very probably on the rapid hieroglyphics of his great master, Styles, off the blackboard, as if there was a possibility of our making use of them. "Now close yer books and do it yerselves," he would say, already fuming at the possibility that any single one of us might now fail.

In the thrall of time, now, the clock would hold us all, master and pupils, in its gluey grasp. We bent over sheets of paper while Bill would stare over our heads into some distance where he saw jolly gatherings of men in pubs or country meets (or his imagination of them), possibly hunting or shooting men, very frequently beagling, free, open-air and hearty, a society in which he had never really been even when he went to stay with his sister in Sussex, but a life to be admired and wanted; and one for which he almost looked fitted, with his big and naturally jolly red face.

Bill's was a class in which I shone. With the possible exception of Norreys, I was the only one to realise that Prop. 7, Book IV (or wherever it was that we had been told to open the book) was explained with all the usual clarity in Euclid's terms on the printed page in front of us. If I could stop my ears to the outpourings, the paralysing confusions of Bill's explanations and read the book instead, I would find each stage in the argument tapped home in the highly satisfactory Euclid pattern.

As a new boy, I had triumphantly been the first to break into Bill's dream of fields gleaming with frost (or sleepy sun in meadows according to the season) with a correct answer. Bill had checked it quickly, written a barely decipherable 10/10 at the bottom and handed it back to me without a word or a blink of acknowledgment. I learnt later that to finish my work early was as unpopular as making a noise in one's prison cell after Sunday lunch—that it upset Day-Dream Hour and made everybody clock-conscious, and that this hurt Bill more than it hurt any of us.

I believe, but am not sure, it was in Bill's that I was first able to look with, instead of merely at, a master—first dimly realised that he could have feelings, wishes and semi-human thoughts.

There was nothing terrible about these masters. After all, there was no beating, no physical cruelty in this school, which once had been celebrated for merciless flogging, in the Busby tradition. Scottish little Mr Liddell was warm and gentle. He glowed like the small gas fire in his study. By contrast with the other masters, too, the friendly sarcasm of Rudwick, the only youthful master was like a friendly grasp of the hand. But there really was something a little horrible about "Squelch the Corruptor." He was a virtuoso of the keep-'em-down technique, with attack aimed at new boys who had been placed in a class above their age because of scholastic ability and precocity—small, white-faced creatures who were likely not to be popular with older boys anyhow. Squelch made a tremendous point of seeing good in the big, athletic boys—J.B.W. Jones, for instance, Vice-captain of Cricket before he was seventeen, a record, but never promoted above Squelch's, also a record. Squelch was openly admiring of him, and helped him through awkward bits of translation. I never saw quite how Squelch made the little good boys feel miserable. He never rapped their knuckles. One saw him standing over them with a look of distaste; then suddenly they burst into tears. After a really satisfactory sob from one of these boys, Squelch would pervade us with a rancid form of geniality.

Moral bullying was the weakness of Westminster at this time—a sort of weary, impersonal reproof, which emphasised the hopelessness of the unsuccessful, an attitude which reached its height in the ritual of the gravest punishment of all, the "Up School Beating," when in the big historic hall, in front of the assembled boys and masters, some ashen-faced criminal would be summoned to answer for some unnamed crime and would receive two strokes of the birch on each palm, the birch held in the hand of the Headmaster, and allowed to drop with its own weight, falling with a deadly softness—no physical pain, just a lifetime of remembering.

Would it ever get better for me? Would I ever get really clear of ruck status? There were no disasters. I was never miserable. But 1915 dragged slower than 1914, and at the end of 1916 I was still only just scrambling into the Shell. Would I never get going? By the time, six years earlier, my sister had reached my age she was entering the top form of her school: three years later she had taken a scholarship to Oxford and was half-way towards her First. Obviously I had no hope of a scholarship or Oxford for myself. It was taken for granted that after Westminster and the Army I should go straight into Father's office—splendid opening, wonderful chance. Anyhow, what a heavenly contrast Father would be, as a mentor, to any of my Westminster masters. Besides, I should be a man, with a briefcase and a bowler-hat, and have lunch in a restaurant every day. But was I never to get anything out of Westminster? I was dimly aware that there could be something actively negative about the failure to learn a subject. There was such a thing as anti-learning. Looking back now, I can see there were areas of incipient interest from which many of us were sealed off for years. So far as school was concerned, a natural English interest in English words and poetry was corked up firmly until my last year. Natural history, if it was ever mentioned at all, had to appear in the guise of a "science side" subject, and Science was in the inexpert hands of the Roach, so far as we Classics were concerned. Once a week we had to watch the Roach's laboratory demonstrations. I remember that these were generally unsuccessful. Sometimes they ended in explosions, and a furious "Stand up anyone who laughed." The penal drill queue was always extra long after these Friday mornings.

There was a considerable amount of anti-learn about Art also. Art meant drawing—endless drawings of a dusty plaster-cast of the Discobolus executed under the eye of an unsuccessful water-colourist stonily determined that his class should not be regarded by his pupils as a place to lounge and slack.

One of the most extraordinary anti-learning feats which Westminster performed on me was to put a stopper on a natural passion for games-playing. True, I very soon separated "games" from "school games" in my head—a conjuring trick made easier by the fact that Westminster's grim word for games was "Station." Station had two sides to it, equally compulsory. Actively it meant taking up one's position on the soccer or cricket field at the time stated for the practice game to begin. Inactively it meant attending First XI matches against other schools.

Games life was rather like work life at Westminster in this respect. One could rise to the blessed circle of the accepted and successful only by a combination of natural talent, dogged drive and a gift for catching the favourable eye of the master. Perhaps for me

there is some rough justice in the fact that as I was myself lacking
in all three characteristics, I never received from any senior boy or
master a single word of advice on how to hold a cricket bat or how
to kick a football. Football I did enjoy in spite of everything: but
cricket without coaching was pure unpleasantness; and I used to
pray for the Wednesday afternoon to be wet so that I could slip
home and eat my way through a column of dripping-toast fifteen
inches high in the glorious peace of No. 36, with the dog whining
for sugar and *The Cloister and the Hearth* open by my side.

Every Saturday afternoon we all had to watch the First XI.
Forty years later I am able to sit through even the most unyielding
Lancashire *v.* Yorkshire match, or the most quicksilver Junior
Prep. School match, with delight and absorption; but the must of
"Station" cast a cloud over the cricket-watching (which I had so
much enjoyed with Uncle Percy) for ten years. The football in the
winter was better: though unfortunately it was a point of honour
among us juniors of the ruck not to wear warm clothes. Dimly in
the river mists of Vincent Square we stood shivering on the touch-
line in our miserably inappropriate top-hats, moaning from time to
time the melancholy cry "West-min-*ster.*" But Westminster is a
famous soccer school, and we had a fine eleven in 1916. Two of
my most admired heroes were in the team. True, Marchmont,
looking fresh and bristling even on the muddiest day, splendid
clouds of steam rising from his head, had no great brilliance; but
he always looked so serious and dependable that it was generally
agreed that he was a tower of strength. Carless was the great one;
and it was well known that he was brave. It was said that he was
the best goal-keeper Westminster ever had. I understood that on
two occasions he had carried on through the game after cracking a
rib, or breaking a collar-bone, or both. Not being very certain of
the anatomical aspects of these injuries, I used to stand as close to
the goal he was defending as I politely could, admiring his wonderful compact play and scrutinising him closely for some sign of
cracked collar-bone or a broken rib, which I imagined should be
sticking out under his jersey like the point of a billiard cue. Carless never spoke to me or looked at me, and I never dared to look

directly at him; but I used often to boast of being at Westminster with him. So, except for soccer, there were no games pleasures for me at Westminster. Feeling that I was doomed to permanent ineptitude, and unwilling to expose this to the world, I had no heart to try Westminster fives or rackets. These were enjoyments for the future.

The biggest stopper of all, though I was mostly unaware of it at the time, was on the side of life which is ruled by the planet Venus. The causes of this were about equally divided between Home and School. No kind of mention—to say nothing of explanation—of the sexual functions was ever encouraged, nor ever arose at No. 36. Perhaps my generation of urbanites was unique in the degree in which this whole side of life was cancelled from consciousness. Freud, instead of being taken for granted, was just beginning to be heard of, as a sort of joke word, a scare, a cue for an amused and amusing leading article by the great W.M. of the *Daily Mirror*; but nevertheless my own family were really and truly of the age when nobody mentioned anything. A generation or two earlier, when farm life and town life were all mixed up together, such a scrubbing out of the essential means of race-survival would have been impossible. The mechanics of sex were never explained nor mentioned in any book which could conceivably be seen by me or by any member of my family. Of course, there had been a good deal of talk among my prep. school friends which had shocked me, bizarre hints of extraordinary uses to which various parts of the human body were sometimes put. For myself, I didn't believe a word of it. I thought it was one of Weddington's silly jokes. He used to pass me little drawings of the most unbelievable nature during the *Henry V* period. I was too timid or cagey to join in with these sexual-parts drawings, nor was I going to admit that I couldn't get the hang of them. As a counterblast, and in order to play my part, I used to contribute drawings which displayed a right angle submerging into a wavy straight line which was supposed to be the sea, thus

The idea was to pass this drawing on and then, in a voice which was imitation Cockney but full of eeriness, whisper, "Titanic sinking." This was a topical joke (1912) repeated endlessly, and the little scare about sexual parts was momentarily forgotten. Yet early sexual feelings alarmed me. I thought they were peculiar to myself, very probably unique, possibly caused by some malformation. Yet to whom could I speak of this? Mother—impossible. As for Father, I personally thought it unlikely that he would ever have heard of this whole peculiar little business.

Bottle up . . . never mention it . . . something nasty . . . beware. At Westminster girls and sex were a huge inaudible whisper, the rumble of an earthquake five miles beneath the deep sea floor. If Westminster was completely unfemale, then even more remarkably was No. 36. No pretty girls visited us in No. 36 land; with the exception of Gwen, Muriel's great friend at Oxford, who had a jolly, clear-skinned prettiness, always bursting with laughter and pleasure, livening up the whole house. I loved her, but she was six years older—a generation at that age. There was one decidedly lovely girl, with a delicate face of soft curves and shadows, and wonderful thick chestnut hair, which hung in clusters like Jacobean table-legs—great twists of rich brown plaited barley-sugar, glistening and soft, yet dry and springy. These splendid arrangements of hair hung down below her shoulder-blades, and so prodigal was it that two or three extra consignments of it hung down towards her breast as well. This girl lived at No. 48, and she used to catch one of my trains in the morning—the nine-eight electric to Victoria. This shook my loyalty to the steam nine-ten. I never knew her name. I used to think of her as the electric-train girl. I liked to try fairly hard to sit opposite her in the carriage. When I saw Gwen I used to feel cheered up and I poured out talk and good jokes at her, showed her a new way of getting down our staircase, etc. But when I saw the electric girl I seemed to freeze and my heart felt like stone. Having dodged and pushed my way down the platform to get into a carriage with her, pounding after this wonderful hair, which left behind it the very faintest scent, I would contemplate her censoriously, with a face of earnest gloom.

Once she smiled at me. It may not have been a smile, but she had a way of sitting impassively, never moving her hands, much less rubbing her nose or making frowning faces or fumbling with books and the ridiculous umbrella, as I did. She turned her completely unembarrassed, her entirely uncoquettish eyes full on me, as if asking me, quite kindly, why I was staring. I would not admit it fully to myself, but I knew well enough that I should speak to her. How? What to say? We were at Victoria now, a fact which emphasised that this was not Home world, but School world, where things went wrong, where everything I did I did badly. I was pushed beside her by the crowd, and gave her, I suppose, a ghastly smile. I opened my mouth to speak—but what?

"Could I . . . wasn't . . ." What was I doing? Yet some sound like this was all that would come from my mouth. A sort of click. "Cl . . ."

The electric girl smiled rather abruptly and turned away. She was gone. I was of the opinion that no pretty girl, of the kind I particularly admired, would ever wish to speak to me. This confirmed it.

Not long after, Mother, knowing by some hundredth sense that I had noticed this girl, told me in a worried whisper that she wasn't really very nice, not really nice. Lowering her voice, she allowed me to know that she had seen her being kissed by a man under the street-lamp opposite Miss Braid's, No. 47. It was a sort of relief to hear this. I guessed that for Mother to say such a thing was wrong; I also knew that I could never disagree with her on this. I probably backed her up. If ever I was near the electric-train girl again, I looked as stern as a judge passing sentence.

After this event I used to look at myself in the glass very much more frequently, convinced that I did this not because of conceit but for unconceit. Indeed, I occasionally explained this to Muriel or Fizz. There would so often at that time be the annoying spot on the chin—a bad part of my face anyhow, because it was still retreating too far behind my nose. Mother, because of her military up-bringing, insisted on my cutting my hair close to my head, like a convict. I felt, erroneously, that a frowning, look-people-in-the eye expression was becoming. I was completely healthy, but in no way particularly attractive to boys or masters. I disliked the dingy smartness of the ridiculous clothes we all wore, though on Corps days, O.T.C. days, thank heaven, we looked much better. I hated the smells of the changing room, the various boy-odours in crowded corridors. There was plenty of scope among the boarders at Westminster for the kind of love in which Apollo was the substitute for Venus; but in so far as I understood these activities, which was dimly, they were made horrifying if not unbelievable to me by the fact that apparently they took place in the unpleasant and by no means perfectly clean lavatories just behind the Cloisters.

I had never heard the word "homosexuality" and never thought there could be any connection between such grim doings and the fact of my curious delight, my pleasure whenever D. was in class, and the happiness I felt when, standing on the top floor of the staircase, I saw the cropped head of young D. beginning to climb the stairs towards me, his strong and pudgy hand on the iron railing.

But there must be no touching. At home, Mother's good-night kiss was pleasant; Father's hand on my arm endurable; but I held my breath and glazed my eyes when I had to kiss the quite reasonably comely face of Auntie Rose. As if her head had lost all bone, my mouth seemed to sink on and on into her face for ever. I felt as if I was drowning in cheek. Touch was my enemy.

At the end of term came the School Report. *Potter, S. Could do better . . . does not seem to take much interest in . . . fair . . . it is a pity that . . . could do well if he tried . . .*

Mother could read all kinds of optimistic and even flattering meanings into such words as "Fair"; but these reports must have been bewilderingly disappointing to Mother and Father and the uncles and the aunts. Father and Mother, anyhow, believed I was next door to brilliant. Father, never of course hinting at the financial hardship of it all, pretended to make a joke of these rebuffs.

"This—ah—Mr Willett—of the indistinct signature—seems to have an extraordinary strain of denseness——"

"Failure to appreciate genius——" (I must try to keep up Father's joke.)

"Not without a tinge—shall we say—of jealousy? 'Two stars keep not their motion in one sphere'?" Father, standing wide-legged and small in front of the fire, eased his shoulders, as if forgetting the gloomy cause of the conversation in the satisfaction of an apt quotation while somehow making fun of this satisfaction and his attitude at the same time.

Later on Mother and Muriel had a more serious discussion on the subject of my reports in general.

"He's outgrowing his strength."

Mother had the perfect phrase for it, and my sister loyally agreed with her, indeed unquestioningly believed it. It is true that between thirteen and sixteen I changed from that wonderful weightlessness enjoyed by the little boy running about in gym shoes to a stalky lengthening of limbs and torso. "Look at those shins," Muriel said. "Like scaffolding." It was a Corps day, and I was winding on my puttees.

"'Neither delighteth he in any man's legs,'" said Mother, upset by the slightly caustic tone of Muriel's remark. "Great Uncle Walter was an outstandingly tall man," she continued, though in fact tallness, except for my cousin Leonard, who was really tall (much too lanky, Mother said), was not an ingredient of either side of the family.

"People used to turn round and look at him in the street," Mother began to elaborate, no doubt imagining that very shortly it was on me that people would be turning their admiring glances.

But though I never remember a trace of growing pains, the suggestion that they existed came in conveniently during that unhappy year in Sam's form. I could take comfort in the fact that his nasty little remarks were the jealous impertinences of a stony tyrant, not able to recognise a semi-invalid when he saw one. It was certainly difficult for everybody, in those days, to maintain the myth of myself as the wonderful son, the promising boy. I seemed half the time to be trying to eradicate myself, to disappear. In term-time, though I lived at home, I would try to shut myself off and bury myself in the newspaper or Kipling. No sooner was I home than my spine became semicircular, curved over a book or the piano. The contrast between school and the admiring kindness and encouragement of Family was too depressingly ironical.

"Of course, it is a very trying time for a boy——"

Mother would be using her knowledgeable voice to Muriel, releasing this confidence as if trying times for girls were either irrelevant, exaggerated or unknown. But my term reports got worse. I used to dread them. And of course the complete absence of recrimination at home made me all the more uneasily conscious that I ought to provide Mother and Father with some slight sign that I was doing something at school which might have some slight chance of pleasing them.

CHAPTER EIGHT

Side-door Education

LESSONS. Period Three. History 11–12. If only there were other words for these things, one might learn. Or if only I could start one of these subjects again from the beginning, so that I could make certain which was left, which was right, which was top and which was bottom. Too late to ask such questions now: so all must ever remain doubtful and obscure. The result was that I could only learn outside learning hours—round the corner, so to speak: a sort of education sideways.

Some of this was done through the uncles. Some of it was at home. Here, in the evenings and holidays, I automatically changed my role from the unsuccessful schoolboy, from "Potter," the surname I disliked (sounding as it did curt, humdrum and unsympathetic) to "Stephen," which much more suggested the promising repository of undeveloped talents which I was supposed to be.

Unconsciously I was growing up to agree with this almost completely unsubstantiated estimate. My only doubt was just exactly which form my talent was going to take.

Drawing, I thought, first of all. While Muriel was at Oxford I filled my weekly letters to her with caricatures—I was certain these were exceptional—of Father in Paris, or Leonard in his new Tank Corps uniform. Even when I was eight, Mother had been certain of my talent. That drawing of her umbrella and Father's walking-stick, done with a 2B pencil, which became more and more smudged as it was shown to more and more relatives, was after all pinned up in the corridor of Clapham High. In fact, a drawing of a poppy filled in with red chalk was exhibited in the White City Exhibition, although it is true that as this was one of 12,000 drawings packed indoors in the long shed next to the pavilion which housed a model of the Prince of Wales in New Zealand butter, neither I nor anyone else, perhaps owing to this other attraction, was ever able to find it. Except for my day in Boulogne with Uncle Jim, I had never been farther abroad than Whitby; but I travelled tens of thousands of miles by copying maps of foreign countries, the more complicated the coastline the better. The coastline of Bernard Partridge, the chief cartoonist of *Punch*, was almost equally intricate: yet I could never successfully imitate the dignity of his lions.

But immediately after the lions, it had come to me with equal force that I was going to be a great author. This feeling of certainty was first manifest during one of those supreme intervals of my school life, the Bad Cold. Once a term I had to have a bad cold or burst. For at least one week it made me free. For the first two days of it I was being looked after with absolute and perfect attention by Mother, for the rest of the time I was being a genius. Everything seemed clear to me. It was not only the writing, there were the things I wrote with—pencils ranging from 3H to 3B. "It was then he realised he was going to be a great story-writer." Mother used to tell me stories about her most admired authors— this one I think may have been George Meredith, her favourite novelist, whom she had discovered before she was pregnant with me, hoping for a son to give him "Meredith" for a second name. Within a week of hearing this story I realised that I myself was going to be a great story-writer.

I certainly liked writing long letters, but as I didn't know anybody outside the family, and as nobody ever went away, there was nobody to write letters to until Muriel went to Oxford. She has kept a bundle of these letters. Never for a second do they relax, or say anything straightforward or simply. I had a romantic view of Oxford. I knew Muriel read books outside my ken. I thought of her life as a mixture of the intellectual and the gay, mixing on equal terms and enjoying boating parties with under-graduates. My picture of university life was dependent on *Charley's Aunt*. The word "undergraduate," with its fascinating abbreviation, at No. 36, to undergrad., suggested a being full of desirable perfections. I wanted to show in my letters that this level was by no means impossibly high for me.

The great Fowler phrase "polysyllabic humour" had not then cast its damper on my writing. But what matter? It was taken for granted that my letters really were exceptionally amusing.

Whether this general family support was always, or indeed ever, a good thing for me is difficult to say; but I do know that I enjoyed one huge advantage through my home, one which though far from universal outside the families of professional artists and writers, was yet something I took for granted. Everybody at No. 36, Father, Mother, Muriel and Jim, took reading books for granted. This particularly included reading the accepted classics. My sister, sailing into classical English Literature at Oxford, was already reaping the advantage of this, and she was destined to instil in me a competitive reading spirit. At home Ruskin, Carlyle, Browning and "the great novelists" were always on tap. It was not that I was ever pushed in this direction. A touch of that would have been too much for my lacerated lesson-time surfaces. It was simply that Mother's normal reading was George Eliot or H. G. Wells or Bulwer Lytton; and I cannot remember the time when names like Boswell and Johnson or Milton or Bunyan or Charles Lamb were unknown to me.

Father was the only one to make an effort to improve the occasion. He occasionally thought there should be some kind of reading aloud. Getting into a suitable position, he would put on a certain expression, serious yet slightly smiling, and then, after a little unobtrusive coughing and clearing up and a long stare at the page, say, "This is rather wonderful." Whereupon (after a stare at Mother to suggest or even demand that she kept quiet while he did this for the children) he would begin to read.

This was usually on Sunday, and the book was usually Ruskin. He did not have much chance, with us. Mother would get up at once, to do something unnecessary. This would make Father sit immobile, silent, with his finger on the place. Muriel would listen, I would listen, but with no encouragement. After two minutes Father would get a tickle in his throat and begin coughing.

"Frank, dear——" Mother would say.

Father, speechless, would wave her away.

"Cigarettes," she would say, very quietly.

"Please, Lilla . . ."

Father banged the book down; but his voice had left him completely.

"Now, how many have you smoked today?" There was a fairly thick sprinkling of the stubs of Father's half-smoked cigarettes, early cork-tipped variety and much chewed, in the four main ashtrays. Mother looked at me with a helpless, hopeless, shake of the head. Father, still voiceless, stamped his foot. He swallowed. Tried his voice again. It seemed to have returned. "A city of marble, did I say?" It was a good start, but as so often, after his coughing, he suddenly suffered a real earthquake of a sneeze. This meant always that twelve more sneezes would follow at ten-second intervals, which would be plainly heard through the cardboardy wall when he had rushed from the room to have his sneezes in the drawing-room, burying these explosions in enormous clean handkerchiefs smelling of eau-de-cologne.

Back again, Father would come in, set in order but faint in the voice. "So sorry," he would say courteously, painfully, as if a dying man were asking forgiveness from the child he had most indulged. The Ruskin anthology was thin and soft, bound in light-green calf without boards. Its atmosphere of Sunday depressed me. Father had one more shot at the reading. "This is really rather fine. *Modern Painters*."

"From what dear?" Father's delicate voice had been much weakened by the sneezing.

"*Modern Painters*," he said huskily, lightly tapping his chest and looking as if he was going to sneeze again. Uncle Jim, sitting in his far corner leant forward and put a hand behind his ear.

A city of marble, did I say? nay rather a golden city, paved with emerald. For truly, every pinnacle and turret glanced or glowed, overlaid with gold, or bossed with jasper. Beneath . . .

I could see Father was getting the tickle in his throat again.

Beneath the unsullied sea drew in deep breathing, to and FRO . . .

Father spoke this very loud to prevent the tickle from turning into a cough, and paused for a long swallow.

"Let's see, where are we now?" said Uncle Jim, suddenly wanting to be one of the gathering.

"St Mark's," said Father in a whisper. Mother took advantage of the pause to adjust the wick of the big oil-lamp.

"VENICE." Father had got his voice back in a sudden rush, but the spell was broken, and I knew there wouldn't be any more reading. I knew Mother was going to say, "Your Father and I went to Venice soon after we were married, you know." This had been her one visit to the Continent, the great treat of all time, the last chance before the children became too expensive, the great glorious time which they were to talk about happily ever after. There would be no more reading. Father's cough cleared up completely, but he was offended with all of us. This might mean that he would say "Really!" and sit in his corner reading the *Sunday Referee*, his back a little towards us. Ten minutes later he would have forgotten all about it. It was not through Ruskin that Father and Mother gave my reading such a useful push. It was years before I read *Modern Painters* on my own for pleasure.

There was one author more taken-for-granted in the Potter household than any other. Writers were writers in those days, and although my parents knew nothing of him personally, they told me that the news of his death brought tears and days of mourning. This was Dickens.

This worshipful attitude was somewhat putting off to the younger generation; but in the end I fell just as deeply under the spell. The conversion was a slow one. "I think you'd love it," said Father, wanting to read it aloud.

Nobody thought this was a good idea. "Just try it," said Aunt Ethel. "*Pickwick Papers*."

"Mr Snodgrass," said Mother, beginning to laugh at the mere mention of the name. Father was having the giggles.

"Head in a water-butt; full confession in the left boot." He wiped his eyes.

"Mr Jingle," Auntie Rose began, "Stephen would love him. I'd rather I found you out than found you in!" Everybody laughed, until Auntie Rose looked at me critically, questioningly, as if in my Dickensless state I was scarcely one of the family.

"Anybody who loves fun . . ." she said.

I did have a really serious try at *Pickwick Papers*, but it was no good. This was when I was ten, and the first chapter, which might take me two hours and a half to read in those days, was a stumbling block. It was peculiar, and it certainly did not make me laugh. I had two tries, and then gave up.

The book which converted me is in my hand as I dictate this. Even then the pages were freckled with brown spots, and it looked like an old curiosity. The page is very full of thick type, there is not much margin, and, more intense to me in those days, there is the odour of sour old paper which wafts into my face when I open it. It was not Dickens: it was "by Boz."

Sketches by Boz, an early bound edition (1839), I got to know because Jim liked reading it; and Jim read so well that I preferred listening to him to reading it myself. He had a perfect sense of comedy. My favourite story was "The Boarding House," the respectable establishment run by Mrs Tibbs. The names were so funny—Mr Wisbottle, Dr Wosky. The scene was Mrs Tibbs's dining-room before dinner. "'Julia my love,' said Mrs Maplesone to her youngest daughter. 'Don't stoop.'" Uncle Jim's brisk-soda-water voice was perfect for it. "This was said for the purpose of directing general attention to Miss Julia's figure, which was undeniable." Next morning the poetic young gentleman was down early.

"'Wisbottle—come here a moment. Beautiful, isn't it? The effect of the light on the broken chimney pot of No. 46.'"

How unspeakably and agonisingly funny. Everything in the story was funny. Even the name of the author was funny—Boz.

I soon learnt the real name of the author from one of those little rhymes Father liked reciting:

> Who the dickens Boz could be
> Puzzled many a curious elf
> Till at last 'twas proved, you see,
> Boz, it was, 'twas Dickens' self.

This was a prelude to months and years of Dickens-reading. Most of *Barnaby Rudge* was read lying under the dining-room table in a light by which now I couldn't even see the title of the book. *Martin Chuzzlewit* wiped out school prep. for a term. The style was so fresh and vigorous that one could tell it was Dickens even if it had been a torn-out scrap of paper pasted on the back of a toothbrush. The print seemed to stand out in low relief. It was not only inexpressibly funny, but (and this made it still more wonderful) it was most tremendously sad as well. How I enjoyed sadness in those days. And how I enjoyed clarity, particularly moral clarity. No doubtfulness, in Dickens, of what was mean and what was generous, what was good and what was bad. Uriah Heep was bad through and through—and equally, so was Steerforth. It was either one thing or the other: no doubts, and no confusing different side of the story.

My other big side-entrance to knowledge was through music. In fact I only didn't go in through the front door because although to my blessed good luck Father and Mother encouraged my music and exchanged pleased glances (in which Jim did not join) when I played the piano, conscience cast a slight shadow across the zest of those hours spent in that unzestful drawing-room. This was chiefly because I could not believe that anything I enjoyed so much could be "good," good for me. As late as 1928 it was a surprise and a puzzle to me to read a passage in Bernard Shaw in which he says "My chief education was through the Beethoven Sonatas." Add Mozart violin and piano, I began thoughtfully to say, and that would be me. But even then I wondered how.

All through the dreary school day I wanted to get back, say, to try out the new Beethoven tune I was, by a familiar but delicious process, on the verge of ingesting, incorporating, getting inside myself. Even at Rillo Road I had been able, because I knew it by heart, to make on my desk with the tips of my fingers the shape of the andante of Op. 14, No. 2. Recently I had discovered the tune at the top of page 2 of the scherzo. "Dolce" is the indication but it was more than that. It slipped and slithered about as if it was

148

an airy-fairy little dog on a lead, the lead being the bass, of semi-quavers regularly meted out. I began looking forward to playing it about half way through Bill's Euclid lesson, in the beginning of the afternoon. As soon as I got home, before even I dug into the stack of toast and jam waiting for me, I nicked into the drawing-room to try the new bit over.

CHAPTER NINE

King Henry's Chapel

"YOU want to use your eyes."

I still think this is one of the most enfeebling of all the standard stupid remarks made, or made in the old days, to children. "Don't walk along in a dream; use your eyes."

It depends of course on the tone of voice. But I particularly remember one occasion when it was said to me, because the tone of voice was unmistakably not the right one, and because it happened at home, the very place where, normally, I was most carefully shielded from such unpleasant shafts.

This happened one November, a month I was particularly fond of. No. 36, being small, was also cosy; and November is a fine month to be indoors. No sunshine on the carpet to make me feel restless or think of slow-bicycling races with Leonard on the airy lawns of Bryn Cottage. With fog outside, lights on at 4 p.m. and from the oil-lamp—a private tent of light—*Bleak House* or the new Sherlock Holmes story in the *Strand Magazine* seemed twice as good. Moreover, October–November–December was a crescendo phrase leading to Christmas, and Christmas, in my Dickensy family, was gone in for so thoroughly and therefore so enjoyably that I began to feel pleased about it six weeks ahead.

Another nice thing—November was usually a month of planning for the St Luke's Amateur Operatic Society. The war stopped this in 1914, but 1915 was to be a special number, all proceeds to go to Christmas Parcels for the Troops. The words, as usual, were by Mr Clarke the Vicar; a special juvenile lead, not nearly juvenile enough for the Army, was available for the hero; Josh's friend, Mr Child, whose satanic laugh still gave me a delicious chill, was the villain; costumes, always first class, by Mr

Compton Northing (who had something to do with Arding and Hobbs) and Josh himself as Producer and Chief Comic Man.

The music was written by Father. I suppose tastes were under the dominion of family loyalty; but it seemed to me that Father was top, and Uncle Josh second, always, in the final share-out of honours. We were all argumentative critics. The style was closely modelled on the Edward German operettas; but listening to Father's tunes as they evolved at home, they seemed to me to possess a perfection of sweetness—particularly (like Sullivan) in the concerted pieces. Even now I can recall nearly all of them; and even now I cannot be sure whether the enjoyment was the result of family pride or Father's melodic gifts. As a violinist Father was sketchy; as a pianist he "played by ear," which meant in practice that he evolved a method of striking every chord twice—first very lightly, to see if it was right, and then the corrected chord immediately afterwards, very heavily. This sounded all right in the next room through the matchboarding, but in the piano room where I sat listening it took the edge off the musical effect. Father had a weakness, too, for noble hymny effects, and when he had got the notes right he would keep his fingers on them and look up at the shining picture-rail near the ceiling as if he was inside a cathedral gazing at the distant roof. Seriousness was never Father's strong point; but his gay music was delicious, and I enjoyed every stage in the process, from those first peculiar piano sounds to the sight of Father in his dress clothes mounting the rostrum as conductor for the first night, looking solemn and well-mannered beyond the reaches of everyday possibility as he bowed to the audience, while all of us were hoping that next Sunday's *Referee* would contain a little paragraph by Mr Brookfield (a genuine dramatic critic and friend, of course, of Uncle Josh) including the sentence "The music, by Mr F. C. Potter, was once again exceptionally tuneful."

Sometimes the performance itself was a bit of an anti-climax. The seats in St Luke's Church Hall were not too comfortable, and the atmosphere had the clayey quality of unconsecrated buildings which, though never prayed in, had never been smoked in or drunk

in either. But the criticisms, the dressing-up, the mysterious fact
that everybody's imitation of everybody else's amateur acting was
usually better than their own performance in their own part, the
music-copying for the orchestra (which sometimes I was allowed
to do a bit of) and in general the whole world behind the curtain
was all high on the list of my different kinds of side-door education.

It was one day when I was in the middle of all these excitements
that somebody said "use your eyes." I was listening to the grown-
ups talking operetta shop. As long as I kept fairly silent, I was able
to sit in even on discussions and planning. The theme for the 1915
production was *The Merry Monarch*, with Uncle Josh as Samuel
Pepys and the new Juvenile Lead as the King. The heroine was
Sweet Nell of Old Drury; but there was no impropriety in the
script, and to emphasise this fact the scenes between Nell and King
Charles were carried on an unusually wide distance apart. The
casting of Nell was the difficulty. The girl should be irreproach-
ably modest in bearing of course, but Uncle Josh (producer) and
Malcolm Child (the villain, Monmouth), the memory of 1913
strongly in their minds, were both determined that there should
be a pretty girl in the cast this year. In the dining-room Mr Clarke
and Father were discussing the subject with Mr Compton Northing. As a reward for his hard work of designing the costumes, it
was traditional to offer the part of the heroine to Mr Northing's
daughter, a handsome girl with fierce black eyebrows which met in
the middle. But she was remarkably square-shouldered, and so far
as general looks were concerned she was about the size and shape
of a grandfather clock. Uncle Josh had put his foot down, and
wanted Father and Mr Clarke to break the news. Father began by
staring hard at Mr Clarke, and then said, clearing his throat
in the middle of the sentence:

"Mr Northing, we want to discuss a rather delicate matter."

Northing was on to it at once and took slight offence before he
knew the point; but in the end he took it surprisingly amiably (his
daughter was inclined to be irritable with him). At the same time
Northing wanted to make some sort of scoring-point himself,

preferably against somebody else's child. Suddenly he discovered that I was in the room.

"Our friend the son of the house," he said, smiling hard at Mr Clarke.

"Yes, boys are heard when they ought to be seen and seen when they ought to be heard nowadays," he went on. A staggering remark, I thought, to insert into a friendly discussion on art.

"About the costumes," Mr Northing went on in an atmosphere of restraint, "the difficulty is going to be the haberdashery for the men. Now then, Stephen, or whatever it is. What did the gentlemen wear round their necks in King Charles the Second's day? Can you tell me that?"

I never could answer a catch-question. Half-learnt history phrases rattled through my head. Judge Jeffreys, the Bloody Assizes, King Charles's spaniels . . .

"And there's a picture outside in your hall at this very moment. Why don't you use your eyes? You ought to use your eyes."

Of course I knew the picture, a copy of *The Laughing Cavalier* in sepia. "Semi-ruffs" is what I ought to have said. In my promising-artist period I had made a copy of this picture on a twopenny piece of cartridge-paper. Even sceptical Aunt Rose considered I had got the way the laughing cavalier wasn't really laughing at all.

"I thought this school of yours was supposed to be historical. Don't you ever look at the tombs in Westminster Abbey?"

"Oh, he's got a pretty good eye really, Northing." Mr Clarke was standing up for me; but Mr Northing might have planted a seed of doubt in Mr Clarke's mind, and this annoyed me.

What was I supposed to use my eyes *for*? On the pattern, faded almost to invisibility, of our dining-room couch? On the leaves of the syringa in the front garden, dusty and insect-bitten? But what was most annoying about Northing's remark was the fact that by chance he had hit on something, something about Westminster, which was familiar, which was indeed famous, but which had

nevertheless to be discovered separately and was thus being discovered, by myself, at that very moment.

"Sardine-openers" or "tin-openers" I was to nickname such
mental releases later. "Egg-shell-breakers" is really better, because the chicken, unlike the sardine, does make some slight effort
to get out on its own account. Yet the discovery of the Old is
gradual. In my family we grew up to believe that anything old was
good, the older the better. It never occurred to us that any modern
picture, ornament or, above all, building could be beautiful or
(with the possible exception of the Crystal Palace) worth visiting.
No holiday walk was considered too long if it ended up with the
sight of a church pre-1500. Any old cottage, the more derelict the
better, received respectful looks if it was half-timbered or thatched.
New books, new stories, new music and new pictures were in all
their different ways suspect.

In Westminster, in the precincts (as everybody knows), different
kinds of Old grow on every square yard. Old is under foot. On
the way through Cloisters from Little Dean's Yard to the Abbey,
there on the right is the entrance to the Chapter House. Up the
steps—but were there ever such steps? Five hundred years of
monks' feet, visitors' feet, earliest Parliament feet, had worn them
away till huge ruts, a foot deep, had been scooped out of the stone.
The steps have been renewed since, unfortunately, but those fantastic ruts in the solid stone were something I passed every day.
"I should think they're about a thousand years old," I was already
saying in my first year. Westminster School was in fact founded
by Elizabeth; but there had been a monastery school there since
the time of the first Abbey, the Confessor's Abbey; and parts of
the Confessor's buildings still exist near the Chapter House. Even
in the "modern" school, Elizabeth's school, things were quite
respectably old. At the far end of our Big School is a shallow apse
the seats of which form a scalloped semicircle. "Shell" this form
was called; and the fact that this spot marked the origin of all
Shells was something else for me to talk about at home. Somewhere within the curve of this shell-shape there was preserved, in
my time, the oldest remaining bench in the school. If one hap-

pened to be alone it was a good thing to sit on this bench. A pleasant glow of ancientness seemed to permeate the cold, thin trousers of my horrid school clothes. I used to call it the "Slade bench" myself, because in the midst of all the nicks and chips and carvings of initials and overcarvings a huge O. SLADE had been hacked out by some boy with an instinctive feeling that in this way only could his name be preserved. The instinct was a good one, because next to O. Slade, rather small and faint, was "J. Dryden." Slightly earlier than Dryden and far more fascinatingly named was Inigo Jones. Was not the gateway to Up School his work? Though now maybe it is considered the work of a pupil, it was always called the Inigo Jones gateway. Boys who had drawn a recognisable Discobolus in the Art Class were sometimes allowed to sit outside in draughty Little Dean's Yard and make drawings of this gate. The subject seemed to me at first a dull one, so to give it life and character I shaded it with copses of tiny parallel straight lines. I was sent back to the plaster cast of Hercules—another injustice. But I did, very gradually, even if only by passing through it twice a day, begin to feel from the gate that there could be something satisfactory in strictness and balance, and that there might be architecture later than the Gothic which yet was all right to look at.

Feeling of oldness, Stage One . . . and now (because was not Dryden a Westminster boy just like me?) a sense of recentness or newness as well (Stage Two). For a Third Stage I had to wait a little longer. I believe this comes with the thrill of the cross-reference, the clincher. I know this was what helped me to peck the second slight chip in my schoolboy shell. I got it first, I think, on a walk "Up Fields" with Westlake. Going "Up Fields" meant the ten-minutes dodge through crowds and traffic to Vincent Square, Westminster's playing-fields near the river. It was a good day for me, anyhow, because I was wearing my Ashburnham House Football Colours for the first time, and I felt quite a few of the people I pushed past, though apparently thinking of something quite different, had yet probably recognised that I was in fact wearing House Colours and were possibly glancing back after me when I had passed. On this Good Day, then, I was surprisingly joined by Mr Westlake. Westlake had taken Orders and was, I believe, connected with school in some organising capacity. He occasionally taught certain forms Divinity. With his blue chin, white face, eager walk and keen eye he looked like a Benedictine of the old Abbey, and indeed his real life and ambition was for knowledge of the Abbey, above every other sacred and profane pursuit. Westlake had a strong sense of duty about watching house matches; but his conversation was entirely History, and he used to plunge straight into it.

"Do you know why Westminster calls this walk going 'up fields'?" he said.

"No, sir—not really, sir."

"Because the whole area south of Victoria Street was all fields once—between Westminster and Chelsea. 'Tothill Fields' it was called."

Westlake suddenly dived out of sight. It was a funny idea— fields; and now, not a garden in sight. Then I began to tingle, and thought "Vauxhall Bridge Road . . . buried in trams and traffic now . . . but of course it was among fields once . . . I know it . . . *Pickwick Papers* . . . Mr Winkle . . . used to shoot rooks in the hedges of the Vauxhall Bridge Road."

The best of the cross-references came from Westminster Abbey. Abbey and Cloisters were within bounds for us, indeed we had special privileges to wander more or less where we liked. The Cloisters, with their spanking stone pavements, were a fine place for a brisk walk, and we would take the tickle out of our feet ("Shall we make a two round Abbey?") with a four-times-round-rapid as often as we got a break. Perhaps it was a good thing that we never had the Abbey forced down our throats in teaching hours, though we were occasionally made to feel uneasy about it, in the curious exhortations delivered to us by visiting eminent Old Wets on Speech Days:

You boys—all of you

"Tiny tots," said Maycroft, in his splendid ventriloquist voice, his face motionless. In the back row we used to make comments.

All you boys have within the throw of a cricket ball from where I am standing—you possess, as part of your heritage, this splendid Guide, this glorious picture book . . . the very monuments have their message . . .

This set Fizz off, because he was an adherent of the widely held theory that the marble figure of a seated man reading a book on an urn at the entrance to the Dark Cloister farted loud on two notes at midnight every night except Sunday.

The church of Edward, the shrine visited by a million pilgrims . . . this vast pile . . .

Maycroft, pretending to be helpless with silent laughter, whispered "Write out a hundred times."

. . . this splendid legacy of the Third Henry. . .

"1216–1272, he means," said Norreys, who was higher in form than he should have been because of a trick of being able to say the right date even if there was a catch in the wording of the context.

In the Cloister nearby, the little room where sat the first Parliament of mankind——

"He may mean the Monks' japs," said Fizz, using Westminster slang to remind us that he had once been told, by our verger friend Foden, that there were remains of an eleventh-century lavatory near the West Walk.

Of course I didn't realise a tenth part of it. It wasn't till fifteen years after I'd left Westminster that I found out such average facts as that the Hall we used for meals had, before the Reformation, been with its minstrels' gallery the refectory of the jolly monks; and if the long tables on which the boiled beef and synthetic dumplings were served to us did belong to Reformation times, the wood of the tables, black and weather-worn to the hardness of stone, had once been part of a captured galleon of the Armada.

The general design and principal motif of Westminster Abbey reflect the devout spirit of Henry III, its founder.

But there was nothing devout or mediaeval about the atmosphere of the Abbey as we saw it. In Catholic Europe we see these cathedrals, as we limp stiff-legged towards them from our cars after the 150-mile drive. Inside, sometimes they are lonely, "like the lair of some pre-historic monster." Others are like market-places, with three-year-olds shouting and running, visitors talking fortissimo, pigeons flapping along the nave, and before the high altar sulky choristers being rehearsed in a ritual by an exasperated priest. Or we see dim walks and shadowy pillars half-hidden by painted Virgins, glaring altar-pieces and violently coloured saints. These, for all their differences, have in common a kind of wild-animal naturalness, a democratic rawness and friendliness which our great reformed churches never suggest. Exeter and Winchester, so calm and beautiful to our eyes, are not more religious than a woodland glade; and though they may be "for the people," they are not expressly for the commonalty.

Westminster Abbey has this Englishness, but in a different way, much nearer to a more popular way. No miracles, no mystical experiences or spiritual conversions, the visitor feels at first sight, could ever take place in this incenseless air. It is a show-place, a museum. For relics there are the waxwork effigies in the precincts or the slab in the cloisters commemorating the oldest man on record. For religion there is the solemn and romantic association with royalty and royal occasions; or the royal tombs with actual bodies, only a few feet from people like Chaucer and Pitt as well. We used to expatiate on the probable condition of these bodies. Since Gladstone was fairly new, for instance, his skin would still be covering his skull, looking like wallpaper gone damp, according to Amos. It was pleasant to stand on this stone, because according to Foden, our verger friend, a man was murdered here, in defiance of sanctuary, by John of Gaunt's men.

Walking round alone there, as I often did, I liked the friendliness and the crowded muddle which makes the Abbey a sort of national drawing-room mantelshelf. I liked to examine the way in which the virtuoso sculptors had simulated parchment in the marble scrolls, grasped in the aristocratic and slender marble fingers of the eighteenth-century notables. Foden and I used to philosophise about these statues. Like Foden's, my view of right and wrong was perfectly clear in those days—a mixture of Gray's *Elegy* and *The*

Vanity of Human Wishes. "The less well-known the man, the bigger the statue," we agreed, and I philosophically noted the difference between the florid tomb of the Duke of N., leaking marble everywhere, and the simple bust of the great poet, with "O rare Ben Jonson" beneath.

Foden, the verger, seemed ordained to be the friend of newish or unsuccessful Westminster boys. I can see him now in my mind's eye with absolute clarity. His handsome face . . . that long, lean chin seemed specially made to suggest the sensible, clear-cut souls of church officials. His hair was silvery and distinguished. His shoulders were broad; but a quarter of a century of the Abbey had given him a fixed inclination forward, as if he were permanently passing in front of the high altar without precisely genuflecting; and his face usually wore a smile small and subdued as if by the presence of royalty. A schoolboy's estimate of age is about as accurate as a dog's impression of the height of a church tower, but I guessed he was between thirty and sixty. He seemed to me to be a man of great culture. He often quoted. "You won't know the author of that," he was always saying. "No particular reason why you should."

"Who was T. Bolton?" I said to him, pointing distastefully at some undistinguished memorial tablet with the uninteresting date 1780.

"Full many a flower is born to blush unseen," Foden would reply. "Author doesn't matter." He added the formula rapidly, almost inaudibly. In my first year at Westminster, before I had mastered the art of getting to Chapel on time, Foden was able, if he was on duty in that section, as usually he mysteriously was, to get me to a seat unnoticed after the service had begun. Half-concealed behind the folds of his verger's vestment, which he wore splendidly as if it was a toga, he had a miraculous way of pushing me behind the tomb of Dr Wollaston, Founder of Crystallography, so that I could be found sitting under Roubiliac's Handel as if I'd been there all the time. Foden looked especially religious when he was performing such services, and held his fine head at a stained-glass-window inclination.

Sometimes we used to confide in Foden. "Sacred Sam is being absolutely foul to me." I thought my low place in form was partly due to Sacred. Although I had not yet fallen fully under his dominion—a fate hanging over me—Sam was then my scripture master.

"The fault, dear Brutus, is not in our stars," Foden said in a voice, which was rich and muted at the same time, "but in ourselves . . ."

The aristocratic voice of a fine actor, and yet, deep at its core, the vestige of a Cockney accent. I often used to walk round with Foden, and visit with him certain tombs to which he seemed to have an addiction. In the nave of the Abbey, where many of these tombs lay, Foden became slightly less religious and his stoop straightened out a little as befitted an area of the church so removed from the high altar. His step quickened, though in his fabulously thick rubber soles it was as soundless as ever. The Baroness Burdett-Coutts was a favourite tomb theme of his. He was so remarkably *sotto voce* on this subject that I never understood what he was talking about; but, by contrast, some of the other Foden tombs opened my mind to great facts. "If you had been born in the sixteenth century," Foden said, "the probability is that you wouldn't have grown up at all."

We were standing before the tomb of Lord Norris.

"The chances would have been about five to one against." As there was only Muriel and me, I felt I had had a particularly lucky escape. The position of the small figures of the offspring was meant to indicate that only one of six children survived. Except for Pitt, Gladstone and Mr Asquith, the only Prime Minister whose name was known to me in early days was Spencer Perceval, because this was one of Foden's favourite tombs. The scene of his murder by a madman is shown carved in deep relief, and was closely scrutinised many times by Fizz and myself under Foden's guidance.

"Examine the eye of the lunatic," Foden used to say. "It is not like my eye or your eye."

I was not so sure of this, I thought, when I came to take a good look at my own right eye in the soapy looking-glass by father's shaving apparatus in the bathroom. I had many worries, then, about unfavourable prognostications latent in my features. Auntie Rose once said of Geoffrey Flint, not the most promising of the young men who were inclined to call on my sister at this time, that it was "a pity he had rather a *weak chin*." If this meant that his chin was slightly receding, all I could say was that it seemed to me, looking sideways in the glass by a special invention of using two mirrors at once, that my chin was disappearing out of sight altogether. Then Mother, particularly, was always making remarks like "never marry a man with a small nose or one whose eyes are too close together." Well, I certainly hadn't got a small nose, and maybe that was why she said it; but sometimes when I looked at my eyes, in a certain light, it seemed that, yes, my eyes were slightly close together, in fact, my God, they were practically touching. Then just about this period Mother often spoke of the theory that the tops of the ears of criminal types always came below the level of their eyes. Well, I was all right there, I thought. But wait. It might be something to do with the angle of my head. If I raised it to a more natural position, the criminal tendency, though slight, became definite. It was about this time that I got the habit of taking sneaking glances at myself in looking-glasses. "Ah, he looks bee-ootiful," Auntie Herbert used to say to me in her gorgeously sarcastic way. But as I explained to her, it was not because I was conceited, but because I was unconceited that I looked at myself in the glass, trying to take the suspicion of mania from my eye, the touch of crime from the angle of my ears, and the vacillation from the jaw by a determined forward thrust of the chin.

Our verger friend Foden had one weakness. It is just possible that this represented a perversion in himself, albeit a microscopic and a perfectly harmless and indeed charming one. It may simply have been a kindly humouring of a fairly universal schoolboy taste. One of the beauties of Henry VII's Chapel is the carved stalls of the Knights of the Bath with the seats of the Esquires below them. Beneath the seats are the carved misereres, "which should be examined" as the guide books say. Some of these hidden carvings are unreligious in subject-matter, and in fact definitely pagan; and as a very special privilege, which he nevertheless seemed to like to have entreated of him, Foden would show us where the "rude" ones were to be found. I never myself discovered anything worse, that is to say better, than a small carving of a boy with his trousers down having his bottom smacked—which was so much more mild than anything in Cunningham-Wells's celebrated collection of pictures of naked persons, that the thrill of this carving quickly faded. But nevertheless it was understood that from time to time our kind friend Foden ought to be asked "to show us the rude ones," alternately with the tomb of the well-connected Baroness Burdett-Coutts.

After this little ceremony he would talk about the Chapel. Through Foden I was soon on easy terms with phrases like "fan vaulting" and "Late Perpendicular." Foden never slipped into the stale sing-song of the regular guides. All he wanted was enthusiasm. "It looks as if it must have taken millions of years to do," I said, looking at the intricacies of the carving. "How did they do it?" "How does it work?" Foden folded his hands and canted his head back, as he always did when he was going to quote.

" 'Stone seems, by the cunning labour of the chisel, to have been robbed of its weight and density suspended aloft as if by magic.' " Foden half-intoned it. "Dumatter, who wrote it," he threw in automatically. The sing-song continued:

" 'The fretted roof achieved with the wonderful minuteness and airy security of a cobweb.' "

"Robbed of its weight," seemed to me an extraordinary way of putting things. Foden sometimes teased us. Supposing the weight came back. It wasn't long since a suffragette had let off a small bomb somewhere in the area of the Confessor's Tomb. This had not done much damage except to release from ten thousand ledges and crevices six hundred years of dust, which covered the floor of the Abbey with a half-inch-thick carpet of finest felt, its texture the most delicate I have ever touched. Foden made considerable drama of this incident and told us confidentially that since the Abbey was built on a marsh, serious results would be bound to follow. "If you stand by Sir Davenport Inchbald," he said later, "you will notice already a slight but definite curve in the main column supporting the triforium." I allowed my eye to slide up the Purbeck marble column, colour of rhubarb and custard, and I at once saw the bulge which Foden had invented, and it seemed to me to be growing just observably worse every time I looked at it. Foden liked to frighten us in this way.

On the way down from the weightless roof of Henry the Seventh's chapel my gaze was caught by the banners. These are the flags bearing the coats-of-arms of King Henry's Knights of the Bath, which had very recently been restored, after many years' absence, to their places over the choir stalls. Today the visitor sees brand-new flags in brand-new colours. Then the effect of ancient chivalry was enhanced by the obvious venerability of the banners, which were torn and much faded, and curiously mottled, probably by the effect of moth, though in those days I took it for granted it was by battle. The names on some of them were torn off, others barely decipherable. Sometimes only the first name remained. One of these I was just able to spell out for myself. "Alured."

"Alured," as a name, has an ancient look about it. It is in fact derived from a Latinised form of Alfred. I knew nothing about that, but *Alured*? That was the name of our vicar's brother—Mr Erskine Clarke's brother. Here it was—"Sir Alured." The second name was mostly missing, or were there letters hidden by the folds? The funny thing was that two of the letters seemed to be AR. I told Foden about it. Foden took it with great seriousness—and that was the splendid thing about Foden. Except when he was teasing, he never laughed at us. He took me seriously.

"It looks as if there was an A there, somewhere, in the second name," he said. "We'll get up above the choir stalls."

Foden, of course, knew a special passage with a curved stone staircase, which meant a good deal of work with his great ring of keys. Unlocking was always to him a ceremonial action. From above it was easy to see that the letters ARK came together, in the second name, and although there was a bad tear in the middle of it, the letter before could be L. Had I made a discovery? "But the extraordinary thing is," I told Foden, "that I was christened—I really was christened—by Alured Clarke."

When I got home that evening I didn't say anything to anybody. For one thing the dress rehearsal of *The Merry Monarch* was in full swing, and No. 36 was empty. I slipped round the corner to the Hall. I wanted to speak to Mr Clarke urgently. My plan was, to tell Mr Clarke that I had noticed the banner, and to say this, if possible, *when Mr Northing was present* (because he had made the remark about "using your eyes"), but not, of course, to look at Mr Northing while I was saying it. I had worked the scene out beforehand. "I've seen your flag," I was going to start.

This was not how it happened. Round at the Hall everybody was doing something different. Uncle Josh, as producer, was in complete command, but it was difficult to see what of. I believed, but was not sure, that Mr Northing had taken offence at something and gone home. He was partly responsible for the scenery, and apparently there had already been three major stops in the dress rehearsal, one of which was to do with a fixture at the side of stage. Josh, as Samuel Pepys, was going to link the whole thing together and be discovered, at the beginning of each act, seated at his desk and writing in his diary with a genuine quill pen. He had to walk on and sit there. But according to an idea of Mr Northing's this desk, and the chair behind, were made all in one piece to ensure quick removal. Uncle Josh, even in those days, was bigly built and had not yet found a way of insinuating himself into this pew (as it had become) in a graceful, to say nothing of a casual, way.

"Mr Willis," Josh was calling for the stage carpenter.

"Mr Clarke," I said, but my voice was scarcely heard.

It was no good trying to attract his attention in that way. "Yes?" Mr Clarke said, in the calm, level voice of Evensong; but he was not listening.

"Mr Clarke, I've seen your banner in Westminster Abbey."

"Interesting . . . Westminster Abbey." Mr Clarke was perfectly composed, but also he was perfectly unconscious.

It was to be five years, at least, before I was to learn the difference, always difficult for children to understand, between right moment and wrong moment. It was three days before he listened to my story. When he did, it was with perfect gravity. I gained confidence. In fact, the conversation went wonderfully well. He began to ask questions. He gave me a job to do. He got me to make a list of the decipherable names on the rest of the banners. This minute incident was very far from being minute for me. In the end it turned out that the name was in fact Clarke. A missing link in a family tree was established. Alured himself came to thank me. This wiped out a dozen "could-do-betters" in my report. And it eliminated old Mr Northing, and his "boys never use their eyes," for ever.

It was soon after this that I was confirmed, and the fact that this ceremony took place in Westminster Abbey greatly enhanced its prestige for me. The clear-cut division between right and wrong, the simplified ethics of Foden's comments on the tombstones, plus a liking for church music and the mysterious vaults of the roof of the Abbey and Henry VII Chapel, were "religion" to me, and remained so till the end of my schooldays. It seemed to me that this was the religion of my parents, of Dickens and all the proper kind of writers. If God is Love never really meant anything to me as a phrase, yet it was easy to understand: and the biggest word in the new mosaic decoration of St Luke's was FAITH, which convinced me for many years that it was wrong to question such matters.

I got into the habit of thinking of myself as good. This notion had grown from the age of seven, when I first understood and could read the Ten Commandments, none of which I had ever broken. I did not steal, I did not covet my neighbour's ox nor his ass. Although at one time there was an old donkey in the end of the orchard at Bryn Cottage, and I was fond of him, the Goodmans, sixteen miles away at Upper Warlingham, could not remotely be called our neighbours.

I felt also that I could make a very reasonable shot at living up to the words on the new electric-light fixtures in the nave of our church. The metal-work, in blue and gold, was arranged round the names of such Christian qualities as TEMPERANCE . . . REVERENCE . . . CHASTITY . . . HONOUR. I believed that if I closed my eyes, slightly compressed my lips, and thought "temperance" hard, I would be fulfilling the "temperance" suggestion.

While still thinking, at the age of sixteen, that I was good, my conscience was not absolutely easy. How about UNSELFISHNESS for instance? It seemed to me that Mother, to whom I often thought I should be kinder, was so completely unselfish to me, and took such pleasure in this, that it was difficult if not impossible for me, because two people can't be unselfish to each other simultaneously. But I guessed that in other respects there must be some flaw in this good opinion of my goodness. Even though, whenever I read a book, Mother would say "Remember your eyes—they're very precious, you know," I knew that of the admonitory stone angels supporting the pulpit of the church in Worthing the one called LABOUR would have disapproved of me most.

Deficiencies in labour might be made up for by tidying the garden or helping with the knife-cleaner on Minnie's day out. In course of time it was satisfied by a project of "reading the Bible all through," the two volumes of Father's big family edition. The print was big enough to stop Mother feeling anxious about my eyes. "Isn't the book too heavy for you?" she said. I was determined to read every word, including the notes by Dr Kitto and even the collations and cross-references, though I did not look these up. This gave me a feeling of interested calm, and an assurance of safety from possible attack (thunderbolts, tidal waves, San Francisco earthquakes, Norris the strong boy of Ashburnham), although my fear of such things had almost disappeared. Soon I was admiring the language of the Bible, first for its prestige and then for itself. Beethoven had already made it possible for me to like solemn eloquence and even to get a foretaste of deeper mysteries at a time when my personal development was ex-

ceptionally superficial. Just so Isaiah and Solomon and Tyn-
dale and Coverdale between them impregnated me with a first
suggestion of the presence of great poetry at the time when my
knowledge of that subject was confined to *Idylls of the King* and
the *Barrack-Room Ballads.* So far as making me religious was concerned, ten years later at the clear-cut age of twenty-six I was to
say, of these church and prayers and Bible days, that it is impossible for a boy to have an inkling of the meaning of religion
because that faculty or dimension is not even embryonic at that
age. Later, when I achieved a diminution of clarity, I thought it
might be possible for a boy to see these things momentarily, to see
through a glass darkly, to enjoy the refreshing taste of seriousness,
to accept the implication that there is something greater than
himself which yet includes him, to like the sense of plainness, and
certainty.

The sea is his and he made it: and his hands prepared the dry land.

My resolution to read the Bible complete broke down. Too
much of it choked me and it began to taste like Sunday breakfast,
it seemed to me—like bacon and sausage in slices which were too
thick. The Jewish names, Abihu . . . Eleazar . . . Ithamar, began
to stick in my mouth like nougat. Just after this I was doing the
New Testament in the Septuagint with Sacred Sam, and I remember then especially liking the cool carved touch of the Greek
by contrast. But I enjoyed the Bible. Even when I was only half
thinking it made me feel that I was on the right side. Besides, by
the curious double-think of early adolescent reasoning, although I
knew analytically that it was the work of the Hebrews and a completely different civilisation, instinctively I thought of it as something absolutely English—one of us, on the right side.

CHAPTER TEN

Two Toes In

IT was just about the time of the Alured Clarke incident that my Westminster life began to look up. So much so that for a time it looked as if Good Days might preponderate—as if Good Days were going to be the expected thing.

This had nothing to do with the Henry VII Chapel. Mother and Father had been delighted about this, and I backed them up. "You couldn't get this from any other school, you know," I said. Outside the precincts I often boasted about school. "You take in history through the pores," I remember saying. I kept to myself the dimness of my position there, the seeming impossibility of getting a foot in. I kept it particularly from No. 36.

Nobody in authority was interested in me. I got into the habit of trying to merge myself in the background, and perfected a technique of doing enough work to keep me out of trouble, but not an atom more. The Buck and I had a sort of understanding; but could I cope equally well with a new form-master? I was due to move into the chilly atmosphere of Sacred Sam's. I should have Sacred intoning at me three times a day.

Nevertheless, about this time I did begin to prize open one door a little way and get one toe in through a sort of side-entrance.

Whatever athletics meant to me at Westminster, they could never conceivably be thought of as games. The technical Westminster word "Station" exactly described their time-table rigidity. At home the contrast was complete. Games were joyous, totally informal, taken for granted, ardently followed, endlessly amusing. Every night, the instant supper was cleared away, the six-foot billiard table was expertly fitted on to the dining-room table and we were hard at it—Father and Mother, Jim and I. The

non-players watched intently. Every game was recorded, every
break over twenty, average monthly and yearly scores, four different kinds of records—all were entered up in the splendidly
bound Billiard-Book, one of the great cash books from Father's
office. "Big Billiards," as we called it, took place on special holidays when Father and I would walk two miles to the nearest
Temperance Billiard Hall, with its stained-glass-window entrance,
and mortify ourselves with the impossible difficulties, the absurd
distances, the unwelcoming acre of the full-sized table.

No laughter on Temperance Hall days: the pleasure was
solemn. The great game for laughing in that carefree era was, of all
things, golf. Long before we ventured on to a proper golf-course
(but with this majestic future in mind) Father and I used to prac-
tise during August holidays on the hilly meadows, now covered
with Prep. schools, underneath Ballard Down. Helpless laughter
from Father (not so much from me) if there was a complete miss;
awed self-praise for any shot which truly rose in the air. Father
developed a habit which grew on my nerves a little, on these "Golf
Fields Walks," as we called them. If from the top of the slope he
hit a ball which went over 130 yards, he stood gazing at it, stock
still, with noble seriousness as if it was Whiston's comet, gazed until
it had stopped rolling and a little bit longer. Then he slowly paced
the distance while I started with him to pace mine, counting out
loud as he did so, which, of course, muddled my counting. Our
average was about 140 yards; our record long shot, on this favourable slope, was 175 paces. Having absolutely no standards of comparison, we never doubted that this was just about as big a distance
as human strength could achieve. No standards, and of course in
those days, neither in tennis nor in golf, was there any thought that
some kind of expert instruction might have prevented all of us from
making our strokes in the way we first thought of, and therefore in
a way which brought every most inappropriate muscle into play at
the worst possible moment.

Every April the overgrown little garden of No. 36 was plotted
for one of the most complex putting courses in the history of the
game. Hole No. 8 started behind the dustbin. No. 6 entailed

shots through the entrails of the garden roller. No. 9 needed a niblick to carry the ball through the fork of the ilex. This game was played with extreme care, yet would come to a stop when Father and I, after one of us had bounced back ten times off the water-butt, used to begin laughing until our bones seemed to go soft in our bodies. Lawn tennis—how strange this seems now in the age of cars and the universal permeation of these games—was almost entirely confined to these August holidays. It was taken for granted that at sixteen (or indeed eighteen) Muriel and I were much too young to join the Sudbrooke Road Lawn Tennis Club.

Besides games-playing there was, of course, games-watching under home auspices. That endless, dreary, non-participating, duty-watching "Up Fields"—the compulsory Saturday afternoons in Vincent Square—did not put me off games-watching permanently only because I had watched games as the highest kind of treat before the war, before Vincent Square was ever heard of, with the Uncles. It was about 1910 that I began to be taken to Lord's and the Oval.

The Uncle concerned with this, Percy, thus makes his brief but auspicious entry, well up to Uncle standard, into my life. He was the youngest but one of Mother's brothers, and therefore young enough to volunteer early in the war and to die of wounds and trench fever in the base hospital at Rouen. He was the best games-player of two families in which liking for games was fifty times stronger than natural ability. I know he achieved some extra-ordinary games glory, such as playing for Surrey II. But even if his club had been even more splendid, it would not have impressed me nearly so much as the fact that Uncle Percy looked remarkably like the great new Surrey star then on the verge of universal fame —Hobbs. Hobbs was in his sixth season, and just beginning to shine forth at full strength; and Uncle Percy had exactly the same appearance, which one might call *crickety*. Complexion a healthy red-brown, eyes clear and unbothered by intellectual speculation, a general look of extraspection (by which I mean to add the sugges-tion of a generally happy way of surveying the world); and when he was playing cricket (as I used to see him occasionally in the

Caterham area) a Hobbs-like neatness of movement. Percy was a
bat, and he had the habit, which I always particularly admired in
Hobbs, of energetic "gardening" after each ball, of banging the
flat of his bat on the pitch with a vindictive thwack which echo
turned into a double-bump. He then mopped his forehead exten-
sively with his handkerchief, just like Hobbs, except that Hobbs's
handkerchief was blue silk and always stuck an inch or two out of
his pocket.

Of course there were Hendren and Hearne (J. W.) at Lord's,
or Woolley of Kent, who seemed able to send the ball to the
boundary with the trajectory of a bullet by just leaning in that
direction. But Hobbs and Hayward were the men; and whether
Hobbs was bowling or fielding or batting (he was the complete
all-rounder in those days), it was impossible to look at anybody
else. But in fact it was not scores and records which attracted me
so much as the place. I was inoculated for life, particularly, with
a sort of homesickness for the Oval, for the sparrows who make
short, aimless flights just inside the confines of the boundary, the
pieces of newspaper which blow across the ground on a windy
day, the standing around, the space, the gasometers, the lemonade
and rock-cakes, the sameness and ordinariness, and the great Oval
certainties like Tea Interval and gentle hand-clapping for a maiden
over—institutions as permanent, safe and dependable, it seemed
to me then, as Nine Barrow Down.

The other great games-watching occasions were under the auspices of Uncle Jim. Here again it was the place more than the
players, whom, however, I remember more vividly than the Oval
giants, because sometimes they were so near one could almost
touch them. This was the regular visit to Thurston's. (Billiards, of
course. Public performances of snooker at Thurston's in those
days would have been just about as conceivable as French cricket
at Lord's.) There was not then, as now, one emperor of the table
whose exclusive reign was taken for granted; there were three or
four warring kings to maintain a balance of power. Their styles
were sharply different, and somehow seemed to fit their looks.
Stevenson, the classical stylist, looked and played as if he was

delivering a lecture, with diagrams, on Greek architecture. Gray's long, loose limbs seemed perfectly adapted to his all-round-the-table play; his looping chin, which seemed almost to touch the cloth as it curved down beneath his cue, was somehow a part of the perfection of his losers. Reece was in person as small, confined and compact as his top-of-the-table play. Younger than these, and the eventual master of them all, was Melbourne Inman. He had no trick strokes and specialised in nothing; he "just played billiards," with a fixed indifference to his audience and to his opponent and to any other consideration outside the fact that professional billiards was professional billiards. How hard I scanned his face, but in vain, for any look, however fleeting, of pleasure or regret. How well I remember these men, though the familiar profiles were a little later made so obvious in Tom Webster's cartoons that now perhaps the cartoon memory is the stronger. What is more truly distinct in recollection is the sight of Thurston's itself. To sit in the shadows and stare at the rich concentration of light. To glance respectfully at the players in their splendidly starched shirts. To steal a glance at the marker as he steps forward to pick some speck from the impeccable surface of the table. To be in the presence (in those days) also of a referee, who must move from his seat to inspect a Reece cannon sequence at close quarters, such was the delicacy of the impact. To see the Press bench full of real journalists who would make it possible for me to read in print, in late editions of the *Westminster Gazette* and in *The Times* next morning, accounts of breaks which I had actually seen; to sit in the cigar-smoke and the silence—all this was to give me a respect for the sacred pleasures of games from which no amount of compulsory Up Fields could deter me.

Indeed, I had my own private hopes of somehow being a real games-player myself, which were stifled but not killed by my failures at Westminster. I seemed, then and so often as I grew older, to be preparing myself for something unspecified and yet certainly happy in the future. Moreover, I had thought again of that description of the schoolboy—"Corky Minimus with arms like cabbage stalks." I had submitted my arms and legs and shoulders to careful inspection in the big mirror in Mother's bedroom, and considered that though they were becoming long and straight, my limbs were devoid of bulges—like celery I would say. I decided to work on these celery stalks.

At that time the back pages of *Answers* and the *Boy's Own Paper* usually had a picture of an extraordinarily handsome, or at any rate glossy-looking man, with a fine figure and splendid moustaches more curly even than those of Viney, our butcher. His name—Eugene Sandow—was then a household word in advertisements. I was a diligent reader of them, the more long-winded the better; and the Sandow page seemed to go on for ever.

There was scarcely a detail of Sandow's muscular anatomy which was not illustrated by realistic drawings. Even the neck of Sandow was stuffed with great sausages of muscle, whereas my own neck was made of nothing but an Adam's apple poised above two large collar-bones which stuck out like cantilevers.

The Sandow method involved exercises with dumb-bells. I bought the book and some fairly heavy iron dumb-bells and initiated the Sandow exercises carefully, with special concentration on the arms and wrists. Needless to say, and typically, I attempted the impossible task of keeping all this quiet from the family. Father might hear some undefinable clanks, and put his head round the corner with a mild "All well?" which I wouldn't even answer; Mother would come in and find me on the floor doing a difficult leg-raise and I would be looking for something under the bed.

"Was something hurting you, darling?"

"No thank you, Mother." Was he ill? Mother's hand would touch my damp forehead. "Are you sure you're not a little bit hot?"

Once the dumb-bells were fully revealed and accepted, Mother would fall back on her favourite piece of general advice:

"Don't overdo it, darling."

The exercises were useful. Sandow was a benefactor, and his

books did do good. "You too can enjoy a man's glory" would be putting it too strongly; but certain bulges the size of squash balls did appear in my biceps, and my arms and wrists grew stronger. And even this suggestion of muscle, combined with a more business-like set of the shoulders, was now to come in useful.

"Tossing the pancake" is an old Shrove Tuesday Westminster custom, associated in the minds of any Londoners who happen to have heard of it with photographs, in the evening papers, of a ruffled boy being led off in some sort of procession. This is the winner of "The Grease," the first grabber of the tossed pancake, who is led to the house of the Dean, where he is presented with a golden guinea and a set of Maundy money. The affair is generally considered a treat for parents, who are encouraged to attend. Mother and Father had arrived early, looking rather dignified, I was relieved to see. In the school winning the pancake means little or nothing. It isn't even considered to be particularly good form to try too hard. Pethwick, who always wore the most beautifully shining top-hats and whose umbrella was always folded as thin as a walking-stick, saw me changing into battledress before we stood in line—one of us chosen from each form.

"You're going to keep clear of the scrum, I hope."

"Hope so."

"So horribly disarranging to the hair. Though possibly you don't wildly worry about hair?"

The school assembled. Preceded by the Beadle, in came little John, the chef, in white overalls and chef's hat, and traditionally tossed the traditional pancake, which moaned and whirred its way —the sound is unforgettable—high over the traditional bar towards my end of the line. I fell on top of it, forty-five boys fell on top of me, and the pancake was pressed deep into my chest, retaining, when at last I was able to remove it, a recognisable impression of my ribs.

Well, of course school took almost no notice of this feat, though later that morning Marchmont did smile in my direction, if slightly over the top of my head, and flexed his arm in a comical strong-man way, which made me smile swimmily. But at home there was universal rejoicing.

"Tell me, do you get special colours for this," Father said, "a special *blazah?*" Impossible, Father having familiarised himself with the difficult word "blazer," to tell him that at Westminster it was called "shag."

"I'm afraid not."

"Just the honour," Mother said, almost suggesting that if it entitled one to letters after the name, the fact was of such renown that one wouldn't use them.

"I think it was a very *popular* win," Mother said, joyfully creating a new version of the scene in her imagination. I was too pleased to argue. After all (quite soon I was thinking) perhaps she was right. I know that Auntie Rose, hearing about it a month later, had the impression that a cheer went up, from masters and boys equally. After all, there was the incontrovertible fact of my name and photograph in the evening papers—something which I was to take out and look at very often. Mother kept the pancake in a biscuit tin. When she died, thirty years later, the pancake was as hard as the stone slab for her monument.

Of course in Sacred Sam's, next morning, the pancake was never mentioned. On the contrary, I noticed that Sacred, always on the look-out for signs of inappropriate hubris among his pupils, was preparing for one of his little pounces.

"Now take it from ὥς ἔφατ᾽ αὐτάρ ἐγώ—Potter."

I rose to my feet with an annoyed frown. Sacred had asked me to construe only the day before. Sacred and I were quickly becoming open enemies. Twenty to one against two days running, as Sacred well knew.

"Thus he spoke," I rightly began (Homer uses this expression on every other page).

"Correct," said Sacred. As if trying to help me by giving me time, he took a throat-tablet from his desk with special deliberation, put it to his lips with his usual fragile, death-bed gesture and closed his eyes. He had the Perugino look. Was his wind-pipe really made of silver, as Cunningham-Wells said?

"Continue please." He gazed upwards as if at some unearthly light.

Yet the absurd pancake was the slight cause of a major change for me at Westminster, something which began in glory and ended in disaster. But the point is it began in glory.

That daily rite at the shrine of Sandow had something to do with it. About this time rowing was being restored to its rightful pre-war position as a Westminster sport. Brandon-Thomas, a boy of enterprise, was responsible. The start was modest. There was canvassing for recruits. Bare, Ashburnham's "Head of Water," asked me if I would volunteer. I leaped at the suggestion. Anything to get me out of that nerve-racking boredom, that parody of cricket known as form matches.

Twice a week we all trooped to Putney to learn how to row. We had no boathouse of our own—fortunately, because the Thames Boat Club were our hosts and gave us something much more spacious than we could then own ourselves. Here I was introduced for the first time to the curious new realm which I was later to know well: to the smells—of wet on changing-room floors, of the varnish and grease of the boats, of the very thin soup of Thames water, of dirty rowing-vests. I was introduced to the club trophies, which were always on display, never to be talked about; to the graceful groups of nineteenth-century photography. In the club were always one or two Old Members, retired notables, men who were too old to take any part in the war and who liked to die slowly in the scenes of their former glories. Immense, heavy men some of them, who taught us that rowing was the only real sport and that compared to it all other games were tiddlywinks. As an unsuccessful cricketer, I found this attitude by no means unsatisfactory, and certainly began about this time to walk with a stronger, more clomping gait, and hold my shoulders as if they were a few inches wider than they were.

I liked these old men, the muscles of their youth long since

I win the pancake.
Right, John who tossed it over the bar.
Bottom right, my first sight of a press photographer.

Getting my fingers well sunk into Beethoven.

Father used to annoy me by looking solemn when he played solemn chords, but being Father he had no objection, when I complained of this, to my photographing this expression to let him see what he looked like.

softened and swollen into a stiff carapace of gristly fat. I liked their wistful attitude to us skinny novices, destined in their eyes to taste the supreme athletic pleasure of hauling boats, with lungs bursting, between the withered old shores of the London Thames. Every Saturday afternoon eight of them rowed a boat up to Westminster Bridge and back, and one huge, gentle hippopotamus of seventy, King-Bowling, known as "The King," used to put on boxing gloves with us, and gave me my first experience of the total impossibility of even stretching out one's arms towards, to say nothing of hitting, any man who did really know something of the art of pugilism, even if he was practically on his death-bed. The other boys training with me were a pleasant unfanatical lot, as "Water" addicts often are. Young, the Captain, was serious, charming, dependable, single-minded. Tripp and Angerley were born incompetents in a boat, and accepted this fact in a spirit of effortless gaiety. With Rea I had a game of pretending we wanted to show that there was another world beside boats by whistling snatches of Schubert in the locker-room (I knew four snatches) and telling Tripp and Angerley to hang their clothes up quietly while we were thinking of the arts. Our coach, M. Felix Taymans, was of the persuasive, not the shouting kind—a professional sculler, refugee from Belgium, who added gaiety to his strictly classical teaching by his choice of words, telling us to "make a crack at the water," to "let de tail push you forward" and conducting with his hands a finely intoned *"Han swy"* for "hands away" at the finish of the stroke. The Thames B.C. has an undercover "tank"—an invention for teaching the elements of rowing in which the novice hauls at an oar which propels nothing to nowhere, while the coach stands over him and examines his faults at the closest possible range. From the distance of two feet it is easy to prove that no single group of student muscles, during any one of the twelve main sections of the rowing stroke, is functioning as it ought to be.

To my delighted surprise I found, and was told, that I had a natural aptitude for one part of the complex stroke cycle—the finish, or rather the flashing flick of motion just after the finish

M   177

when the wrists drop and snap away in one motion. A tenth of a second—but it was enough to put me above the rest of the first-termers. Incredible fact to be digested—that I could successfully do some games thing more really important than putting golf balls through the garden roller. *"Han swy"*—M. Felix stood over me. "See, he can do it some." What an infinitely better teacher, I thought, than Sacred Sam or Willett. No one outside the happy precincts of home or G.P.D.S.T. had ever told me before that I could do anything some.

I began to look forward to rowing days. True there were slight flies in the ointment. As a vague gesture of wartime economy, crews were limited to fours, although eight-oared boats were available. Then in accordance with one of the current theories of the training of the youthful oarsman, the slides in our boats were fixed. This may have reduced the complexity of the stroke, but the act of moving my bottom over the raised forward edge of the seat began to rub a large permanent red weal in the fold between cheek of bottom and my right leg. But everybody complained of "sore bottoms" as a joke, and this discipline of the flesh was to me part of the pain I believed to be essential to the pleasures of major sport, and I used at first to display my wound smilingly to admiring friends, and laugh jollily when the heroic curative treatment of methylated spirits brought real tears into my eyes. For now already I was a certainty for House Fours, and there was reason to think, though I still couldn't believe it, that there was a real chance of my rowing Three in the Westminster boat.

Here, then, was a first slight dent made on the indifferent heart of Westminster. Dent No. 2 was inspired by the confidence I was gaining from the always admiring heart of home.

Most unexpectedly, this second chance came through music. It is extraordinary now to think of the relatively barbarous nature of music at Westminster in those days. A few years after I left it was quickly changing into one of the best schools, for music, in the country. My own sons, at Westminster a generation later, used to walk about the house singing excerpts from the *Christmas Oratorio* or Walton's *Belshazzar's Feast* with the same familiarity which at their age I had for *Sweet and Low* or Sullivan's version of *Orpheus with his Lute*. True, these are quite charming pieces; but the peculiarity of the thing was that in my time choral singing was a matter of honour, loyalty, keen attendance and a sense of the spirit of the House. There were House competitions; and the choice for 1916 was *Merrie England*. I loved the music, I still think it wonderfully melodious, it was nice to sing something about

> Love is meant to make us glad
> Hey nonny nonny ho jolly little Cupid.

But it would have been nicer if a house monitor had not been in the background making sure that we were being keen. My piano teacher, the elegant Mr Reinbecker, made no pretence that he enjoyed his bi-weekly effort to guide me through one of the Op. 10 Beethoven Sonatas. I myself enjoyed it intensely, and once or twice tried to discuss the reason why a certain chord was so satisfactorily clinching or clenching; but my teacher was too glazed by the wearisomeness of his job to give anything but an impatient response. True, not even Mother could yet say that I had mastered piano technique. Poor Mrs Baines, who lived next door in the undetached side of our semi-detached No. 36, would have agreed kindly but deeply. I had a habit of doing the allegros allegretto, already under the life-long delusion that in the general flurry inaccuracies wouldn't be heard.

But suddenly a new and staggering musical gift appeared in me, needing a re-orientation, for the fifth time, of my activities towards the shape of their final destiny. Mother's very fine contralto voice had decreased in range as she grew older and did not now stretch to an octave: but these remaining notes were of splendid power and of the very finest organ quality. She could, for instance, give a wonderful rendering of "He was despised," the compass of which is not big.

"You try it," she said. I did. Perhaps for the first time my voice was fully broken. Anyhow, the effect wasn't too bad—in fact I had the feeling that I was suddenly able to do it. Moreover, Mother, having herself been taught by the best voice-producers in England at the Academy, was able there and then to begin to teach me certain basic rules. I was soon learning why the second syllable in "Father" had to be tense when sung, and why "spirit" had to be something like "speereet." Among many dodges, Mother was especially keen on the good results achieved by a slightly smiling expression, said to relax the mouth and throat when in full voice; and within a fortnight I was doing a moderately passable "Angels ever bright and fair" at an Uncle Josh who had been specially placed on the drawing-room sofa for this purpose, quietly smiling towards him while I did so.

"Stephen has a very fine voice." Round every Uncle and Aunt the word went. "He shall Feed His Flock," "The Rajah of Bong," "*Kennst du das Land*," the tenor part in the quartet in *The Yeomen of the Guard*—my range was as wide as my versatility in choice of themes. Indeed, perhaps neither Mother nor I was quite careful enough about choosing songs suitable to my age and sex. So long as it was a good suitable tune in a baritone key I would Shake my Greying Locks or Nurse the Babe at my Breast with equal gusto. A slight check to this was associated, I remember, with the arrival of Rex Littleboy, the tall undergraduate friend of my sister, much admired by me. Within half an hour of his entrance to No. 36, Mother allowed him to discover us in the piano room so that I could show off my delightful new talent. The tune I happened to be most fond of just then was already on the piano, and Mother started to play the long, delicious introduction to "My Mother Bids me Bind my Hair." As I began to sing, Mr Littleboy's delicate and discriminating nose sharpened slightly, I remember, at the words:

Tie up my locks in ribands blue

and the shifty look in his eye, which I was watching for signs of appreciation, made me falter and stop as I realised for the first time that this song would possibly not be the perfect choice for my platform début.

That boy: I can see who it is.

In-att-ent-ive.

There we were in Yard by the shop; we all turned guiltily; and it wasn't Sacred at all. It was B.-T. Wonderful B.-T. doing one of his miraculous imitations. His very face became fragile and Sam-like as he spoke. Even the timbre of the voice had acquired Sam's thin cathedral echo.

Boys have a much fresher and more responsive ear to intonations than grown-ups; but of all the fifty brilliant parodists of the manner of Mike, Bill, Sacred and Co., B.-T. was universally acknowledged the winner. Later he came into high prominence in the school as the leading light of the O.T.C. and a school monitor. And whenever he entered for the speech competition, "Orations," he was always far the best, surely. His voice was crisp and clear, his gestures definite. No one could do a more confident, more eye-flashing "Friends, Romans, countrymen" than he. His expression was always a bit sharp or pernickety, as if he were at a wine-tasting but pleased that the wine was good. Mysteriously to me, he seemed to enjoy every hour of his life at Westminster, like so many of these leading and successful boys only a year or two older than myself yet already somehow young men—these larger-than-life figures from a world I could not touch. In his case there was the extra glamour of his name: for B.-T. stood for Brandon-Thomas, a great name in the theatre, as I knew. His father was the author of *Charley's Aunt*, a play which everybody knew was marvellous, and which the B.-T. family lived, acted, played—and could recite backwards and forwards if necessary.

The undeveloped boy is the last person to realise what is missing in his education. I realise now that one of the safest and surest ways of letting in a little light, opening up a crack or two, is through drama. Let him act the tiniest part; or if he has no talent for acting whatever, let him be somehow concerned with the production of a play, even if it is only switching on the house-lights. Westminster had its famous annual Latin play; but, Westminster-like, this was exclusively the preserve of the resident scholars, a small group and the least backward, the least needful of intellectual encouragement, in the school. For the large majority, therefore, there was then no acting whatever. B.-T. must have felt the frustration of this; and he had the authority and character to do something about it. He couldn't do much, but it was a little. It was B.-T. who had already earned respect by reviving rowing at Westminster. It was B.-T. who decided to revive the Westminster School Glee Society. Wanted—performers: and here at once was a chance for those who shone neither at games nor at work, a chance to sidestep school ranking. Our aim was ambitious. Under the inspiration of B.-T. this was to be no mere musical recital, but an all-round entertainment combining the best elements in the Co-optimists and Pelissier's Follies. The serious note could be provided by a serious recitation from B.-T. or a good straight song by Andrews based on the general effectiveness, as Counties, of Devon or Somerset. Our first opening chorus, words and music by the organiser, was so repeatedly rehearsed that I can still remember it:

> We are a very serious troup
> To common puns we rarely stoop . . .

And here was I on equal terms with B.-T.—and Andrews too, a Double First Eleven. Indeed, at our first performance I actually sang a duet with Andrews:

> Tenor and baritone
> We are respectively
> We can in merry tone
> Sing most effectively.

The next part of this duet was tremendous, musically:

> Song or duet
> Each takes his part.

It was in canon, to which, on first impact, I thought no form of musical harmony could be superior:

> Trio, quartet:
> We have our art.

Andrews came in with his trumpet of a voice two notes after me to sing those words in harmony while I had already got on to the next lot. The practice we put into this feat was rewarded by measurable applause from the school on the first night. For the second edition, which came in the spring term, Andrews and I sang Offenbach's "Bold Gendarmes," well coached by B.-T., who added a lot of business to our act. This was the success of the Glee Soc., and I was quickly learning to like audiences and applause. With my rowing progress to back it up, I felt I had now got two toes in at Westminster. I even tried to make a bit more of an impression in my work; but Sacred Sam remained my enemy, and was certainly not going to allow me any privileges because of any meddling of mine with comic songs and activities at Putney. Yet this didn't matter, because in the school I was now something. Auguries for the future were almost promising.

CHAPTER ELEVEN

The Shadow of Sacred

BUT it was not to be. Good term did, after all, mean bad term to follow; and the summer of 1917 was not good.

The term started well. A selection of parents was to be asked to a special performance of the Glee Soc., and rehearsals began early. All this coincided with big events at Putney. My best hopes were realised. I was chosen to row in the School Four and was given my pink-and-whites, only one degree below the "pinks" which had seemed so utterly beyond my grasp a year ago. More incredible still we actually won our first race of the season, against a crew superior to St Pauls, our rivals in the schools championship event, who were inclined to take rowing in a light-hearted spirit.

At the same time it was quite rightly agreed by everybody, particularly the Thames Club Old Men, that we must not slack off in our training by a fraction. In the world of rowing, whether expert or novice, however careful one is not to reveal a hope that there might be a chance of taking things a little bit easily, this thought is always followed, and at once, by an excess of toughening exercise. Westminster prospects were discussed in the boat-house area. Prolonged hours were recommended. The advice was even sought, not directly of course, but through various intermediaries, of the Royal Bargemaster himself, the great Bossy Phelps, who was enthroned deep in a nest of boats of his own building five Houses down river. He was understood to suggest that besides the customary Long Row, a good deal more work on the towpath was advisable. This meant running to Hammersmith Bridge and back, or at any rate trotting. Of all forms of exercise, running has always seemed to me to be the lowliest and the most dreary; but the honour of rowing for Westminster meant that all such suggestions should be received with alert keenness. In particular, we ought to be positively licking our lips in anticipation of the Long Row.

Normally, I should have quite enjoyed it. There was the long paddle up beyond Westminster Bridge, perhaps caught sight of by some admiring juniors, and on the way back, swinging somehow fairly well together, out of fatigue, or allowing ourselves a little bit to use our instinct, the timing would come right and we should feel good, and look good, and then surely everybody, seeing the pink blades of the oars, must know that we were Westminster First Four. But in fact I was dreading this row. Last year's scar from the front edge of the fixed seat had opened up again vengefully. The edges of the weal were permanently parted slightly, like lips; and I knew it would hurt. I found it impossible not to flinch at the end of the stroke. Bossy Phelps watched us coming up the last stretch and came over to speak to M. Taymans and the Old Men about us.

"Falling away from their work in the middle of the boat," he said, looking straight ahead.

Well, there's no "middle of the boat," technically, in a Four. The nearest thing is No. 3, and No. 3 was me.

It was perfectly true. My body was moving away from the oar at the finish, to ease the rub on the raw patch. I was no longer joking about my bad place. In fact, I was most careful not to mention it, or let anybody see it. My motives for this must, I suspect, have been mixed. For one thing, complaining about some physical ailment just before a race is an example of what might be called an Impossible Thing; and Impossible Things do crop up, especially where school is concerned. There may be people in the world who could have said, addressing the thick roll of muscles at the back of the neck of Bossy, formerly sculling champion of Britain, that they had "rather a sore place between their bottom and the top of their leg," knowing that the inside of their shorts was stained with blood.

I couldn't—and I wouldn't. "Well, we must bring in somebody else," I could just imagine the sudden coldness and formality of the voice of Young the sincere, friendly, Captain of Rowing.

Because of storms, there was little practice before the race. I longed for it to be over. Half frightened of the race and half distrusting the auguries, I shielded from Father and Mother the fact that a special launch for parents was following the race.

It was a drizzling day, and the Thames was full of rain and the muddy rubbish of flood-water. It would be a long pull, upstream, whatever the state of the tide. "Take the finish right through," the Old Men had been telling me; but paddling to the start I was still wincing at each stroke. I could feel that my blade was somehow getting buried at the finish. I had lost my special and essential gift of "hands away."

The most unpleasant moments of my whole life have been those spent waiting for the start of a race, taking sickly and unnecessary looks at the blade of my oar flat on the water. Yet after a minute all pains are forgotten, or merged in the struggle. But not in this particular race, for me. Even in the heat of it I could feel the back of my leg being probed by a scalpel at the end of the stroke. We were leading by a length; but at the start of our first spurt, I was leaning right away from the pain. I felt as if the stroke would never end. Then suddenly a great swath of water curved back from my oar as it dug in. A big "crab" can wind you physically and morally in one moment. I was hit by a double shock. A lead of two lengths was turned into a deficit of four. Young somehow steadied us, and got us through to the finish. We even drew up on them a little. But how, I thought, as we paddled back to the club-house in silence—how face the rest of my day—term—year—life? I had let everybody down—Young, crew, House, School, M. Felix and the Old Men. How dreary, how like the Thames on a rainy day it is to lift the boat out of the water after defeat. No sarcastic jokes. No "Well-rowed, bow." No one allowed to smile. No cheek from cox. M. Felix coming down the bank silent, looked smaller than usual. No one spoke. School and visitors hung respectfully back. We hoisted the boat out of the water on to our shoulders, and climbed the slope like coffin-bearers. I saw "The King," the old man. He looked indignant.

"'Straordinary bad luck."

186

He was speaking to me. Silence all round, especially of course from me.

"'Straordinary bad luck. All those snags everywhere. They ought to have stopped the race."

I only half understood rowing talk—half saw that he meant some excuse for me. But I was diving for the changing-room, hurrying to get away, to get out, to be alone with that most sympathetic and understanding of old friends, myself. On the platform at Putney Station I let the extent of the disaster drift over me like a wave. It was almost pleasant. I looked at the railway lines, I remember, and thought "this is the kind of moment which some kinds of people think is the kind of moment to commit suicide. But not me." I felt suddenly as if I had sunk so low that I had fallen through into the room below, so to speak, and that the room below wasn't so bad. "It's perfectly all right," said my friend myself to me. "It wasn't your fault."

Then, in the train, I thought of that well-intentioned Old Man, trying to put in a word for me. What was it exactly he had said? He spoke of "snags" (which means surely bits of driftwood); and he was—yes, actually he was suggesting it was a snag I had caught, not a crab at all. Was it possible? *Was it conceivably possible?* There were certainly good-sized branches floating in the flooded current. I gazed out at another friend of mine—the railway lines. But changing trains at Victoria, I was *sure* it was a crab—ten to one? Five to one anyhow: and anyhow, also, not truly my own fault. Whichever and whatever it was, I decided on the front doorstep of No. 36 to state the two possibilities—the two explanations of the event, and never to give any opinion on this matter, one way or the other. Nor do I now.

Next morning came one of those extraordinary pieces of luck which have so often pulled me back from disaster by the scruff of the neck. Father's *Daily Telegraph* described the race in a small paragraph low on the sports page. "Floating debris" was mentioned; then came the phrase I was to remember:

But for the excellent watermanship of No. 3 . . . the boat might well have overturned.

There it is, printed for ever to be found, whether one is in the Bodleian or in Cardiff, or Colindale, or in whatever place friendly *Telegraphs* are preserved for ever. All the same, for me it was the end of Westminster Water. Next day my raw and ragged posterior surfaces were shown to Dr Oram. For the first and only time, Dr Oram was really interested in my symptoms. Blood poisoning was spoken of. Deep antiseptics were thrust into the wound. I was forbidden rowing for three months.

The second set-back of that term was a pin-prick by comparison; but Sacred Sam had a way of making his pin-pricks hurt like the sting of a wasp.

Planning the special Glee Soc. meeting at the end of term, B.-T. (who was now Captain of the School and whose word was therefore law) decided, since parents were going to be present, that there ought to be a strongish mixture of "good" music in the programme, and that once or twice a fairly serious note should be struck.

The chorus were to sing a Mendelssohn quartet of delicious sweetness, "Good night, my love" (commonly referred to as "Sleep tight, my love").

It was suggested—or possibly I suggested myself—that I should supply a serious solo. Then if B.-T. or Winkleman did a Shakespeare recitation out of *Richard II*, we felt that that should strike enough solemn notes to satisfy any parent. I was quite glad to be doing this solo, because Mother had paid for me to have half a dozen singing lessons (although she in fact was a better teacher than Mr D.), and by a great piece of luck, at my special request I had been coached in a song, the unusual modernity of which should, we thought, contrast well with the slightly old-fashioned sound of the Mendelssohn. This was called "The Temple Bells" by Amy Woodforde-Finden; and I began hard work on this song, though my singing-teacher did not quite share my liking for it. Still, Mr D. trained me well in the enunciation of the words, and in a week or two vowels and consonants were approaching a fine state of audibility.

The Temple bells are rrreeenging
The young green corn is sprrreeenging . . .

All the same, I was still finding it difficult to manage the pronun-
ciation of the syllable on the high note of the first verse

And the month of marrry JEZZ is drawing neeeer.

I was looking forward to the concert. A minor point, unexpectedly in my thoughts, was that Amos's sister would probably be
there, in the three rows reserved for parents and family. I thought
she was a very pretty girl, and that meant there was going to be a
small patch in the audience I couldn't quite look at, and that
unexpectedly gave me a twinge of my before-the-start-of-the-
race feelings. True, so far on my visits to the house of Amos I had
scarcely spoken three words to her. Yet I felt especially pleased
that members of the O.T.C., with parades now, in war-time, daily,
had been able to discard the top-hat and tails uniform which I so
disliked and wear uniform for all occasions. Moreover—still somehow relevant—I had at long last and after months of being passed
over, received, besides my marksman's badge, my first stripe.

It was quite a successful concert: but I felt nervous, waiting to
sing my song. Of course, suddenly getting up and singing a serious
song at a concert, a song about love, was universally acknowledged
to be something absolutely right and proper—a custom in honour
of which everybody had to look glum and sit silent. But was it
not equally, I was also thinking, with a clear-sightedness born of
nervous tension, something absolutely ridiculous and hopelessly
idiotic? My mind flashed back to Rex Littleboy, and his fixed
expression when I began to sing the Haydn:

My mother bids me bind my hair
In bands of glorious hue.

But this time I was supposed to be a man, so that was all right. As
the piano prelude started I walked into position. I remember
wondering why I was making myself walk with a slight limp. My
face was a little smiling to relax the mouth. . . . And my teacher
had told me to remember my posture.

"This is a love song," he had said, "and you are standing rigidly to attention."

I did a stand-at-ease.

"No, no. Lean forward a little, relax, try putting your hands half in your pockets . . ."

So now I was relaxing tremendously. Yet how absurd the song seemed—and what a time to have such a thought now that I was singing it in public.

"The Tem Pull Bulls are Reeenging." What was I doing? I wanted to giggle.

"She is young and very sweet . . ." Why was I here? Mr D. had made me linger over the word "she" a little; and I now did so, slightly overdoing it, even making it a little leering, so that the long three-line, twelve-bar "Ah-ah-ah" at the end of the verse sounded suddenly to my ears as if I was wagging my finger at myself, archly, or "trying to get off," as we said then.

Of course, as soon as I felt this, so did rows N to W, reflecting my feeling; and very faintly, but audibly, somebody echoed my "Ah" from row V. I thought it was Fizz. I felt a giggle coming: and my relaxed position froze solid. In the end it was a failure without absolute disaster. There were a few polite hand-claps.

I seemed to have got away with it; but the stab came later. I could see next morning that Sacred Sam was in a bad mood. But I scarcely noticed it. Personally, what with one thing and another, I was in a good one; and on the whole I had got away with this, my first solo. Amos had asked me over for Saturday, and Miss B. Amos would be there. One by one, Sam was calling us up to his desk to show us his corrections of our work. I had absolutely no expectations of any good coming out of this so far as I was concerned, but still was not prepared for what was coming. Delicately crunching a throat-tablet, Sacred kept me standing silently before him until he had finished the last atom, swallowing with a visible effort, as if he only had a week to live. Then he started.

"You realise you disgraced the school yesterday."

He was using a special fluting voice, audible to the whole class. There was a silence.

"Do you realise there were visitors in the audience? And if so, do you realise that to stand on the platform and lounge with your hands half in your pockets is an insult to the audience, an insult to the school, and an insult to your uniform?"

Could this small drama be enacted today? Are not masters more perceptive, and are not therefore schoolboys more comprehending, at this age? How much was I to blame for the situation? My mental age may have been only a little below my physical (seventeen), but put my character development at this time back to fifteen-and-a-half and still I marvel at my inability to see Sacred even momentarily with a compassionate eye. Let me plead—if this catches the eye of a contemporary Westminster sixteen-year-old—the out-of-date tradition of schoolhood, still then so universally accepted, of masters and boys ranged against each other. Of compulsory lessons, compulsory seriousness, compulsory play and compulsory moments of the day to eat one's favourite type of biscuit, followed by compulsory agreements to agree with anything the master says. Even so, after you have made all allowances, you will agree that I ought to have seen in Sacred the war-worried man, possibly with close relations at the Front in fearful danger, perhaps a man not particularly well supported by his headmaster, conceivably feeling that his chance of being himself a headmaster was evaporating finally this very year; a classical scholar forced by his profession to see regurgitated annually the whole stale stock of grammatical errors and textual traps, to see the beloved charm of Herodotus turned into a pile of school-book selections, a deformity on a desk, scribbled over with witless schoolboy drawings. Horace defaced by rampageous agnostics—and to see all this with the aching clarity of ill-health. But whatever the truth, I never once so thought of him. Sacred was a "master," and the most masterish of them all.

Yet just then, at the very moment of Sam's most despicable insult (as it seemed to me), the whole thing seemed to be melting away. To my surprise, I was saying something.

"But, *no*."

What had happened? Was I answering back?

"No, I didn't." Unheard of to defend oneself, if there was a reprimand.

"My teachers—that is, I had one singing teacher"—it was difficult to get it out straight—"told me to stand like that."

Sacred Sam stared at the book on his desk and made a correction. No sound from Sam. I felt bolder.

"It wasn't fair at all, what you said."

Sam bent over the exercise-book.

"Next, please," he said. He was smiling slightly.

I went back to my seat. I felt good, I think. All is absurd, I began to feel. This little room is absurd. Then a lot of other thoughts came, as I sat doing nothing. I took a look at that funny note from Amos with the funny drawing. Then—what about Leonard in France, in the Tank Corps? And Uncle Percy, in hospital at Rouen? . . .

After the concert Amos had passed me a note. "My sister says can you come to her dance on Saturday? Her twenty-first something or something."

"It's a dance," Amos had repeated, in a ding-dongy voice, when he gave me the note.

"I can't dance," I said.

"But you've got to come," Amos said. "She specially asked you or something. You can stay with us if you like."

I'd never been asked to a dance, never had an invitation from a girl, and the girl was pretty, too pretty to *see* properly. She actually noticed me? Was it possible?

I had almost forgotten Sacred. He dismissed us rather mildly, wanly smiling. The atmosphere was growing end-of-term. My school report had already arrived when I got home. Sacred's comments on me were more coldly depressing than usual. But this time it hardly mattered. I had determined to tell Mother and Father all about the hands-in-the-pocket incident, and for the first time I revealed my case against Sacred in general. At once they were on my side, as I knew for certain they would be. Father even talked of writing to the Headmaster as if poor old Gow could by that time have been capable of defending anybody against any-

F. C. Potter, of Bird and Potter, taken when I worked in the room
with him as his most junior office-boy.

Mother, photographed by me, wearing the clothes I most admired.
She is sitting in Jim's Corner. Behind the curtain at the back is
our slip-on billiard-table.

I get the uniform at last.

thing. It was generally agreed that Sacred was almost a kind of criminal.

On the last day of that term Sacred came up to me while I was standing surveying the scene on one of the little pedestals of the Inigo Jones gateway. On his clerkly little face was the suggestion of a smile. He clapped his hands behind his back and lifted his heels twice in imitation of geniality. It made me feel somehow powerful. I remained on my pedestal, nearly three feet above him. Sacred's going to be friendly. Batten down all hatches.

"I see we're to congratulate you on your Thirds. Well done." (Piddling, unimportant kind of football colours awarded to me for something or other.) I realised this was Sam's way of half apologising.

"You will be joining Mr Hignett's next term. I wish you luck." New form. That I didn't know. Everything seemed unlike life. Sam had never used quite this voice to me before. But I was just going to be absolutely polite, nothing more, nothing less. As for Hignett, he specialised in trig., as far as I knew, and was only interested in the maths geniuses. It meant nothing to me. I felt extraordinarily happy. Algebra? I guessed that before spending five minutes in one of Hig's maths sessions my mind would feel as if it were turned off at the main. I had no kind of mind for numbers. A single spasm of chess turned my brain as solid as the old sponge in the bathroom.

I walked over to the notice-board to see my name on the list of "Thirds have been awarded to the following." Next door to it was the usual little list of Westminster casualties

Missing: believed killed
L. G. Harriman
A. J. K. Harris
W. R. Sprott.

I had had two terms of Sprott. He had been an Ashburnham monitor; but much less stuffy than our present lot. He was not such a good mimic as B.-T., but he was original to the point of madness. I once heard him imitate the whole of Latin prayers,

including the sounds of coughs, the scraping of chairs, Big Ben
striking five o'clock and Gibbs whispering something filthy all at
the same time. I smiled, considering Sprott, because I was glad to
be made to think that all the things happening to me here at Westminster, good or bad, were minute, microscopic, in comparison
with what happened to grown people like Sprott (as indeed they
were) and something to be forgotten (as indeed they never were).
Back on my pedestal, I conceived a big plan for the future. It was
strange that no one was taking any notice of me, but in a way that
pleased me too.

CHAPTER TWELVE

Der Dichter Spricht

"I'M going to do something rather interesting." I was talking to Flap about four weeks after the end of term. Phil the Flapper was so-called because of the tender pink-and-whiteness of his complexion, although at this moment his face was matted with sweat and smeared with dust.

"As a matter of fact," I said (as he was paying no attention), "I want to ask your advice."

It was the end of August, and I had had a good August. The O.T.C. camp at Tidworth had been cut to ten days; and though the Corfe Castle holiday had been cut to a fortnight, and had a 1917 "last time" atmosphere about it, I was enjoying Dartmoor, where ten Westminsters were helping with the harvest at Bovey Tracey. The last comb-out of men had hit the farmers badly, and the schools had been asked for volunteers.

"I'll show you something really tremendously interesting," said Flap.

"Where?" Hay Tor, over his shoulder on the hill, was looking benign in the sunshine. I took a brief glance to make sure that the top, the pinnacle of the Tor, had not suddenly turned, as it sometimes did turn, into the image of the face of Miss Amos. Miss Amos was engaged to an officer in the Royal Flying Corps, and since hearing about this it seemed to me I had seen her face on rocks, two or three times an hour, in the most extraordinary way.

"I have here—an example—yes it is . . ." I said.

"What, you don't mean——?"

"Yes, I don't think it would be wild exaggeration——"

"Fanciful diagnosis——"

"To say that this is——"

"My God. A Small Potato."

We had picked up two thousand potatoes that morning, sorting them into big and small. It was Saturday, two-thirty, and nearly time to knock off. The potato business was quite hard work, and the happy thought of the week-end made us laugh weakly at practically nothing.

I packed up with Flap, but before we left I turned to pull up one of fifteen thousand weeds from the patch before us. I stood up straight and took another look at Hay Tor. It was full in the sun, and the extraordinary thing is that there she was, only it wasn't Miss Amos at all, but Phyllis. Phyllis had a wide smile and a long, loose pigtail and eyes which shot sparks through a nest of lashes. She was a new friend. We had met at Corfe Castle.

"But stay, an unclean intruder," I said.

"Not—not charlock?"

"*Charlock*."

It was possible to say it in eight different cadences, all funny. We could hardly move with laughing. Even the pods of the charlock, lumpy and hairy like the neck of Slime, our least favourite Westminster master, looked extraordinarily funny. The next thing to do was to go to the landing-stage by the Big Pond and eat our sandwiches before bathing. We found a cosy bit of Dartmoor granite to sit on. Eating stopped giggles. We got through the big pack of sandwiches, staring at nothing. Giggling periods were usually followed by earnest-talk periods in those days. On my side this generally meant being shocked that Flap wasn't interested in what I was interested in, and wanting to convert him. Flap was high in the Chemistry Seventh contingent, hard-working, and I was high nowhere; but he knew nothing about Beethoven whatever, and the fact that he never worried about this piqued me. The only music he knew was out of *The Bing Boys*, and since I didn't know *The Bing Boys*, but only *The Bing Boys on Broadway*, its successor (which we went to together), Flap was able to imply that he knew more about music in a way than I did, and to emphasise this he was always singing *The Bing Boys*.

There was a little hen and he had a wooden leg
The best little hen that ever laid an egg.
He laid more eggs than any in the farm . . .

Flap was whistling this now, through his teeth. It annoyed me,
though of course I liked this tune.

"You've got quite a nice whistle," I said. "It's a pity you use it
on such ghastly bilge."

Flap made no reply, except to chew with exaggerated sucking
noises.

"How's the poetry library?" he suddenly said. He began eating
a twopenny bar of chocolate—or rather licking it off the inside of
its wrappings, it was so hot. I was feeling sleepy, but Flap woke
me up.

Again Flap was irritating me, if only because he was speaking
lightly of an important event. Back in our tent lay the first volume
of poetry I had ever bought for myself, bound in half-calf, in my
haversack. Already there was a diagonal smear of pink toothpaste
across the ends of the pages, which were painted gold: but the book
was an Oxford edition and had cost 11s. 6d.

Flap and Watkins, in my tent, had noticed the title—*Poems of
John Keats.*

"I mean, do you really read it, or is it just show-off?" As the
orange I had just been peeling seemed to me to be made of a
cotton-wool, I threw it hard at Flap, and hit him. Flap was being
sort of damned *clear*, in his scientific way. That was how he was
senior sergeant in the Corps—never a hair nor a finger nor a
blanket out of place, I thought. Oh, yes, he was jolly good, I used
to tell him. Next year he would wake up the Army, I said. They
put down the red carpet for people who had done an hour a day in
an O.T.C.

"Poetry is marvellous," I said.

" 'Clothed in white samite, mystic, wonderful.' "

There he goes. That's what poetry meant to Flap.

"For - so - work - the - honey-bees - creatures - that - by - a -
rule - in - nature - teach."

School Rep. Truth to tell, in a way that was what poetry had meant to me, till two months before this incident. The others at No. 36 took it for granted that poetry was marvellous. There were thin volumes of Christina Rossetti and thick volumes of Browning; Muriel read Rupert Brooke even at the crises of her Oxford struggle with the ancient English poets. I had been an addict of the great novelists for ages. I had spent the total cash proceeds of last Christmas on the India-paper Thackeray; but privately I still thought of poetry as warmed-up stuff which had to be learnt by heart. The Buck had a passion for making us learn some obvious Shakespeare speech, or the *Idylls of the King*. "Then loudly cried the bold Sir Bedivere." It was like Mr Northing dressing up for the pageant at the Church Fête. It was too *good*, too church. Sometimes it was too physical—a little disgusting, or clogging, like being chocked up with stuffy church clothes:

> Pale was the perfect face;
> The bosom with long sighs labour'd; and meek
> Seem'd the full lips, and mild the luminous eyes.

It made me disgusted, it was like Miss Greenslough in church, when it was a fine day outside. Her lips were meek enough, when she was singing the Magnificat, and looking down hard at her bosom as if nobody was supposed to look at *her*. Pretty but disgusting, I should say she was. Not like Phyllis, with the raindrops on her face after we had biked down the Rempstone Road. No poetry about Phyllis—nothing you would ever want to say.

Poetry called Poetry I didn't like. But if that unpleasant word, difficult to pronounce pleasingly, was out of sight, there was much more of poetry pleasure in my life than I admitted. Corfe Castle, for instance, or the uninhabited upper realms of the Abbey beneath its roof. Nobody called these things "poetry" in that special voice, as muted as a drawing-room carpet, so respectful that one scarcely dared move, and sounding like one of the deadest patches in Divine Service. Nobody in an extra-modulated voice recited Corfe Castle; nor did I have to learn by heart the view from the golf-course across Frome Heath. When Muriel and I got up at four-forty-five one morning to bike towards Studland and see our early-morning shadows fantastic and long behind us as the sun sucked up a skyful of coloured mist and rose above Ballard Down, there was nobody to add a footnote on the classical origin of dew. The smell of the mist could be enjoyed free, as it were; and so, for that matter, could the description of fog at the beginning of *Bleak House,* because anyhow it was Dickens, and anyhow also it was prose. Even the Psalms and the Bible were prose in my category; and perhaps therefore the Bible began for me enjoyment of poetry by instinct.

The nations are as a drop of a bucket, and are counted as the small dust of the balance: behold, he taketh up the isles as a very little thing.

Not only rhythms as complex as that, but metaphors as boldly poetic as "How beautiful upon the mountains are the feet of him that bringeth good tidings, that publisheth peace." Valleys laughing and singing . . . it was a much better, more "super" way of saying things than anyone ever found in poetry.

Plenty of poetry was drifting in my direction in those days, although I did not know it, or so name it. I did not then read Shakespeare for pleasure, but scraps of Shakespeare are always floating in the English air, and like wind-blown pollen, they attach themselves one by one to the indifferent stigma. For the schoolboy in those days the Bible turned up much more frequently than it does now. But for me the real drift towards the pleasures of poetry came through music.

A boy can advance much earlier, much faster and indeed surprisingly deeply into this realm through music. Later, when I studied conventional literary criticism at Oxford, I used to dislike the constant references to "word music." Give me the music of music, I used to think. The "poetry of music" I could love unconsciously, and can still more readily accept. In that embryonic intellectual period when thoughts of lyricism and love seemed unmanly, I could easily get enjoyment from those very elements in Chopin or the early Beethoven Sonatas—or long before that, from say "Solveig's Song," or *Moments Musicales* played on the Assembly Hall piano. Sawing and stumbling, Father and I ploughed our way through the Mozart violin-piano sonatas: yet the pleasure was not less appreciated because we mangled them: their purity was the embodiment of the attraction of music—the poetry stripped of the flesh of words, and the lumber of associations which to a boy are mostly incomprehensible. Best of all, perhaps, for these early years were the short Schumann pieces, the true Songs or Talking Without Words (Mendelssohn the softly feminine was really Feelings Without Words) because Schumann seems and intends to talk, as I knew. Sometimes I found a page of Schumann I could play—and then I lingered over it, and soaked it up through the fingers. Such a piece comes at the end of the *Kinderszenen*—"*Der Dichter Spricht*"—and, because it was in German, there was nothing to warn me that the suspect word "Poet" came into it at all, though I must have known, clearly enough, that while I listened the poet spoke.

Only hobbling along at first, in the wake of pleasure in music, came pleasure in words. Light verse started me on the journey towards making the feeling conscious and cumulative. No "poetry voice" here: not even from Father. He was a great quoter of Tom Hood and *The Ingoldsby Legends*. Indeed in childhood, as in the evolution of a literature, verse rhythms come before prose. We used to make it up ourselves on Corfe Castle area holidays, before I can remember:

> Uncle Jim
> At Tilly Whim
> Been and gone and loss himself
> Folks say of him
> His sense is dim
> He isn't fit to boss himself.

" 'Twas brillig" certainly got into my head for ever the metre of the elegiac quatrain: and perhaps the pleasure of words disassociated from meaning as well. Words as entities to be enjoyed for themselves emerge out of the very boredom of Greek and Latin grammar books. "Oimeen oio oito" one repeats sarcastically, learning the Greek optative case, yet there is enjoyment

about the very glueyness of the sound. The Latin-verb tags sometimes make perfect little couplets, impossible to forget:

> If diligent, intelligent, not negligent you be
> Remember lego, lexi makes the perfect of these three.

It was a pleasure to speak it, for the trenchancy: just as for the
Browningesque lack of flow it was nice to say "Hic haec hoc.
Hunc hanc hoc. Hujus. Huic." What did it remind me of? Not
Browning, which was then (except for "The Pied Piper," a
splendid tin-opener for verse appreciation) two particularly solid
volumes stuck to the varnish of Father's bookshelf. It was:

> Awaiting the sensation of a short, sharp shock
> From a cheap and chippy chopper on a big black block.

Big black block. Hic haec hoc. In other words, while the tram
was taking us back from the Kennington Theatre to the corner of
Nightingale Lane those marvellous word-tunes or tune-words—
for I never separated them in my mind—were hammering into my
theatre-heated mind the structure of English verse.

But a considerable jump had to be made before I could say "I
like poetry" and be proud of having my eleven-and-sixpenny
volume of Keats with me, and parading it before the sceptical eyes
of Flap and Watkins in our tent at Bovey Tracey.

There were two authors who for me could do no wrong in those
days. Dickens and Kipling. They could even write poetry so far
as I was concerned, and this of course is where Kipling came in.
Not that I would ever read the volume of his collected poems; but
the lines were insinuated into the body of the text, whether it was
a Mowgli story, *Just-So*, one of the grown-up stories, or a child's
History of England. They were of the nature of magic charms,
they were not concerned with such clogging poetical subjects as
love, or spring, or wild flowers; they were, on the contrary, connected with machines, modern battleships, tough soldiers, and the
tone of voice was not poetical at all. True, I often didn't understand it at ten years old; but it was not poetry-incomprehensible,
it was explaining-how-a-magneto-works incomprehensible:

China-going P. & O.'s
Pass Pau Amma's playground close,
And his Pusat Tasek lies
Near the track of most B.I.'s.

Sometimes the mysteriousness was quite easy to understand.

Five and twenty ponies,
Trotting through the dark—
Brandy for the Parson,
'Baccy for the Clerk.
Them that asks no questions isn't told a lie—
Watch the wall, my darling, while the Gentlemen go by!

If there were images or descriptions, they were something I could
understand at once. The Roman legionary ordered back to Italy
from England—what was it that "he would ne'er forget?" The
smell of hawthorn in the sun and bracken in the wet. Well, that is
right, they did have an extraordinary smell, especially bracken.
And even if the verse was not "light," that did not matter. Indeed, how splendidly *sad* the Lukannon poem was: "*The Beaches
of Lukannon—before the sealers came!*" Here was another thing.
When Kipling was talking about the Army and the Navy he made
you feel, especially in the war, that our army and navy were
worth more than anything else in the world. It made you feel
personally dignified. Those *Sea Warfare* pieces—the one about
minesweepers:

Dawn off the Foreland—the young flood making
    Jumbled and short and steep—
Black in the hollows and bright where it's breaking—
    Awkward water to sweep.
    "Mines reported in the fairway,
    "Warn all traffic and detain.
"*Sent up Unity, Claribel, Assyrian, Stormcock, and Golden Gain.*"

Week after week, at the London Coliseum those songs used to be
sung, a special turn, by three men in oilskins standing in front of a
backcloth representing very rough water (the sound of which was
well imitated by a special machine) and the whole thing illumin-
ated by a searchlight. The music was good, too. And "*Sent up*

202

Unity, Claribel, Assyrian" . . . how was it that the sound of the names in Kipling was sometimes more important than the sense? "I am the Most Wise Baviaan." Why, didn't matter. "Eddi, priest of St Wilfrid." Who, didn't matter. Sometimes even, if it came in a favourite book, like *Puck of Pook's Hill*, I would skip a poem, and then go back to it afterwards, and read it after all. Not understanding it didn't matter:

> What is a woman that you forsake her,
> And the hearth-fire and the home-acre,
> To go with the old grey Widow-maker?
>
> She has no house to lay a guest in—
> But one chill bed for all to rest in,
> That the pale suns and the stray bergs nest in.
>
> She has no strong white arms to fold you,
> But the ten-times-fingering weed to hold you
> Bound on the rocks where the tide has rolled you.

The notion that poetry is not a piece of material, smelling slightly of the drawing-room couch, that it is not best clothes on Sunday, but that it is on the contrary alive all over, like skin, being part of a person—this I first came to understand from the reading of Keats.

Did I like poetry? Certainly, I said, meaning I liked Kipling, and privately certain that this was about as far as poetry could go and that Kipling was the most original writer who ever lived. And no wonder I thought so, because it never occurred to me that Kipling had not himself invented all the exciting or comical metres and rhythms which I admired, or that anybody else had ever chosen his words so tellingly.

Kipling, yes; but still, Poetry, no. Until in May 1917 it was Kipling himself who made me say, "Poetry, yes," who hauled me suddenly up the last steps of the ladder to the discovery that poetry could be written by other people as well; a fact which once learned, made me discard, with the ingratitude typical of such mental events, the very man who had guided me, so that I was seldom to read Kipling again for twenty years.

These volumes of Kipling short shories were still coming out, though already there was a feeling that each new one "wasn't quite so good." The latest was *Traffics and Discoveries*, and one of these stories, "Wireless," was certainly one of Kipling's weakest. A young chemist with poetical inclinations is suffering from tuberculosis. Late at night he is experimenting with the new miracle of the wireless receiver and he "gets" a voice which is distant in time as well as space—the voice of Keats, in fact; and the phrases he hears come from the "Ode to the Nightingale." *Beaded bubbles . . . sunburnt mirth . . . the same which oft-times hath charm'd magic casements.* . . . The fact that they were some of the most famous words in English poetry meant nothing to me. I doubt if I had ever taken them in before. The important fact is that they were here presented to me as great poetry by the voice of the absolute authority I was so glad to accept, Kipling.

Through the door into the new world—and I was suddenly able to understand it, and enjoy it. So now I was reading Keats from beginning to end.

It was not possible to explain all this to Flap while we were eating thick egg-sandwiches underneath Hay Tor, though I had thought of doing so. Now for the pool (always remembering that it was dangerous to bathe too soon after a meal).

"You ought to try him," I was still saying feebly, meaning Keats. Flap looked at me with screwed up eyes.

"I doubt whether you've ever read a word of it," he said. "People only like it because it's the right thing."

I had tried lecturing Flap on this before. "What I simply do not understand is why you should be so *pleased* about not liking it." But we were longing to get our boots off.

On the landing-stage I took a photograph of Flap in his shirt only and successfully performed the comic trick of making him retreat two steps backwards "to get into focus." He fell with a perfect splash into the pool. I remember this because it started one of those laughing-giggle-pain sequences which happened every other day in those times. Laughing shades off into giggling and goes on till it turns into distressful aching in the throat. This sequence was a particularly bad one, and I remember it. We were giggling after the bathe, because Flap couldn't wear his shirt, and we had been asked to tea at the vicarage. Then we were pushing our bicycles up a Devonshire hill, "practically perpendicular." This action always increases giggling: the steeper the hill, the more the giggles. Why? The vicar's name was a curious one—Verity Stiggle. This was ominous for us, and we began to feel a sense of dread. The door was apparently opened by a large square dog, behind which was a not very beauteous young lady with enormous spectacles and strangely shaped legs which were somehow concave rather than convex in shape, it seemed to us. She stood as if thunderstruck and said, or so it sounded, "I am Miss Tickle." Absolute explosion from Flap and me. These explosions were more or less suppressed by us during tea, but only at the expense of aching pain and cramp-like contraction of the roof of the mouth. They were kind people. It would be misery to laugh. Finally, I began laughing wildly—it was impossible to hold it in—and as a last resort I pointed into the garden and said, "Look at the dog." But by great misfortune, the dog, large, unhealthy and white, was performing one of those elaborate de-worming operations on the grass, a sort of horizontal-bars act, scraping its bottom along the ground. This of course could not have put me in a worse light. It removed all desire to laugh for about three hours.

Going home, we had to wheel our bikes across country over rutted fields set to a plaster-cast by the sun, yet acres of uncleared thistles were thriving on it. We were rather tired, and Flap and I had a long, fairly serious conversation starting with Miss Tickle and ending with girls and love. The tin word "sex" was not used in those days. I knew that Flap had a girl, and I had seen her one Sunday in a red silk dress—she was very small, tiny, with minute feet, and really extraordinarily pretty. She had held Flap's arm in a way which gave me a pang. I knew he had taken her to *The Bing Boys*. Her name was Sally. Flap introduced her name. I more or less realised that he was doing this as a revenge for my special knowledge of Keats; and although I was quite certain that this still left me in an unassailable position, and that every kind of right sort of thinking would agree that Keats was better, and the closest members of my family would be behind me to a man, I was conscious as well of the uneasy feeling that in Flap's mind there were no doubts of any kind whatever. Flap had a sort of leather purse for his money with a pocket in it, and inside he had a miniature photograph of his girl which he produced for me to see; and I was bound to say that the girl still looked extraordinarily pretty, even in a photograph. On my side I could easily have mentioned that I had a photograph too—of Biddy Amos. I did—but unfortunately this photograph, taken by my own No. o Brownie, made Biddy look as if she had an extraordinary lump on the side of her neck, really the bulb of an electric light on the shelf behind her—rather a comical effect. It didn't look like her, and anyhow Flap would have found out that she was already just over twenty-one and engaged to a man in the Air Force. I did mention Phyllis, and meeting her at Corfe Castle, but Flap felt, and I felt, that this did not really alter my position *vis-à-vis* Flap. So I came up with something different altogether—something which I had been planning earlier in the day.

It was the surprise remark I started when we were doing the potatoes in the morning. "What do you think?" I said. "I want to leave School and get on with the Army."

I was interested to see what Flap would say.

"What are you getting at?" he said.

"I mean I'm rather tired of playing about at Westminster. I want to get on with it."

This idea was developing on the spot—as I was talking to him. I got to like the sound of it.

"I mean I'm not going to get anything out of hanging around." It would be all right for Flap, I thought. He would probably be sergeant-major, head boy in the Corps, next term. A school monitor for certain. Doing chemistry work so high up in Plum's section that it practically amounted to research. Perhaps Ben Willett would be so gracious as to make me a full corporal at the end of another long term of right-wheeling and being about to advance in column of fours. If I joined the Army now, anticipating conscription, it might save me eight or nine months of this ping-pong-playing waste of time which at seventeen—and in 1917 of all years—was beginning to make me realise that so far, though I might at various times have thought myself a genius ten different ways at once, there was nothing whatever to show for it.

"What will your pa and ma say?" Flap was making a facetious thing of it. Later on he called it "swank" in mock schoolboy language yet meaning it at the same time. I had obviously given Flap something to think about. I was beginning to persuade myself that Keats and my Army talk together were a little better than, in fact decidedly put in the background, his photograph of the pretty girl in the red dress.

CHAPTER THIRTEEN

Breaking Fate

THE possibility of "breaking fate"—the fact that the fate which seems inevitable can frequently be turned aside and avoided—is something I was to learn from my betters in the years to come. My Army decision was a good one. I did save myself from eight months of time-wasting and shameful inactivity. After the Army was over Fate was broken again, in a way which I could neither anticipate nor control.

An advantage of anticipating conscription was that it gave me some choice of regiment. As a result of family discussions, advice from friends and the sympathetic concern of O.T.C. officers at Westminster (I found the fact that I was longing to leave them gave me new status in their eyes) the first choice was Cavalry. There had been a call to make up new drafts for cavalry regiments. True, in my countryless existence I had never been on a horse in my life, except for the ponies which trotted up and down the front at Sandown, for sixpence a time. This was something which could be put right before going up for interview. I bought a book on horse-management and learnt how to cure "jaws" (a disease of the hoof). Six times I went to the riding school at Robin Hood Gate, where there was a special course under military supervision. I rode round in a circle, with reins, without reins, bareback with reins, bareback without reins, on a horse with a special flat back which moved in a dream, never varying its pace or its rhythm. It was exactly like a horse in a roundabout; indeed, it would have been perfectly easy to ride it standing on its broad buttocks, facing the tail. This, I thought, was getting me nowhere. There was a Mr Fawcett who advertised riding lessons on Tooting Bec Common. By now I knew how to hold the reins, and I was just beginning to be able to trot without jarring my teeth out of their sockets when there was an accident. My horse stumbled, fell, I was on the ground, and Mr Fawcett was standing beside me, his face pale. To my incredulous astonishment it was the horse, not me, which seemed to concern Mr Fawcett. There were certain quite small scratches, as I saw, on the horse's knee, whereas I had a bump on the elbow which already felt sore. Then Mr Fawcett lost his head, "Why didn't you hold him up?" his voice seemed distorted with emotion. I kept my head. How could a falling object "keep up" an object it was falling *with*? I started a clear little lecture on this point, but Mr Fawcett was not listening. He was saying something about "three hundred pound." It was obviously better just to leave. Mother, of course, understood and was wonderfully sympathetic about the graze on my elbow. Later on I was more relieved than disappointed when after coming up before Brigadier-General Sir Lionel Vane-Templeton, of the 15th Hussars, I learned that there was no vacancy for me. And this in spite of the fact that when I told him of my week's riding experience on Tooting Common, I never mentioned the accident.

The Army was the first big event in my eventless life, yet this is a time which I find most difficult to remember. Life passed in a dream of placid obedience. I moved in my circle complacently, like that old training horse at the riding school. Because the day was filled with a hundred worries, there was no anxiety. Because everybody was equally put upon, there was no injustice. The good-day-bad-day sequence disappeared.

It was to be infantry, after all, and the training battalion was that of the most ancient and honourable Inns of Court, at Berkhamsted. My family took their April holiday at the hotel in the High Street. The war was going badly, and people used to regard me and my colleagues with a faintly posthumous look. I occasionally felt uneasy on this score myself. My bravery had never been tested, but my guess was that it was below rather than above the average. However, there was no time to think deeply of such things, nor of the fact that the average expectation of life of subalterns in the regiment I eventually joined was, in the front line, not more than six weeks. All such glooms were lost in the euphoria of complete and raging good health (instead of just being well) which I was getting out of army life. I was also fortunate, in a way, that at the age of seventeen to eighteen, no doubts about the rights and wrongs of the war, the slaughter or the kind of patriotism involved had struck me with anything heavier than the most glancing blow. Muriel had doubts, I knew, and there was that Siegfried Sassoon poem. I understood just enough not to be scornful of pacifists. And yet the Inns of Court then was the very centre of a new toughness in get-your-man-by-any-methods training.

If a man dropped his rifle on battalion parade there was no second chance. It was the end of his prospects of a commission. There was a little company sergeant-major there, thin and pale. He was as tingling, straight and taut as a guitar-string. His words of command cut like a knife, and he seemed to be coldly on fire with an abstract passion. We were all pretty scornful of him, yet utterly obedient. In private life he was a schoolmaster. His boys must have trembled. He used the word "discipline" a hundred times a day with the accent on the second syllable. As we watched his de-personalised raging through those six months he seemed to be withering away before our eyes as if with a cancer. He was in fact, after years of shouting at school-children and cadets, gradually losing his voice; and this sent him into a rage of frustration. We talked cheerfully of the possibility of his dying. His high moments, his orgasmic climaxes, came in bayonet drill, where his detailed instruction on how to aim first at the loins did horrify us: I shall never forget the frenzied mania of his "at the gut, *in*"; in fact, one of the older recruits, brought in by a late desperate round-up of the over-forties, took a transcript of his words, which later became the subject of a Question, even a Debate, in the House of Commons.

But the sterner the bark, the more tender the bite. That was the rule, with sergeants. I liked the discipline and throve on it. The Westminster O.T.C. had been well run, especially the drill; and this gave me a good start. I had always enjoyed arms drill as conducted and performed by experts.

The Public Schools Camps had been much more unpleasant to me than living under canvas at Berkhamsted. If the rest of the year is mostly comfort and cosseting, ten days on a straw palliasse at Tidworth Pennings are difficult to bear; and such details as the use of latrines amateurishly made and more or less open to the public eye are quite disproportionately unpleasant. Deems minor, always particularly shy about this kind of thing, used to go the whole ten days without a single evacuation. But at Berkhamsted I was happy. Indeed I learned the ropes. Some of the more etiolated areas of my personal development, kept back by my shan't-and-won't attitude at Westminster, were brought to life just in time. No longer did I stand on the edge of things with one toe in the water, so to speak. I was *in* it; I grasped it; I worked, for the first time in my life, very hard; I was working for something (April 1918 was the month of "Gough's disaster," the great break-through of the Germans, and there was nothing to tell us it was the last disaster). I was losing (if only it could have been completely—and for ever) a streak of irresponsibility, and I was learning to give commands and to speak in front of other people. This speaking may have been no more than a five-minute discourse on Lewis-gun tactics; but even this is worth gold for the future. I was learning also that it was possible for me to do well in something immediately and commonsensically useful. At the end of the six months I passed out top of my Company. I was even asked to stay on as an instructor. I know that anybody who has known me since then will regard this as the wildest traveller's tale; but it happened, and I am grateful for it.

This was the most militarist part of my career, when my head was cropped closest, my chest most unnaturally protruding, my rifle-management at its nimblest, and my behaviour, for the first and only time in my life, approaching the exact and the clear-cut: the time when my leisure was most rigidly rationed. It was therefore a great time for reading. The sales of Anthony Trollope always go up in war-time. Barchester is the perfect antidote to a battalion parade. Instruction in the new Lewis-gun made the pleasure of *Sense and Sensibility* all the sharper by contrast. For the only time in my life I was under the Jane Austen spell: but I was even then much more deeply involved with Keats, now that I had discovered he had a Life. Keats never for an hour forgot the moment when he first saw unmistakably the blood on his handker-chief. "It was arterial blood . . . it was my death warrant." And I shall never forget reading those lines lying on the grass outside my tent. I felt I had to pass it on instantly. I told a man called Royle.

Now my regiment had to be decided, and this time the family were unanimous. It must be Grandfather's regiment. I must try for the Coldstream Guards. A good report from Berkhamsted helped; but it was Grandfather, eighteen years dead, who got me in.

The official Brigade training headquarters was not then (as it is now) my grandfather's Caterham, but Bushey Hall; and it was at Bushey Station, next to Watford, that I was told to detrain. There had been a week's leave at No. 36, where I had been gloriously petted, fattened and well basted at every meal with my favourite kind of cream-cheese, braised onions, dripping, toast, stewed steak, ginger biscuit, milk chocolate, ginger beer, raisins, ginger pudding and treacle, pyramid creams from the Army and Navy Stores, and even the Christmas pudding specially kept over from last year's batch. Brigade cadets wore special officerish-looking uniforms with leather belts, and for two days, after a quick fitting from a military tailor, I was able to walk about for the first time in a uniform with a shape, instead of the bunched-up floppy mess which was the ordinary private's tunic of the time. This caused me to glance at myself increasingly in plate-glass windows as I went round with Mother, both of us feeling light-headed with pleasure, my back preternaturally straight as I stretched myself up to be even taller, relatively, than she was.

But by the time I was in Baker Street Station, ready to entrain, with kit-bag and steel helmet and gas-mask, all alone in charge of myself, so to speak, I was feeling apprehensive. If the Inns of

Court discipline was ten times stricter than that of the average cadet unit, it would be natural to expect Brigade discipline to be ten times fiercer still.

At Bushey Station I detrained myself ready to be escorted in—with a suspicion of frog-marching, perhaps, from the N.C.O. in charge of me. Yet there was something vague and dreamy about the platform of Bushey Station. The war news was good, almost unbelievably so; and it made one sleepy, somehow. The sun was so hot that it brought out the smell of the wood and released the suggestion of ozone from the live rail. Soon the train had clacked mildly into oblivion, the signal had clonked back into place and the handful of passengers had wandered abstractedly out of sight. The platform was empty. Why no escort? I felt a pang. Had I already done something unsoldierly, like catching the wrong train? "You will be met," my instruction sheet said.

Suddenly I felt there was someone behind me.

"Excuse me . . ."

God! A man in uniform.

"Is your name . . . ?"

"Sir?"

The man in uniform cleared his throat.

"I'm sorry?"

But his gaze was turned towards the distance. I took a respectful look at the profile. No neat military back of the neck here. On the contrary, his hair was longer than any I had seen for months. No bulging chest—the shoulders were a little drooping. Good aristocratic nose; but the rest of the features a little meagre—a sketch of a man. He seemed to be in a dream, as I had been. Perhaps he was trying to think of my name.

"Potter?" I suggested.

"Of course—S. M. Potter." He felt in three of his pockets and then out of the fourth pulled a crumpled sheet of typed paper.

"I have, I believe, to escort you to the Hall. . . . I'm sorry there is no actual drum to greet you. No flourish of trumpets." He wasn't being sarcastic. His lean face was turned upwards. He was enjoying the words. "Drum"—very brief, almost onomatopoeic.

o   213

"It's quite unnecessary. It's only ten minutes walk. You will not find it aggressively unpleasant. A hundred lashes before breakfast. . . ."

I had some difficulty in keeping in step with him as he walked. There was no "left, right" about his gait whatever. "Meals of blackened bread," he went on.

"Are we in tents?"

"Tents? *Tents?* At the Bushey Hall Hydro? Tents, where only man is vile? You will have a choice of shower-bath or swimming-bath, foot-bath, salt-spray or the compromise of the tepid douche —Turkish vapour, or Hungarian hot spring. The English are a most remarkable people. My name is Collis. J. S. Collis." He cleared his throat and repeated more clearly, gazing with a rather crucified look towards the sky, "John Stewart Collis."

What was interesting me was the peculiar intonation. There was a slightly rhetorical sing-song—a sudden attack on individual words, not necessarily those which needed emphasis for the sense. "Douche," for instance. And according to what system of anglicising did he pronounce it "dowtch?"

Bushey Hall Hydro had been turned into a pleasantly un-barracks-like barracks for cadets whose ages ranged from eighteen to forty-five. The drain on officers had been so overwhelming that the Brigade was running very short. Tough, battle-worn majors, with D.C.M.'s alongside their D.S.O.'s, were here to learn Brigade drill, Brigade words and customs, side by side with the normal 1918 crop of very young men of impressive, or like myself of un-impressive, family names. With those were older men, over forty, who had never seen the Army before. They were late call-ups, or volunteers—writers like C. C. Abbott (Claude Colleer, the poet). The old countryman who tried to get through our lines on the field exercise against Blue Force turned out to be Gerald du Maurier in a beard and a wig filled with bits of straw. Officers from other regiments had come to learn Brigade terminology, most of them men who had miraculously survived three years of front line. They looked like ghosts and seemed to be embers only—old men, we very young ones thought uncomprehendingly, not able to feel much about such things one way or the other.

All this gave to those Bushey days the quality of a dream. A deeply respectable and commodious hotel housed a load of shell-shocked veterans and puzzled innocents. Training and discipline seemed unreal. The Company Commander, of course, was impressive, and gave us frequent little pep-talks. "You can do it" he was always saying with a peculiar accent on "can" which he pronounced "kahn."

"If you do your share—and you kahn do it. . . . Work hard, and you'll be as happy as sand-boys." He was like a figure in a war play. My platoon commander was Nigel Ronald, tall, elegant, diffident Coldstreamer who taught us how a Brigade officer should behave, never raising his voice even when giving commands (a little difficult to hear), always punctilious, never relaxing his gentle discipline or his half-concealed amusement at the gymnastics of arms drill. In Self-Expression classes he would suggest essays on "Gothic Revival Architecture" or—a lucky break for me—"Keats's *Ode to Melancholy*." I remember he complimented me on my attempt, though he corrected some of the spelling.

My desire to excel in the Army or to work hard was fading. The good thing about Bushey for me was this different kind of dream figure, Jack Collis. He was one of those men whose personality was cancelled out by army uniform. His body could never fit the army shape. But in P.T. clothes, or playing tennis, he emerged as gracefully athletic, with the subtle physique of a long-distance runner who had won Rugby's difficult cross-country Crick. In time off, we played golf on the Bushey course, or watched Ted Ray, over from Oxhey to play with his friend J. B. Batley, Ted leaping in the air as he smashed his driver into the ball with the most unorthodox swing in golf history. Jack and I were unorthodox too, and slowly developed a style which was destined to produce the shortest-length ball in golf. Jack was becoming my friend, and I realised the interesting fact, now for the first time, that at Westminster I did not know what "having friends" meant. I had by now identified the slight strangeness of his accent as Irish.

Before meeting him I had thought that all Irishmen inverted the sentences into an "Is it after coming you will be now" structure. Jack had been a star in the debating society at Rugby, and while I was stoking up with Meredith and Hardy, he was full to the finger-tips with Macaulay, and used to quote Macaulay's speeches during pauses on the golf-course, when we were looking for the ball. Suddenly he would stand erect.

"What then, it is said, would you legislate in haste?" Jack's face was tilted upwards, I noticed. I was caught as if by chance in the wide orbit of his gaze. The answer came like a thunderbolt: "I allow that hasty legislation is an evil. But reformers are compelled to legislate fast just because bigots will not legislate early."

Then he suddenly got quieter, in order to bring out the word "bigots" with an effect which stunned me.

"Reformers are compelled to legislate in times of excitement, because bigots will not legislate in times of tranquillity."

The long grass was tufted and wet. It was nearly autumn. Even as early as July we had seen from the casualty lists that the war was truly dying. We were in the beginnings of the most gigantic relaxation in history—of a sigh of relief which filled Europe like an inundation. Yet it was a sigh which marked with sadness for ever all those whom it touched, not least the boys like Jack and myself who gave no thought to it, but were to feel the sadness and the tragedy, mixed with nostalgia, all through their lives.

On 11 November 1918 the usual early morning detail was cancelled. Instead, a battalion parade was called for 11 a.m. We were careful not to lift an eyebrow at this announcement, but the unpopular G— who never would and never could acquire the correct Bushey attitude, rushed about, his red face a-shine, chanting "wind up . . . wind up" in his attempted army slang, already out of date by two years—the climax of a lifetime of misplaced friendliness.

Colonel Pyke had the finest moustache in the Grenadiers, and he announced the Armistice in a tone of voice which differed in no way from the one he used when presenting the prizes after a boxing competition, or delivering a reprimand for unsoldierly behaviour. We let off steam with a specially loud "God Save the King," and then wandered off to talk to each other casually of other matters.

"Let us observe, let us record the scene," said Jack Collis. We had the rest of the day free. To be different from everybody else, we thought it would be a good idea to go to Trafalgar Square. There might be some demonstration. We would take notes. I was also inclined to feel that history would some day be grateful for our notes of the events of this day. "There might be various manifestations, certain behaviours: a suggestion of *genre* . . ." Incredibly, Jack pronounced the last word "jong-ry."

Standing on the paws of a Landseer lion, we watched curates and waitresses, marines and district nurses, riding astride the bonnets of buses. "This," said Jack, speaking from the heights of undemonstrative rationalism of the Irish peoples, "could only happen in England." My private sensations were of the nature of delicious excitement and joy. God and the Right had triumphed. God was on our side. We were the best nation in the world. No other thought was possible.

We had all been given leave till midnight, and we were surprised in the huts to find a number of the Old Ones, as we called the over twenty-fives, drooped about in various stages of exhausted debauch. F. and V. were being slowly and carefully sick. Tiny D., the platoon stallion, was understood to say he had "seen off eight." Only one of them had journeyed farther than Watford. From the heights of our virginity we felt that such temptations or pleasures would never at any time in our lives so disarrange the composure of ourselves. We felt cool, we felt superior, and yet in some internal core or heartspring we felt uneasy.

When Bushey came to an end Jack went off for ever, I guessed, so far as I was concerned. There was no one, except Muriel, with whom the talk had gone so deep. There was mention of his coming to see me at home; and I began apologising a little in advance, thinking of the photographs he had shown me of his house on the beautiful slopes of Killiney Bay, and then having a vision of that sticky box hedge stretching five yards across the front garden of No. 36, whereupon I became irritated by the thought that Mother would tell Jack how delightful I had been at the age of four, how specially talented at eleven, and that then she would ask me to play the piano to him—to Jack, who hadn't a note of music in his head anyhow. I started to explain.

"You needn't worry about that when you come to us," Jack had said in effect.

What did he mean?

"You won't be told about *my* exploits. Not by *my* mother." Why the look of real grimness? Well, it must remain a mystery, I thought. Jack was due to go to Oxford. He had got into Balliol. I, of course, was going (as it had always been taken for granted) in the totally opposite direction—to learn double-entry book-keeping in Father's office—Bird and Potter, 28 Victoria Street.

After the Armistice it took a long time to bring the training battalions to a halt. Recruits kept pouring in well after November 11. Then at the beginning of 1919, W.D. suddenly realised they didn't want us any more. After six months of Bushey I was duly gazetted. It was in *The Times*—"2nd Lt., Coldstream Guards, Special Reserve," and I waited instructions. There was a curious lack of reaction to this event. I found myself fitted with the uniform and the glorious hat with the golden peak. A special studio photograph was taken. For six weeks I walked London in these fine clothes, occasionally succeeding in getting a fatherly salute from some battle-scarred old N.C.O. I spent every waking moment in this uniform. Most of my pay went on conspicuous front-row seats in theatres. The music of *Chu Chin Chow* was as wonderful as the white skins of the not very Far Eastern maidens. I saw Jack Buchanan and Phyllis Titmuss do their songs and dances together in *Tails Up*. "I'm very fond of wild thyme," sang Phyllis. "I've had a wild time too," replied Jack.

Sow it in your garden—won't you make a note?
I'll sow it in a line wherein I sowed my wild oat.

The not too healthy pallor of Buchanan's face, the well-groomed poise, the daring ease, the faint madness of his cupidinous ogling, all seemed to me the unapproachable model of the kind of man I would like to be: I gazed at the silk legs of the chorus with feelings of wistful desire and an expression of angry solemnity. Girls of this degree of prettiness were outside my orbit. I tried to feel that I was having a wild time too, just by sitting in the audience.

In a last blind desire to make one final impression at school, I turned up in all this uniform at Westminster, ostensibly to watch the Pancake Grease. After all, in 1916 or '17 Cranston and Phillimore had so turned up in their uniforms, soon after being commissioned. It was not a success. As I expected, Flap was breezing round, still at school, and, also as I expected, he was in the uniform of the Corps Company Sergeant-Major. But by chance B.-T. was visiting too, and I noticed with a pang that he was in plain clothes, without a hint of uniform about him. He was the centre of a small knot of boys and masters. B.-T. had crammed a lot into his year in the front line, having been blown up, gassed, and buried alive on three separate occasions.

Still, there was Flap, outside in the Yard. As he had his cap on, if I were to move in close to him he would be forced to salute me—would probably be delighted to salute me, I thought. Times had changed. He saw me, but to my surprise he made no attempt to salute me whatever. Instead he sidled up, murmured "Good show" and turned away. It was his old sarcastic voice, and he obviously meant "swank," or "show-off." It was true, I said to myself. 1919 was not 1917: it was completely different. Heroes were limping back, and here was I showing off my uniform after enjoying the safest war on record.

After the Grease was over, B.-T. joined me and we walked down Victoria Street together, talking about school. Typically charmingly, he congratulated me on my commission. I moved up the pavement, to avoid a salute.

"I suppose Sacred Sam was all right really," I said. "A sort of unsatisfied scholar, I suppose."

"Not a bit of it." B.-T. was quite brusque. "He had a crib

under his desk for every lesson he took. I'm sorry Jimmy Gow is retiring."

"He wasn't much good with boys, was he?"

"Marvellous. He was marvellous," said B.-T. "Ah, but you didn't see him before the war. So *amusing*—he understood us. But his son was killed in 1915, you know. After that he shut up shop—wanted to retire altogether, but they wouldn't let him."

My golden cap felt desperately hot and uncomfortable. At home, I took it off for the last time. Later, Mother fished it out of my room and surrounded it with tissue paper for preservation in the top drawer of her wardrobe.

I realised that my last chance of splendour had gone. The age of Sam Brownes shining like satin had suddenly disappeared as completely as the age of wearing pink-and-white blazers of a lustre and significance to strike one dumb. Next week I would be catching the morning train from Wandsworth Common once more. This time it was to work for my living. I was going to start in Father's office.

The premises of Bird and Potter, Chartered Accountants, were the familiar ones I knew—one of the up-to-date office suites at the Westminster end of Victoria Street. Mr Bird, the senior partner, sat in one of the smaller rooms on the sunny side; Father, who did more work than anybody, had the large triangular room over-looking the inner yard. There was plenty of space for me to sit at a subsidiary table. Father reigned over a tremendous roll-top desk, sitting in the middle of a swelling surf of papers foaming in what appeared to be the maximum of disorder; but in fact Father had discovered what I was later to learn—that it is this very dis-arrangement of the study or desk which makes instant finding and identification possible. The best filing system is discontinuity of position and heaps of contrasted configuration. It is only in deserts that compasses are necessary. I admired the look of Father at his desk, so much more effectively definite than he was at home, in complete charge of his work, clearing up problems which were endlessly renewed. In moments of chill and doubt it seemed to me like trying to mop up the sea-shore; but to Father it was an unendingly satisfactory shaping of raw materials, something not far different from the pleasure of a sculptor or an architect. I believed I would get the hang of it—get the taste for it. It was a totally new thing. As for the work, half my army acquaintances were already in business; and it might be mentioned that Perks, the office boy, was only fifteen. Even Muriel was now earning money, though it was work of a special and responsible kind. She had achieved an alpha-studded First in her English Finals, and was now an English teacher at St Paul's Girls' School under the celebrated Miss Gray. It was different for Jack Collis, of course. He was sending me postcards from that airy bay just south of Dublin, he had been entered for Balliol, and he was going to Oxford in the summer. I was in the middle of a first, half-comprehending study of *Jude the Obscure*, and I could not help identifying myself, though in quite a cheerful way, with Jude's wistful longing for the university spires. Perhaps I wouldn't have been any good at it, I thought. Perhaps it would have been like Westminster.

All the same, after twelve months more or less in the country out of doors, it was strange to be sitting in Father's room. Though big, it was neither sunny nor airy, and it was often too warm. Father had a strong nineteenth-century aversion to "draughts," which meant air. I had spent hours, at No. 36, perfecting the art of pulling down windows without being noticed. Father on a mild June day could suddenly put his hand to his throat as if an arctic wind of death had smote him; but he would breathe in cigarette-smoke and the smell of old ledgers as if he was standing on Beachy Head. I remembered that sun did sometimes shine into this room, but it was only on the window-sill, and only from four to four-thirty, on the afternoons of June.

It was bad having to wear a good dark suit every day and a stiff white collar. Westminster had made me hate putting on town clothes in the morning; but I liked having lunch with Father in his special restaurant ("Let's go round the corner") or at the St Stephen's, the first club I entered.

There was a feeling among the uncles and aunts that Father was pleased to see me in the office—no, more than that, delighted, proud as Punch. Uncle Josh had a permanently satisfied look. Step was getting on with it. He probably put me down for a special £500 in his will, just for the sight of me with inky fingers.

"And you've let your hair grow a bit since leaving the Army, Step," he said. "It's natural up to a point; but you mustn't put on too much hair, you know—all this yellow stuff sticking out from under your hat."

He laughed encouragingly. Here was I at the bottom of a ladder Josh was already briskly climbing. He was three-quarters of the way up. There were going to be moments when Josh was going to irritate me.

Josh thought that before I was thirty-five, say, Father might take me in as a junior partner. It was a wonderful opportunity for me. True, but one had to remember that equal partner was what Father was at this moment, and he was just sixty-three.

Most of the time I was supposed to be studying accountancy, which meant that I sat at my table by the window and read an advanced manual on double-entry book-keeping. It was comprehensible; indeed the explanations, helped out with many a (i) (ii) (iii), and liberal doses of black letter for emphasis, were just a little too clear for me to be able to take them in. Very frequently, in another text-book, words like "goods" were made the subject of calculations, and my difficulty was to get an image of what this word "goods" was meant to stand for. One thought of bolster-shaped bundles tied up with broad canvas bands and smelling of cornflour. Occasionally Father and I would have a break.

"What precisely," I would say, "would you understand by 'mean dividend residue?'"

Father would get up, pretend to pull his moustache judicially, and say

"Personallah, I would describe the term as extraordinaralah misleading."

"They do not wish to infer 'mean' in the sense of 'stingy'?"

"By no means. By *no means*." Then we would start one of those long laughter-giggle matches, and go out to lunch.

Father used sometimes to give me covert looks, when I was working. I had to learn the use of round rulers, for ruling columns in ink; but after a lot of experimenting I came to the conclusion that flat ones were best, and told Father why. I used to watch Father in my turn, in absolute concentration on some intricate problem of balance, columns of pencilled figures all round him on his desk, calling for Mr Spong, who hovered behind his chair, leaning delicately over Father's shoulder with a sort of dignified deference. Father, so much less mild than he was at home, would ferociously sign or counter-sign columns in a frowning rapture, till his cigarette burnt a hole in the middle of his moustache. I tried to take part, and have ideas. After three weeks I put forward the suggestion that a thimble made somehow of blotting-paper would be useful for writing in figures, because you wouldn't have to pick the blotting-paper up. It would only save a quarter of a second, but think of 50,000 quarters.

One evening after about eight weeks of this Father sent me off from the office early, at four-thirty. He "had something to do."

What should I do with my extra hour? I had more money than usual—about three pounds ten, part of my month's pay from the office. I might slip into the Army and Navy Stores, over the way. I hadn't been since before the Army. It would be nice to revisit these scenes of past treats with Mother. Inside the entrance I enjoyed once more the bracing, major-key smells of groceries and provisions. I nipped up the stairs and through to the back building for the menagerie, which had always been rather a long tramp for Mother. I was my own master. Back to the book department, where I had decided to buy. I already had eight poets in the Oxford half-calf edition. These were ten-and-six or more each: but they certainly seemed the best edition you could buy. My eye was caught by a bigger, more luxurious kind of volume: Shelley's *Lyrical Poems and Translations*, complete. It was in light green half-calf, with light green boards, and the print the best I had ever seen, and obviously valuable. It made the book look even more expensive than it was. Right at the end was a special notice "Printed in England by the Florence Press for Chatto and Windus and published by them at iii St. Martin's Lane." Then at the end was the date, M.CM.XVIII. It was this way of doing numbers which made it seem especially costly. Sometimes if the poems were fragments there were only about two lines and the rest of the page was blank. It was thirty-two-and-six, a good deal more than I had ever paid for a book.

I supposed now I might as well go home. It must be after five already, for there was Morgan and Pierce Minor.

Why should they remember me? Even if I was in the Westminster boat that was eighteen months ago. Nobody was interested now in anybody's army career, least of all mine. They would remember B.-T. all right, and so it should be. They would probably have read that he was starting on the stage as a professional. Or Harrod, head of Ashburnham, who had got a gigantic scholarship and was going thundering up to Christ Church. Pierce Major, typically, was stopping on in the Army, in some regiment specially interesting for something. Flap had this red-silk-dress girl, a sort of monomania.

Of course Westminster had been a wonderful school (certainly it was a wonderful school). Needless to say I wasn't going to give up my reading and writing and music ("Give up." What a strange phrase even to think of). How typical, Pierce in the Army (in a curious way, that was something I had been good at). I bought a quarter of a pound of pyramid creams to eat in the train.

When I got back to No. 36, to my surprise Father was already there, in our front room, looking grave, and therefore as if the top half of his face was nothing but that deep furrow, that congenital frown, and the bottom half nothing but moustache. Mother was there too, with her finger on her chin and looking abstractedly out of the window at No. 34. The whole scene meant that somebody was going to "say something." A chilling thought flashed through my mind that Father was going to send me to some Business College to learn the elements.

"Your Father wants to say something to you, darling."

"Lilla—*please.*"

"I was only going to——"

"Yes I know, but just——"

Father sighed twice, deeply. It had obviously been decided that he was to say it.

"It's nothing nasty, darling," Mother said, trying to look as if she wasn't speaking.

"*Lil.*"

I didn't like the sound of this. Father sighed again, and went over to the couch, leaned back and put his feet up.

"What your mother and I have been thinking is this. Have you ever thought that you would like to go to Oxford?"